I0528282

# CHRISTIANS HELPING ADDICTS PURSUE SOBRIETY

Mark Tabata
(Evangelist)

(More Bible Studies Available @ www.marktabata.com)

Charleston, AR
COBB PUBLISHING
2024

*Christians Helping Addicts Pursue Sobriety*
is copyright ©2024 by Mark Tabata.
All rights reserved.
No portion of this book may be reproduced in any way without the prior written permission of the author or publisher.

Published in the United States of America by:
Cobb Publishing
704 E. Main St.
Charleston, AR 72933
CobbPublishing.com
Editor@CobbPublishing.com
479.747.8372

ISBN: 978-1-960858-37-5

# INTRODUCTION

When I was twenty-five years old, I was blessed to move to the town of Hazard, and begin working with some great people in Eastern Kentucky. Before I knew it, I had been there nearly twenty years! During that time, I was blessed to work with several churches of Christ. One of the most saddening facts that I encountered was the powerful hold that addiction-especially in the form of recreational drug abuse-had over so many. Indeed, when my father learned that I was moving to this area of the country, a coworker told him:

> "Hazard! Tell him not move there. That is the drug center of the country!"

Sadly, it seems my father's friend was correct. Over the years, we have been blessed to work with hundreds of addicts and their families. Many of them have shown so much incredible strength, faith, resilience, and courage in the battle against drugs. Nearly all of the ones I have worked with have encountered setbacks, spiritual crisis, relapse, and family trouble of one kind or another. I have witnessed and personally known many who have lost their war to addiction-some of whom were very close friends and loved ones (even some in my own family). On the other hand, we have witnessed some very difficult situations that drug ministry directly led us into and "dropped us in the soup," as the old saying goes. In this book, you will read about encounters that we had with menacing drug dealers, corrupt law enforcement, and even demonic forces connected with substance abuse. Yet, Jesus and His inspired Apostles have always told us in God's Word that we will face trials in this life as we lovingly preach and teach His Word to others, and do what we can to minister to those who struggle spiritually.

*John 15:18-20—If the world hates you, you know that it hated Me before it hated you. If you were of the world, the world would love its own. Yet because you are not of the world, but I chose you out of the world, therefore the world hates you. Remember the word that I said to you, 'A servant is not greater than his master.' If they persecuted Me, they will also persecute you. If they kept My word, they will keep yours also.*

*John 16:2—They will put you out of the synagogues; yes, the time is coming that whoever kills you will think that he offers God service.*

*2 Timothy 3:12—Yes, and all who desire to live godly in Christ Jesus will suffer persecution.*

*1 Peter 4:16—Yet if anyone suffers as a Christian, let him not be ashamed, but let him glorify God in this matter.*

What has become abundantly clear to me throughout the years is that this is a particular ministry we in churches of Christ need to put more attention and effort towards, because drug abuse is an area that touches nearly every family in one way or another. However, many of our brethren do not seem to be aware of the need for this type of outreach. My mind goes to two examples over the years which have made me personally aware of this.

The first involves an email that I sent to several of our brotherhood preaching schools back in the year 2006, shortly after I moved to this area of the country and began specialized outreach to try and reach out to help addicts. I requested that the schools of preaching consider devoting one of their yearly lectureships to equipping the saints to prepare them to help addicts and their families. Surely one of our schools would be willing to undertake such a lectureship theme! After all, through the years I had seen fantastic lectureships on Bible translations, Apologetics, textual and expository studies, denominational investigations, false prophets and false teachings, etc. In addition, they had done many studies on "church" issues such as orphan homes, eating in church buildings, "one cup" controversies, abuses to the pattern of worship and the plan of salvation, etc. Several weeks passed without any word. Then, one day, I received a response! Of all the fifteen emails that I sent out, I received one response:

> *"Drug abuse isn't a big enough problem to devote a whole lectureship to."*

The second incident involved a fellow Christian who wanted to start a drug rehab ministry in the surrounding area. He went around to churches of Christ asking for help with funding and resources. One congregation that he spoke with told him: "Helping addicts is not part of the work of the church."

As discouraging as these incidents were, I have learned that the attitudes of local Christians often do not reflect that mentality. Two churches that I have been blessed to work with have been very eager to be involved in ministry to addicts, and we have been especially blessed to use CASA (Christians Against Substance Abuse) literature put out by New Life Behavior Ministries (more on that later). Many of the Christians I have known have been extremely eager and willing to participate in outreach such as this. Several want to know how they may minister individually to addicts, and others would like to know how their churches can be involved in working with those ensnared to substances. It is primarily for these individuals and congregations that this book is being written.

Please understand that I am not a licensed counselor or professional. I am a Gospel preacher with more than twenty years of full time ministry experience and belief in the all-sufficiency of the Word of God. With the help of the Lord, I have been able to set up addiction outreach programs over the years (one-on-one, family environments, churches, jails, and rehabs). Please take this information and use it accordingly, and may it be a blessing to you. I am praying for you in whatever situation this book finds you in!

The grace of the Lord Jesus Christ, and the love of God, and the communion of the Holy Spirit, be with you all. Amen.

# CONTENTS

# Chapter One

# THE ROOTS OF ADDICTION

## Physical Roots

There are many theories about the underlying roots or causes of addiction. Frankly, I don't like the word "causes" because that seems in my mind to alleviate responsibility from a person. The word "roots" implies something which is a factor of addiction that may be (and likely is) very deeply ingrained within a person. When I speak about the "physical" roots of addiction, I am referring to the idea that sometimes there is a biological factor (or factors) that may impact a person in their vulnerability to drug addiction.

It is helpful to understand that the body itself may become physically dependent on substances. The introduction of a pharmaceutical can affect the body in ways that it was never designed to exhibit. As an illustration, I remember a good friend of mine in West Virginia who used to drive a Crown Victoria that her father left her when he passed away. She always bragged on that car, telling me how it was especially good during night time conditions because of the good headlights and wiper blade system. One day, she went out and started her car up and let it warm up to the cold before setting out. She activated the windshield wipers in order to clear the glass, only to discover that instead of windshield wiper fluid coming out, there was a barrage of bubbles! (She had accidentally filled the windshield wiper container with dish soap)! The soap was fine, when used in the proper circumstances. However, the introduction of that soap into her car's systems created all kinds of problems for the car.

In the same way, when a person introduces drugs into their

body, it can create all kinds of physical disruptions and problems that may last for years, even if treated. The substances don't just cause the body major problems, but they can also make the body physically dependent upon them. This is seen especially with the drug known as alcohol. Many have witnessed how addictive alcohol can be on a person, and how withdraws from alcohol can be very dangerous (even deadly) unless handled under proper medical care. The Bible discusses this addictive nature of alcohol:

> *Proverbs 23:28-35—Who has woe? Who has sorrow? Who has contentions? Who has complaints? Who has wounds without cause? Who has redness of eyes? Those who linger long at the wine, Those who go in search of mixed wine. Do not look on the wine when it is red, When it sparkles in the cup, When it swirls around smoothly; At the last it bites like a serpent, And stings like a viper. Your eyes will see strange things, And your heart will utter perverse things. Yes, you will be like one who lies down in the midst of the sea, Or like one who lies at the top of the mast, saying: "They have struck me, but I was not hurt; They have beaten me, but I did not feel it. When shall I awake, that I may seek another drink?"*

The Bible understood what medical science has confirmed in numerous ways: alcohol and other drugs can be physically dangerous and addictive.

## The Question Of Genetics And Disease

Many prefer to use the word "disease" when discussing drug addiction. Indeed, this is the standard word used to describe a physical addiction, claiming that this disease is inherited from one's ancestors. The relationship between genetics and drug addiction is one that is hotly debated in some circles. Most have concluded that genetic factors may play a role in a person's struggle with drug addiction, but there are other factors that also come into play. As an example, consider the following:

*"Studies of alcoholism in twins have been far more strongly suggestive of a genetic factor.' And several skillfully designed studies of adopted children have provided some insights into the nature versus nurture question. Representative of these studies is the pivotal work of Donald W. Goodwin and his associates.' Goodwin's study is based on a simple idea, though one arduous and complex to implement: Find children who were born to an alcoholic mother or father but who were put up for adoption very shortly after birth and thus were not raised by their biological parents; then see whether these children in later life show a higher rate of alcoholism than a comparable group of adopted infants whose biological parents were not alcoholics. Any difference in the rates of alcoholism between the two groups could be attributed to heredity rather than rearing. And since both groups of children were adoptees, any relationship between alcoholism and being an adoptee should be the same for both groups and will, in effect, cancel itself out in comparisons between the two groups. Goodwin chose to study only male children, and in 85 percent cent of the cases the biological alcoholic parent was the father. This experimental design followed the lead of earlier studies, which suggested that father-son relationships were likely to show the strongest genetic influence. The difference in the incidence of alcoholism for Goodwin's two groups was statistically significant. The rate of alcoholism among the adoptees who had an alcoholic biological parent was 3.6 times greater than that among the adoptees whose biological parents were not alcoholics. What added extra persuasiveness suasiveness to Goodwin's results was that for the*

*subset of sons whose adopting parents happened to be alcoholics, no statistically significant difference was apparent. It was consistently the case that only alcoholism in the biological parents was a statistically significant factor. Somewhat similar results have been obtained in several other studies.[o] But taken together, these findings do not come anywhere near warranting the conclusion that there is a unique disease of alcoholism which is genetically determined. Besides the question of the differing definitions of alcoholism used by the various research teams, at best the studies suggest gest that heredity is one factor, among many, that pertains in a minority of cases. A second look at the data shows why these qualifications are necessary. In Goodwin's study, about 18 percent of the sons who had an alcoholic parent became alcoholics, compared to 5 percent of the sons of nonalcoholic parents. The hypothesis is that the difference between these groups is attributable to heredity. But to see the full picture, let's turn the numbers around: 82 percent of the sons who had an alcoholic parent-more than four out of five-did not become alcoholics. So if we generalize from Goodwin's results, we must say that about 80 percent of persons with an alcoholic parent will not become come alcoholics. Either the relevant genes are usually not transmitted or the genes are transmitted but are usually outweighed weighed by other factors."
(Herbert Fingarette, Heavy Drinking: The Myth of Alcoholism as a Disease, 496-513 (Kindle Edition): Berkeley, CA: University Of California Press)*

From a Christian point of view, it is certainly plausible to suspect that there is some kind of genetic factor regarding a person's physical attraction to and dependence upon certain substances. The Bible is clear that the Fall and introduction of sin into the world caused several terrible consequences especially to the physical body of mankind. We are told, for example:

*Genesis 3:17-19—Then to Adam He said, "Because you have heeded the voice of your wife, and have eaten from the tree of which I commanded you, saying, 'You shall not eat of it': "Cursed is the ground for your sake; In toil you shall eat of it All the days of your life. Both thorns and thistles it shall bring forth for you, And you shall eat the herb of the field. In the sweat of your face you shall eat bread Till you return to the ground, For out of it you were taken; For dust you are, And to dust you shall return."*

The physical Creation described in Genesis 1:31 as "very good" was now subject to suffering and death, as a result of mankind's sin. Furthermore, the continuing wickedness and sin of mankind in the world unleashed the Flood that completely changed the Earth itself:

*Genesis 7:17-24—Now the flood was on the earth forty days. The waters increased and lifted up the ark, and it rose high above the earth. The waters prevailed and greatly increased on the earth, and the ark moved about on the surface of the waters. And the waters prevailed exceedingly on the earth, and all the high hills under the whole heaven were covered. The waters prevailed fifteen cubits upward, and the mountains were covered. And all flesh died that moved on the earth: birds and cattle and beasts and every creeping thing that creeps on the earth, and every man. All in whose nostrils was the breath of the spirit of life, all that was on the dry land, died. So He destroyed all living things which were on the face of the ground: both man and cattle, creeping thing and bird of the air. They were destroyed from the earth. Only Noah and those who were with him in the ark remained alive. And the waters prevailed on the earth one hundred and fifty days.*

Who knows what the Earth was like before the Flood? Moses records that there was a canopy of water that surrounded the Earth before the time of Noah.

---

*Genesis 1:6-8—Then God said, "Let there be a firmament in the midst of the waters, and let it divide the waters from the waters." Thus God made the firmament, and divided the waters which were under the firmament from the waters which were above the firmament; and it was so. And God called the firmament Heaven. So the evening and the morning were the second day.*

---

What would have been the apparent effects of such a water canopy?

*"Many early creationists interpreted the "waters which were above the firmament" as a layer of water vapor above earth's atmosphere. Probably gaseous water, it was thoroughly transparent, neither made of liquid water (like clouds) nor of frozen water. This invisible layer of water in gaseous form would have acted as a canopy surrounding earth, producing a "greenhouse effect" on the surface below. Numerous speculative benefits to life and the environment have been ascribed to this canopy. Just as in a greenhouse and beneath the canopies of other planets, it is postulated that the temperature within would have been evenly distributed—no polar regions, and no deserts. This would make the entire earth habitable and warm, probably similar to our modern subtropical zones. In the present world, temperature differences produce today's weather patterns, but without temperature gradients, no storms or wind would ravage the land. Without wind, there could hardly even be rainfall. Evaporation that occurred during the daytime would condense in zones directly above as*

*nightfall cooled things off, falling back to earth as dew near where it evaporated. Most importantly, the canopy would form a great shield surrounding earth, filtering out incoming cosmic and solar radiation. These cause mutations to living cells and to DNA. Over time, great damage builds up in cells and bodies. Damage to our organs and skin by radiation is responsible for many diseases and the aging process we all face. Scripture doesn't give much detail for such a canopy and we can't be dogmatic, but several hints are given and cannot be ignored." (John D. Morris, The Global Flood: Unlocking Earth's Geologic History, 666-680 (Kindle Edition): Dallas, TX: Institute For Creation Research)*

The Bible certainly teaches the idea that our physical bodies deteriorate over time. Add to this the influences that mankind has made throughout the years to the environment such as pathogens, viruses, germ warfare, Agent Orange, radioactive waste from nuclear reactors, jet streams, and so many other things, and we should certainly be able to consider the possibility of several consequences to our physical bodies and environment. Certainly, there would seem to be some strong evidence that there is a physical root to addiction.

With that all being said, we must be careful not to overstate the physical roots of addiction. As noted above, the evidence suggests that there may be several factors involved in a person's struggle with drug addiction, which we will notice in detail throughout this book. For now, please notice the danger of extremism in regards to an improper view of the physical roots of addiction. Some may claim that because their addiction is rooted in physiology, then there is nothing morally bereft in such a condition. While it is true that a person is not responsible for their physical makeup, it is not true that a person is not responsible for their actions. Consider a parallel from the Word of God.

At one time, God declared that the people were "not sound" from the head to the foot.

---

*Isaiah 1:1-6—The vision of Isaiah the son of Amoz, which he saw concerning Judah and Jerusalem in the days of Uzziah, Jotham, Ahaz, and Hezekiah, kings of Judah. Hear, O heavens, and give ear, O earth! For the LORD has spoken: "I have nourished and brought up children, And they have rebelled against Me; The ox knows its owner And the donkey its master's crib; But Israel does not know, My people do not consider." Alas, sinful nation, A people laden with iniquity, A brood of evildoers, Children who are corrupters! They have forsaken the LORD, They have provoked to anger The Holy One of Israel, They have turned away backward. Why should you be stricken again? You will revolt more and more. The whole head is sick, And the whole heart faints. From the sole of the foot even to the head, There is no soundness in it, But wounds and bruises and putrefying sores; They have not been closed or bound up, Or soothed with ointment.*

---

The people here were spiritually unhealthy, from the top of the head to the bottom of the foot. Yet they were still responsible for their actions!

One author has well noted on this passage of Scripture:

*"Not surprisingly, Scripture does use illness as a metaphor for our spiritual condition. In fact, one of the best known passages in Scripture uses the imagery of sickness and healing....Have you (or has someone you know) been captivated by a disease model? Here is the point of contact. Scripture, indeed, emphasizes that sin has many things in common with a disease. For example, it affects our entire*

*being, it is painful, it leads to death, and it is absolutely tragic. Yet there are also ways in which sin is not like a disease. It is something we do rather than catch, we confess it rather than treat it, the disease is in our hearts rather than our bodies, and only the forgiveness and cleansing found in the blood of the Great Physician is sufficient to bring thorough healing." (Edward T. Welch, Addictions: A Banquet in the Grave, 61 (Kindle Edition): Greensboro, NC: New Growth Press)*

A person is not morally responsible for the parts of them that desire what is morally wrong. Jesus Himself was tempted in all points as we are, yet without sin (Hebrews 4:15). James reminds us that desire itself is what leads to sin, and not that desire itself is sinful (James 1:13-15). Yet while a person is not responsible for whatever their personal desires and attractions are, they ARE responsible for their conduct.

As such, we must be careful not to allow the idea that there are physical roots to addiction become a crutch to aid an addict in irresponsible living and decision making. Addictions are not sinful: actions are. Personal responsibility for personal actions must be acknowledged and embraced.

Yet the other extreme must also be acknowledged and avoided: that of denying that there may be a physical root to addiction. Many well-meaning Christians through the years have looked at addiction as merely a moral failure, and as such do not take seriously the impact that the abuse of drugs (and possible genetic disposition to addiction) may have on the body of the addict. We must remember that Jesus-when ministering to people from whatever background they came from-ministered to them in every way: spiritually, physically, socially, psychologically, etc.

We need to realize that there is a legitimate place and use for medicine in right contexts. This is especially true in regard to helping addicts. Indeed, the Bible itself makes this clear in numerous ways.

---

*Mark 5:13-15—And at once Jesus gave them permission. Then the unclean spirits went out and entered the swine (there were about two thousand); and the herd ran violently down the steep place into the sea, and drowned in the sea. 14 So those who fed the swine fled, and they told it in the city and in the country. And they went out to see what it was that had happened. 15 Then they came to Jesus, and saw the one who had been demon-possessed and had the legion, sitting and clothed and in his right mind. And they were afraid.*

*John 6:5—Then Jesus lifted up His eyes, and seeing a great multitude coming toward Him, He said to Philip, "Where shall we buy bread, that these may eat?"*

---

**Please don't forget that Jesus fed even those who were just following Him for the food!**

---

*John 6:26—Jesus answered them and said, "Most assuredly, I say to you, you seek Me, not because you saw the signs, but because you ate of the loaves and were filled.*

---

Again:

---

*Acts 10:38-how God anointed Jesus of Nazareth with the Holy Spirit and with power, who went about doing good and healing all who were oppressed by the devil, for God was with Him.*

---

Christian, there is no shame in a person needing medical treatment for a medical problem! Indeed, this is one reason why God has allowed nature and medicines to begin with: for the healing of the body and mind from physical problems. Remember the example of Hezekiah:

> *Isaiah 38:21—Now Isaiah had said, "Let them take a lump of figs, and apply it as a poultice on the boil, and he shall recover."*

Did you notice that?

God instructed Isaiah to make medicine to heal the king.

The Scriptures are full of references to medicines of various kinds.

For example:

> *"In the figurative account of the evil case of Judah and Israel because of their backsliding (Jer 30:13), the prophet says they have had no rephu'ah, or "healing medicines." Later on (Jer 46:11), when pronouncing the futility of the contest of Neco against Nebuchadrezzar, Jeremiah compares Egypt to an incurably sick woman going up to Gilead to take balm as a medicine, without any benefit. In Ezekiel's vision of the trees of life, the leaves are said (the King James Version) to be for medicine, the Revised Version (British and American) reads "healing," thereby assimilating the language to that in Re 22:2, "leaves of the tree.... for the healing of the nations" (compare Eze 47:12). Very few specific remedies are mentioned in the Bible. "Balm of Gilead" is said to be an anodyne (Jer 8:22; compare Jer 51:8). The love-fruits, "mandrakes" (Ge 30:14) and "caperberry" (Ec*

*12:5 margin), myrrh, anise, rue, cummin, the "oil and wine" of the Good Samaritan, soap and sodic carbonate ("na-tron," called by mistake "nitre") as cleansers, and Hezeki-ah's "fig poultice" nearly exhaust the catalogue. In the Apocrypha we have the heart, liver and gall of Tobit's fish (Tobit 6:7). In the Egyptian pharmacopoeia are the names of many plants which cannot be identified, but most of the remedies used by them were dietetic, such as honey, milk, meal, oil, vinegar, wine. The Babylonian medicines, as far as they can be identified, are similar. In the Mishna we have references to wormwood, poppy, hemlock, aconite and other drugs. The apothecary mentioned in the King James Version (Ex 30:25, etc.) was a maker of perfumes, not of medicines. Among the fellahin many common plants are used as folk-remedies, but they put most confidence in am-ulets or charms, which are worn by most Palestinian peas-ants to ward off or to heal diseases." (Alexander Macal-ister, "Medicine," in James Orr, The International Standard Bible Encyclopedia, 117347-117366 (Kindle Edition); Os-nova)*

Again:

*"Medical care in biblical times frequently employed the use of different kinds of salves and ointments. Olive oil was used widely, either alone or as an ingredient in ointments. The use of oil for the treatment of wounds is mentioned in Isa. 1:6 and Luke 10:34. Oil also became a symbol of medi-cine, and its use was coupled with prayer for the ill (Mark 6:13; James 5:14). Herbs and various products obtained from many different plants were among the most popular of ancient medicines. These were applied to the body as a poultice, or, in many cases, taken by mouth. Frankincense and myrrh—gum resins obtained from trees—were com-monly used to treat a variety of diseases, although their*

*main use was in perfumes and incense. Wine was com-*
*monly thought to have medicinal value. One of its uses was*
*to alleviate pain and discomfort. Wine, mixed with gall and*
*myrrh, was offered to Jesus prior to His crucifixion, but He*
*refused to drink it (Matt. 27:34; Mark 15:23). Wine also*
*was used to sooth stomach and intestinal disorders (1 Tim.*
*5:23) and to treat a variety of other physical problems. Beer*
*was also widely used as an ingredient in several medicines,*
*especially by the Babylonians....When Leah suffered a tem-*
*porary period of sterility, she sent her son, Reuben, to the*
*field to obtain mandrakes. Her barren sister, Rachel, also*
*asked for some of the mandrakes (Gen. 30:9-24). The root*
*of the mandrake was widely used in the ancient world to*
*promote conception, although there is no reason to believe*
*it was truly effective. It was also used as a narcotic." (Ken-*
*neth Eakins, "Diseases," in Holman Illustrated Bible Diction-*
*ary,14729-14755 (Kindle Edition); Nashville, TN: Holman*
*Reference)*

The writer of Proverbs teaches us about the importance of alcohol as a remedy for those who are suffering (physically and mentally):

*Proverbs 31:6-8-6 Give strong drink to him who is perishing,*
*And wine to those who are bitter of heart. 7 Let him drink*
*and forget his poverty, And remember his misery no more. 8*
*Open your mouth for the speechless, In the cause of all who*
*are appointed to die.*

When Jesus told the story of the Good Samaritan, He instructed
us about the important medicinal use of drugs:

*Luke 10:34—So he went to him and bandaged his wounds,*
*pouring on oil and wine; and he set him on his own animal,*

*brought him to an inn, and took care of him.*

The Samaritan used oils and wines to bring healing to the man who had been injured.

When Paul wrote to Timothy, he instructed him about the importance of using medicine:

*1 Timothy 5:23—No longer drink only water, but use a little wine for your stomach's sake and your frequent infirmities.*

I believe these words from the apocryphal book Wisdom Of Sirach are helpful here:

*Sirach 38:1-2, 4-8, 12-15-""Honor the physician with the honor due him, according to your need of him, for the Lord created him; for healing comes from the Most High, and he will receive a gift from the king... The Lord created medicines from the earth, and a sensible man will not despise them. Was not water made sweet with a tree in order that his power might be known? And he gave skill to men that he might be glorified in his marvelous works. By them he heals and takes away pain; the pharmacist makes of them a compound. His works will never be finished; and from him health is upon the face of the earth... And give the physician his place, for the Lord created him; let him not leave you, for there is need of him. There is a time when success lies in the hands of physicians, for they too will pray to the Lord that he should grant them success in diagnosis and in healing, for the sake of preserving life. He who sins before his Maker, may he fall into the care of a physician."*

In a future chapter, we will look at the use of medicines in helping addicts in much greater detail.

## The Environmental Roots Of Addiction

Another root of addiction is environmental factors. It is a well-known fact that a person's environment may be a powerful factor in regards to their struggle with addiction. We realize this from Scripture, and of course also from science.

The Bible provides many examples of how environmental factors can lead a person down a dangerous path. The first example in the Bible of sin among humanity was a direct result of our parents allowing themselves to be influenced by environmental factors. God had placed a tree in the Garden of Eden that Adam and Eve were not supposed to partake of-for in the day that they ate of it, they would die (Genesis 2:14-17). That tree was necessary for allowing Adam and Eve the freedom to choose good from evil. One author has well said:

> *"I used to be very angry with God about that tree. Tempting them like that? It was only a matter of time before they wouldn't be able to restrain themselves. And then what? He blames them ? How long did God expect they would make it before, to their ears, the "you can eat everything but that one tree" became "you can eat everything but that one tree"?...I have come to appreciate the risk of that tree for God— and the necessity of that tree for us. Simply put, that tree made us real: it gave us choice. God wasn't looking to make some complicated hamsters that he could set up in a sweet cage. He created us for real relationship with him. Real relationship simply cannot exist if you cannot choose something else other than that relationship. We pity a woman whose husband or boyfriend keeps her locked in their house, monitors the few phone calls he allows her to have, and keeps even her family at arm's*

*length. No one would call that love. Had God not offered the tree and with it the opportunity to rebel against him, he would have been that guy. Love that isn't chosen is forced. In giving us that tree and making the warning very clear, he gave us choice, even the option to reject his guidance and companionship. He knew very well that decision would cost him dearly, but it was what was best for us."* (Jim Pace, *Should We Fire God? Finding Hope In God When We Don't Understand,* 829-842 (Kindle Edition); New York, NY; FaithWords Hachette Book Group)

Yes, that tree was meant to be a blessing! Yet Adam and Eve chose to use it for evil. Notice where the Bible indicates where they were when they were tempted:

---

*Genesis 3:1-6—Now the serpent was more cunning than any beast of the field which the LORD God had made. And he said to the woman, "Has God indeed said, 'You shall not eat of every tree of the garden'?" And the woman said to the serpent, "We may eat the fruit of the trees of the garden; but of the fruit of the tree which is in the midst of the garden, God has said, 'You shall not eat it, nor shall you touch it, lest you die.' ". Then the serpent said to the woman, "You will not surely die. For God knows that in the day you eat of it your eyes will be opened, and you will be like God, knowing good and evil." So when the woman saw that the tree was good for food, that it was pleasant to the eyes, and a tree desirable to make one wise, she took of its fruit and ate. She also gave to her husband with her, and he ate.*

---

Notice that the woman saw that the tree was good for food, that it was pleasant to the eyes, and a tree desirable to make one wise. What is the implication? She is right there near the tree!

Again, she took of its fruit and ate. Adam and Eve didn't need to hightail it back to the Tree of Knowledge! They stretched out their hand and ate from it!

What's the point?

Adam and Eve had chosen to be in the environment where they would be vulnerable to sin. Not only that, but they had chosen to listen to the wrong person-Satan himself!

In the same way, we are reminded about King David's terrible fall from grace in 2 Samuel 11. In that passage, David chose to commit adultery with Bathsheba (it is even possible that he raped her). Later, when it was discovered that she was pregnant with his child, David summoned her husband Uriah the Hittite back from the front lines where he was stationed in fighting with the Philistines. David wanted Uriah to get drunk and sleep with his wife in the hopes that people would think the child was Uriah's and not his. When this failed, David had Uriah murdered!

Now, how did the whole terrible mess begin?

---

*2 Samuel 11:1-3—It happened in the spring of the year, at the time when kings go out to battle, that David sent Joab and his servants with him, and all Israel; and they destroyed the people of Ammon and besieged Rabbah. But David remained at Jerusalem. Then it happened one evening that David arose from his bed and walked on the roof of the king's house. And from the roof he saw a woman bathing, and the woman was very beautiful to behold. So David sent and inquired about the woman. And someone said, "Is this not Bathsheba, the daughter of Eliam, the wife of Uriah the Hittite?"*

---

David had chosen to be in the wrong place, at the wrong time.

His choice of environment led him to downfall and ruin.

And many other examples from Scripture could be cited! The point is that our environment has a huge impact on our decisions and actions. This certainly is true also in the situations of many addicts. Perhaps the greatest example of this may be seen in what in known as "Rat Park."

> *"As I said earlier, the strongest evidence for the pharmaceutical theory of addiction had, for years, been a series of experiments on rats. A famous advertisement that ran on U.S. TV in the 1980s, paid for by the Partnership for a Drug-Free America, explained it best. It shows a rat in close-up licking at a water bottle, as the narrator says: "Only one drug is so addictive, nine out of ten laboratory rats will use it. And use it. And use it. Until dead. It's called cocaine. And it can do the same thing to you." The rat runs about manically, then—as promised by the scary music—drops dead. Similar rat experiments had been run to prove the addictiveness of heroin and other drugs. But when Bruce looked at these experiments, he noticed something. These rats had been put in an empty cage. They were all alone, with no toys, and no activities, and no friends. There was nothing for them to do but to take the drug. What, he wondered, if the experiment was run differently? With a few of his colleagues, he built two sets of homes for laboratory rats. In the first home, they lived as they had in the original experiments, in solitary confinement, isolated except for their fix. But then he built a second home: a paradise for rats. Within its plywood walls, it contained everything a rat could want—there were wheels and colored balls and the best food, and other rats to hang out with and have sex with. He called it Rat Park. In these experiments, both sets of rats had access to a pair of drinking bottles. The first bottle contained only water. The other bottle contained morphine—*

*an opiate that rats process in a similar way to humans and that behaves just like heroin when it enters their brains. At the end of each day, Bruce or a member of his team would weigh the bottles to see how much the rats had chosen to take opiates, and how much they had chosen to stay sober. What they discovered was startling. It turned out that the rats in isolated cages used up to 25 milligrams of morphine a day, as in the earlier experiments. But the rats in the happy cages used hardly any morphine at all—less than 5 milligrams. "These guys [in Rat Park] have a complete total twenty-four-hour supply" of morphine, Bruce said, "and they don't use it." They don't kill themselves. They choose to spend their lives doing other things. So the old experiments were, it seemed, wrong. It isn't the drug that causes the harmful behavior—it's the environment. An isolated rat will almost always become a junkie. A rat with a good life almost never will, no matter how many drugs you make available to him. As Bruce put it: he was realizing that addiction isn't a disease. Addiction is an adaptation. It's not you—it's the cage you live in. Bruce and his colleagues kept tweaking the experiment, to see just how much your environment shapes your chemical compulsions. He took a set of rats and made them drink the morphine solution for fifty-seven days, in their cage, alone. If drugs can hijack your brain, that will definitely do it. Then he put these junkies into Rat Park. Would they carry on using compulsively, even when their environment improved? Had the drug taken them over? In Rat Park, the junkie rats seemed to have some twitches of withdrawal—but quite quickly, they stopped drinking the morphine. A happy social environment, it seemed, freed them of their addiction. In Rat Park, Bruce writes, "nothing that we tried instilled a strong appetite for morphine or produced anything that looked to us like addiction."" (Johann Hari, Chasing the Scream: The Inspiration for the Feature Film "The United States vs. Billie*

*Holiday" (The Opposite of Addiction is Connection), 171-172 (Kindle Edition); New York, NY: Bloomsbury)*

Environment is thus shown to be one of the greatest factors of addiction.

## The Traumatic Roots Of Addiction

Many addicts turn to drugs for comfort in an effort to medicate themselves from some pain or trauma which they endured.

> *"History of trauma and adverse experiences. Some people turn to substance use to cope with the ongoing psychological impact of traumatic events, either recent or in the distant past. Many survivors of trauma—especially deliberate trauma at the hands of others—live life with a deep sense of insecurity and mistrust. They don't view the world as a safe place, and they put up walls that prevent closeness with other people. Their pain and haunting memories are a source of deep anger and resentment, which is understandable, given that life has been so unfair. Some experience intrusive thoughts and memories of their trauma, including nightmares and flashbacks, which keeps the pain fresh. These haunting memories, and the assortment of negative feelings (such as anger, guilt, injustice, fear, anxiety, and shame) become a daily source of pain and unhappiness for them, and they may find temporary relief through substance use to be a welcome break from their tortured thoughts and feelings. The condition known as post-traumatic stress disorder (PTSD) has become a household name because of its life-disrupting symptoms. Given the severity of the psychological symptoms of PTSD, it's not surprising that there's a very high association between PTSD and addiction. There's very little medical science can do to heal PTSD, so affected people are prone to seeking refuge in*

*drugs or alcohol. True PTSD isn't nearly as common as people would believe by the amount that the term is bandied about; in fact, only about 20% of people who experience severe trauma will go on to develop PTSD. However, people don't have to develop full-out PTSD or even experience severe trauma to develop significant disruptive and painful symptoms related to past experiences that elevate their risk of addiction. Significant trauma may not be from just from one horrible event, but may result from a pattern of events over time. For example, being bullied in school over a prolonged period of time, being subjected to repeated workplace harassment, living in poverty, or being neglected over an entire childhood can cause the same psychological trauma as can a single significant event. What matters is how it affects the individual's thoughts and feelings, not the specifics of the trauma. Identifying and confronting past trauma is a significant part of addiction therapy, so that the individuals will no longer be attracted to "escape and avoidance." Too, we must recognize that living through addiction is, in itself, a deeply traumatic experience. It destroys self-esteem, self-confidence, and disrupts normal brain function. It's associated with great loss: material wealth, employment, family and friends, health, and happiness. It's a miserable and prolonged experience, a struggle of a lifetime." (Andrew Proulx MD, Understanding and Helping an Addict (and keeping your sanity), 18-19 (Kindle Edition): Recovery Folio Publishing)*

The research documented here is fascinating in demonstrating that the environmental factors of addiction are extremely powerful.

## The Spiritual Roots Of Addiction

There is a powerful case to be made for the way that a person's viewpoint of God shapes his decisions in regard to how he chooses to deal with the issue of drugs. Simply stated, many people who choose to use drugs do so out of a sense of spiritual confusion, depression, hopelessness, and doubt. Our culture has so de-emphasized the reality of the spiritual that it has left a huge void in the lives of many people. The issue of God's existence and nature is so paramount to every choice and action of our lives that we often do not even realize this connection. Blanchard points out:

> *"It has often been said that the most important questions anyone could ever ask are: 'Who am I?', 'Why am I here?' and 'Where am I going?' As they deal with the issues of a person's identity, meaning and destiny, they are obviously of great significance, but even these are secondary when put alongside one which is both fundamental and inescapable: 'Does God exist?' This is the question, and every debate about human life and death, and about the universe in which humanity lives and dies, ultimately revolves around it. Several years ago, Encyclopaedia Britannica published a set of fifty-four volumes marshalling the writings of many eminent thinkers in the Western world on the most important ideas that have been studied and investigated over the centuries. The subjects covered included law, science, philosophy, history and theology; the longest essay of all was on the subject of God. Addressing the question as to why this should be the case, co-editor Mortimer Adler wrote, 'More consequences for thought and action follow from the affirmation or denial of God than from answering any other question.' 1 The outstanding Latvian philosopher Isaiah Berlin, who died in 1997, elaborated the point in his book Concepts and Categories: The world of a man who believes that God created him for a specific purpose, that he has an immortal soul, that there is an afterlife in which his sins will be visited upon him, is radically different from the*

*world of a man who believes in none of these things; and the reasons for action, the moral codes, the political beliefs, the tastes, the personal relationships of the former will deeply and systematically differ from those of the latter. Men's views of one another will differ profoundly as a very consequence of their general conception of the world: the notions of cause and purpose, good and evil, freedom and slavery, things and persons, rights, duties, laws, justice, truth, falsehood, to take some central ideas completely at random, depend entirely upon the general framework within which they form, as it were, nodal points. 2 If Adler and Berlin are right, looking into the subject addressed in this book is hardly a trivial pursuit. Those who disagree over the question of God's existence are not merely crossing paper swords over some interesting but ultimately irrelevant point of science, philosophy or theology. They are disagreeing over the greatest issue of all." (John Blanchard, Does God Believe in Atheists? 240-266 (Kindle Edition): Carlisle, PA: EP Books USA)*

One of the most powerful factors of addiction stems from these questions and issues that addicts struggle with. As Christians, one of the most important aspects of our ministry (to everyone) is defending the Christian faith. As I have noted elsewhere:

*"God has declared: Isaiah 1:18—Come now, and let us reason together," Says the LORD, "Though your sins are like scarlet, They shall be as white as snow; Though they are red like crimson, They shall be as wool. Notice how God calls upon people to "reason" together. This reminds me of what the Apostle Paul said about "rationality." When he was presenting a defense of Christianity, Paul was accused of being "mad" by the Jewish high priest Festus (Acts 26:24). Paul responded: Acts 26:25—But he said, "I am not mad, most noble Festus, but speak the words of truth and*

*reason. The word translated as "reason" in the NKJV is the Greek sophrosunē, which has an interesting meaning of that which is logical and rational.[ 2] Paul wants us to understand that Christianity is not based upon "insanity," but rather on "sober truth." This is especially interesting when we consider that throughout the New Testament, the Apostles and early Christians were seen as those who often "reasoned" with their unbelieving neighbors. Acts 17:2—Then Paul, as his custom was, went in to them, and for three Sabbaths reasoned with them from the Scriptures, Acts 17:17—Therefore he reasoned in the synagogue with the Jews and with the Gentile worshipers, and in the marketplace daily with those who happened to be there. Acts 18:4—And he reasoned in the synagogue every Sabbath, and persuaded both Jews and Greeks. Acts 18:19—And he came to Ephesus, and left them there; but he himself entered the synagogue and reasoned with the Jews. Acts 19:8-9—And he went into the synagogue and spoke boldly for three months, reasoning and persuading concerning the things of the kingdom of God. But when some were hardened and did not believe, but spoke evil of the Way before the multitude, he departed from them and withdrew the disciples, reasoning daily in the school of Tyrannus. Acts 24:12—And they neither found me in the temple disputing with anyone nor inciting the crowd, either in the synagogues or in the city. Acts 24:25—Now as he reasoned about righteousness, self-control, and the judgment to come, Felix was afraid and answered, "Go away for now; when I have a convenient time I will call for you." The word translated in these passages is dialegomai, and Mounce reminds us about the important implications of this word for every Christian: "If we are to emulate Paul's preaching and teaching, we must do much more than just talk. dialegomai involves preaching and teaching that harnesses reason and logic into a defensive and positive exposition of God's Word to persuade and edify." (William D. Mounce (General Editor, Mounce's Complete Expository Dictionary of Old and New Testament Words, 1103 (Kindle Edition); Grand Rapids, Michigan; Zondervan) This shows us that the Christian is to be prepared to show logical and rational evidences to his friends and neighbors." (Mark Tabata, Old Apologetics for a New Age: Volume One: The Existence of God, 5-7 (Kindle Edition): Charleston, AR: Cobb Publishing)*

This means that the Christian must spend time preparing himself adequately to help the addict with issues and questions of faith that will arise. At the end of this volume, I will provide you with many evidences that will be helpful for you in ministering to the addict regarding these and related subjects.

## **The Demonic Roots Of Addiction**

Here, we enter into one of the roots of addiction which some in the churches of Christ are uncomfortable in acknowledging and preparing themselves for. This is due in large part to the erroneous and seemingly widespread belief among many in our churches that Satan, fallen angels, and demons are somehow locked away in Hades until the Second Coming. Simply stated, the Bible does not teach this and-as we will see-it teaches that these forces are still at large and at work in the world of man today. Furthermore, we will notice that these demonic forces sometimes play a role in the suffering and struggles of addicts in one form or another.

Let's start by noticing that the forces of darkness are indeed still at work in the world today. Some believe that the words of Zechariah the Prophet claim that these forces were "locked up" when Jesus died.

*Zechariah 13:1-2—In that day a fountain shall be opened*

*for the house of David and for the inhabitants of Jerusalem, for sin and for uncleanness. "It shall be in that day," says the LORD of hosts, "that I will cut off the names of the idols from the land, and they shall no longer be remembered. I will also cause the prophets and the unclean spirit to depart from the land.*

Let's notice the words of author Timothy Packer regarding this text of Scripture:

*"Zechariah 13:1-2—In that day a fountain shall be opened for the house of David and for the inhabitants of Jerusalem, for sin and for uncleanness. "It shall be in that day," says the LORD of hosts, "that I will cut off the names of the idols from the land, and they shall no longer be remembered. I will also cause the prophets and the unclean spirit to depart from the land. It is often claimed that the phrase "in that day" is a reference to the day that Jesus died on the cross, and that the "unclean spirit" (a reference to demonic spirits it is argued) would be forced to depart from the land on that day. However, even a cursory study of this passage shows several problems with such an approach. First is the interpretation of "in that day" as a reference to the day of Christ's death (or, as argued by some, to the day of Pentecost). When we study the phrase "in that day" throughout Zechariah, we learn that the reference may be to several things, depending on the context. Let's notice every example of "in that day" in Zechariah. Zechariah 2:11—Many nations shall be joined to the LORD in that day, and they shall become My people. And I will dwell in your midst. Then you will know that the LORD of hosts has sent Me to you. This refers to the events of the First Coming and the Christian Age. The prophecy of "many nations" being joined to the Lord and becoming His people began to be*

*fulfilled on Pentecost of Acts chapter 2. During the Christian Age, the people of God are all those from every nation who turn to the Lord. Acts 2:38-39—Then Peter said to them, "Repent, and let every one of you be baptized in the name of Jesus Christ for the remission of sins; and you shall receive the gift of the Holy Spirit. For the promise is to you and to your children, and to all who are afar off, as many as the Lord our God will call." Zechariah 3:10—In that day,' says the LORD of hosts, 'Everyone will invite his neighbor Under his vine and under his fig tree.' " This applies to the events of the First Coming and continues on throughout the Christian Age. Notice that in context, these events occur when the iniquity of God's people is removed. Zechariah 3:1-4—Then he showed me Joshua the high priest standing before the Angel of the LORD, and Satan standing at his right hand to oppose him. And the LORD said to Satan, "The LORD rebuke you, Satan! The LORD who has chosen Jerusalem rebuke you! Is this not a brand plucked from the fire?" Now Joshua was clothed with filthy garments, and was standing before the Angel. Then He answered and spoke to those who stood before Him, saying, "Take away the filthy garments from him." And to him He said, "See, I have removed your iniquity from you, and I will clothe you with rich robes." Joshua and his companions were a 'sign' for what was to come to pass during the Christian Age. The Angel of the Lord is Old Testament phraseology for Jesus in his preincarnate Form, 33 and He is able to provide forgiveness of sins to His people. Zechariah 3:8-9—Hear, O Joshua, the high priest, You and your companions who sit before you, For they are a wondrous sign; For behold, I am bringing forth My Servant the BRANCH. For behold, the stone That I have laid before Joshua: Upon the stone are seven eyes. Behold, I will engrave its inscription,' Says the LORD of hosts, 'And I will remove the iniquity of that land in one day. Throughout the Old Testament, the phrase "the*

*BRANCH" was a prophetic title of the Messiah, Who would be the Offspring of David (cf. Isaiah 11:1-2). "However, another medieval Jewish sage, David Kimchi (Radak) took the messianic interpretation, following the most ancient sources, such as Targum Jonathan (see below), saying the day described is when "the Messiah, son of David, will arrive." Additionally, the sages employed the messianic term ṣemaḥ to the concept of resurrection and salvation (acts envisioned for the Messiah in the end of days) in the daily prayer: "You are a king who causes death and resurrects, and you make salvation sprout forth (ṣemaḥ). Blessed are you LORD, who resurrects the dead" (Amidah 2)... Although the nominal use of the term ṣemaḥ is the first usage in the biblical text, the use of the noun appears in a third-century BC Phoenician document from Cyprus with reference to a legitimate royal heir. While this foreign usage may not have influenced Isaiah's terminology, it demonstrates, as Smith observes, "that this imagery was an appropriate term to represent the appearance of a new king in the ancient Near Eastern world." 2 The verbal use, in a messianic context, occurred some 300 years earlier. However, the verbal use of the root ṣmḥ appears in the record of King David's last words in 2Sm 23:5: "Will He [God] not make spring forth (Hb. yaṣmîaḥ) my salvation?" (author's translation). This statement is like that concerning David (probably written by Solomon) 3 in Ps 132:17 (NASB): "There I will cause the horn of David to spring forth (' aṣmîaḥ); I have prepared a lamp for Mine anointed (mešîḥî)." It seems that the psalmist understood David having connected the concept of "springing forth" with the coming of the Messiah from the line of David." (J. Randall Price, "The Branch Of The Lord In The Messianic Age," in Michael Rydelnik & Edwin Blum, The Moody Handbook of Messianic Prophecy: Studies and Expositions of the Messiah in the Old Testament, 803-804 (Kindle Edition); Chicago, IL; Moody*

*Publishers) So again, this prophecy applies to the First Coming and the Christian Age. Please notice that these events began on Pentecost of Acts 2, but did not stop there. They continue on, even today, so that whenever one is saved the blood of the Messiah is applied! Zechariah 9:16—The LORD their God will save them in that day, As the flock of His people. For they shall be like the jewels of a crown, Lifted like a banner over His land—The events of this passage refer to the First Coming and the entire Christian Age. This is made clear because in context, Zechariah contains a Messianic prophecy which was fulfilled during the First Coming of Christ. Zechariah 9:9—Rejoice greatly, O daughter of Zion! Shout, O daughter of Jerusalem! Behold, your King is coming to you; He is just and having salvation, Lowly and riding on a donkey, A colt, the foal of a donkey. Matthew 21:4-7—All this was done that it might be fulfilled which was spoken by the prophet, saying: "TELL THE DAUGHTER OF ZION, 'BEHOLD, YOUR KING IS COMING TO YOU, LOWLY, AND SITTING ON A DONKEY, A COLT, THE FOAL OF A DONKEY.' ". So the disciples went and did as Jesus commanded them. They brought the donkey and the colt, laid their clothes on them, and set Him on them. Again: Zechariah 12:3, 4, 6, 8, 9, 11—And it shall happen in that day that I will make Jerusalem a very heavy stone for all peoples; all who would heave it away will surely be cut in pieces, though all nations of the earth are gathered against it.. In that day," says the LORD, "I will strike every horse with confusion, and its rider with madness; I will open My eyes on the house of Judah, and will strike every horse of the peoples with blindness...—In that day I will make the governors of Judah like a firepan in the woodpile, and like a fiery torch in the sheaves; they shall devour all the surrounding peoples on the right hand and on the left, but Jerusalem shall be inhabited again in her own place—Jerusalem...—In that day the LORD will defend the inhabitants of Jerusalem; the*

*one who is feeble among them in that day shall be like Da-
vid, and the house of David shall be like God, like the Angel
of the LORD before them. ...—It shall be in that day that I
will seek to destroy all the nations that come against Jerusalem....—In that day there shall be a great mourning in Jerusalem, like the mourning at Hadad Rimmon in the plain
of Megiddo.* This prophecy is truly remarkable in that it
takes into account the time frame of the First Coming, the
Christian Age, and even up to the Second Coming! Notice
specifically: "Zechariah 12:10-14—*And I will pour on the
house of David and on the inhabitants of Jerusalem the
Spirit of grace and supplication; then they will look on Me
whom they pierced. Yes, they will mourn for Him as one
mourns for his only son, and grieve for Him as one grieves
for a firstborn. In that day there shall be a great mourning
in Jerusalem, like the mourning at Hadad Rimmon in the
plain of Megiddo. And the land shall mourn, every family
by itself: the family of the house of David by itself, and their
wives by themselves; the family of the house of Nathan by
itself, and their wives by themselves; the family of the
house of Levi by itself, and their wives by themselves; the
family of Shimei by itself, and their wives by themselves; all
the families that remain, every family by itself, and their
wives by themselves.* Zechariah 12:10 itself is applied to
both the First and the Second Coming in the New Testament. John 19:34-37—*But one of the soldiers pierced His
side with a spear, and immediately blood and water came
out. And he who has seen has testified, and his testimony
is true; and he knows that he is telling the truth, so that you
may believe. For these things were done that the Scripture
should be fulfilled, "NOT ONE OF HIS BONES SHALL BE BRO-
KEN." And again another Scripture says, "THEY SHALL LOOK
ON HIM WHOM THEY PIERCED."* The same prophecy is also
applied by John to the Second Coming. Revelation 1:7—*Behold, He is coming with clouds, and every eye will see Him,*

*even they who pierced Him. And all the tribes of the earth will mourn because of Him. Even so, Amen. What is especially interesting is the type of "mourning" that takes place. It has primary reference to the mourning that takes place when people repent of their sin and turn to the Lord for salvation. This is made evident when we consider the rest of the wording of Zechariah 12:10. "Let me, while dwelling on the Jewish interpretation of this passage, reproduce a striking passage from Alshech, which, barring the mention of Messiah ben Joseph, might almost be accepted as a statement of the Christian view of this scripture. "I will do yet a third thing, and that is, that 'they shall look unto Me,' for they shall lift up their eyes unto Me in perfect repentance, when they see Him whom they pierced, that is, Messiah, the Son of Joseph; for our Rabbis, of blessed memory, have said that He will take upon Himself all the guilt of Israel, and shall then be slain in the war to make an atonement in such manner that it shall be accounted as if Israel had pierced Him, for on account of their sin He has died; and, therefore, in order that it may be reckoned to them as a perfect atonement, they will repent and look to the blessed One, saying that there is none beside Him to forgive those that mourn on account of Him who died for their sin: this is the meaning of 'They shall look upon Me.'"" (David Baron, Zechariah: A Commentary on His Visions & Prophecies, 5290-5299 (Kindle Edition): Northfield, Chorley Wood, Herts.) There are also references here to events that took place during the Christian Age. Notice in Zechariah 12:6 there is reference to Jerusalem being inhabited "again." This is significant because Zechariah and the Jews were already living in Jerusalem, having returned from exile in Babylon. There is thus an indicator that Jerusalem would again be devastated, and the Jews brought back another time. In A.D. 70 the Roman Empire destroyed the city of Jerusalem and the Jewish people were removed, being dispersed throughout the world. Then, in 1948, the city of Jerusalem was again rebuilt and the Jewish state was reestablished. Zechariah 13:1-4—In that day a fountain shall be opened for the house of David and for the inhabitants of Jerusalem, for sin and for uncleanness. "It shall be in that day," says the LORD of hosts, "that I will cut off the names of the idols from the land, and they shall no longer be remembered. I will also cause the prophets and the unclean spirit to depart from the land. It shall come to pass that if anyone still prophesies, then his father and mother who begot him will say to him, 'You shall not live, because you have spoken lies in the name of the LORD.' And his father and mother who begot him shall thrust him through when he prophesies. "And it shall be in that day that every prophet will be ashamed of his vision when he prophesies; they will not wear a robe of coarse hair to deceive. The events of this text (like those in chapter 13) describe the entire Christian Age, beginning with the First Coming and concluding with the Second Coming. The fountain opened for sin and uncleanness is reference to Jesus' atoning death on Calvary, and the "fountain" that was there made for sinners to be redeemed. This is made especially clear in verse 7. Zechariah 13:7—Awake, O sword, against My Shepherd, Against the Man who is My Companion," Says the LORD of hosts. "Strike the Shepherd, And the sheep will be scattered; Then I will turn My hand against the little ones. The New Testament applies this to the First Coming of Christ. Mark 14:27—Then Jesus said to them, "All of you will be made to stumble because of Me this night, for it is written: 'I WILL STRIKE THE SHEPHERD, AND THE SHEEP WILL BE SCATTERED.' The reference to the Man Who is the Companion of Yahweh is especially interesting. It had the meaning of Someone Who was of the same Nature as Yahweh, and His Friend. Thus we see an intimacy between Yahweh and the Companion. "Second, as mentioned above, the smitten shepherd is identified as "My associate" (v. 7). He is associated with YHWH (" the LORD"). The Hebrew term geber 'amiti (" the man close to me") implies one united to another by possession of common nature, rights, and privileges. The only other use of this term is in the priestly context of Leviticus (Lv 18:20; 19:11, 15, 17; 24:19; 25:14-15, 17) where it has the idea of neighbor, fellow, associate, or companion, and is closely related to the word 'ah (" brother"), such as in Lv 19:17; 25:14. J. Baldwin defines this as one "who stands next to me," indicating essentially an equal. 16 In all of the early Christian discussions of this passage, the shepherd has a positive function as the one who is on God's side. 17 The Targum translates Zch 13:7 as: "O sword, be revealed against the king and against the prince his companion who is his equal, who is like him ..." indicating the two figures share a royal connection. The shepherd is often used as a figure of the ruling king, as in 1Kg 22:17 where the prophet Micaiah predicts that the absence of the king would result in the sheep (Israel) being scattered on the mountains. The historical interpretation therefore understands this "associate" as a member of the failing Davidic dynasty (Zerubbabel or Elnathan). However, James Smith contends, "It is not likely that God would apply this epithet even to the most godly among men whom He might appoint as shepherd over the nation. Only one man could be denominated God's equal, and that is the Messiah." 18 Since this equates the Lord who struck the shepherd with the shepherd himself, the only shepherd that would qualify would be a divine Messiah. This identification is appropriate biblically (cf. Isa 9:6-7; Jer 23:6; Dan 7:13; Pss 45:6-7; 110:1). In theological terms, the shepherd is a man, but he is also deity, and such a person could only be the God-man, the Lord Jesus (cf. Jn 1:1; 8:58; 14:9-10; 17:24; Rm 10:13; Col 2:9; Ti 2:13; Rev 1:8; 22:12-13 with Isa 44:6)." (J. Randall Price, "The Striking Of The Shepherd King," in Michael*

*Rydelnik, Edwin Blum, The Moody Handbook of Messianic Prophecy: Studies and Expositions of the Messiah in the Old Testament, 1306-1307 (Kindle Edition): Chicago, IL: Moody Publishers) This passage refers to events that would take place during the Christian Age, including the ending of the miraculous gift of prophecy. The Apostle Paul says this took place when the Word of God was completed and the New Testament Scriptures were brought to fruition (1 Corinthians 13:8-10). The text of Zechariah 13 goes on to describe the way that the city of Jerusalem would be destroyed, which took place with the Roman siege in A.D. 70. Zechariah 14:4, 6, 8, 9, 13, 20, 21—And in that day His feet will stand on the Mount of Olives, Which faces Jerusalem on the east. And the Mount of Olives shall be split in two, From east to west, Making a very large valley; Half of the mountain shall move toward the north And half of it toward the south.... 6—It shall come to pass in that day That there will be no light; The lights will diminish.... 8—And in that day it shall be—That living waters shall flow from Jerusalem, Half of them toward the eastern sea And half of them toward the western sea; In both summer and winter it shall occur. 9—And the LORD shall be King over all the earth. In that day it shall be "The LORD is one," And His name one... 13— It shall come to pass in that day That a great panic from the LORD will be among them. Everyone will seize the hand of his neighbor, And raise his hand against his neighbor's hand;... 20—In that day "HOLINESS TO THE LORD" shall be engraved on the bells of the horses. The pots in the LORD's house shall be like the bowls before the altar. 21—Yes, every pot in Jerusalem and Judah shall be holiness to the LORD of hosts. Everyone who sacrifices shall come and take them and cook in them. In that day there shall no longer be a Canaanite in the house of the LORD of hosts. Finally, we have reference here in Zechariah again to the events of the Christian Age, beginning with the First Coming and continuing through to the Second Coming. Notice the reference in Zechariah 14 to the "living water." Zechariah 14:8—And in that day it shall be—That living waters shall flow from Jerusalem, Half of them toward the eastern sea And half of them toward the western sea; In both summer and winter it shall occur. The "living waters" is a reference to Jesus and the Holy Spirit. John 4:10—Jesus answered and said to her, "If you knew the gift of God, and who it is who says to you, 'Give Me a drink,' you would have asked Him, and He would have given you living water." John 4:14—but whoever drinks of the water that I shall give him will never thirst. But the water that I shall give him will become in him a fountain of water springing up into everlasting life." John 7:38-39—He who believes in Me, as the Scripture has said, out of his heart will flow rivers of living water." But this He spoke concerning the Spirit, whom those believing in Him would receive; for the Holy Spirit was not yet given, because Jesus was not yet glorified. The nations gathered together against Jerusalem (Zechariah 14:1-3) were fulfilled when Rome destroyed the city in 70 A.D. Yet there will be a day when the Lord returns. Notice the reference to His Second Coming in Zechariah 14. Zechariah 14:6-7—It shall come to pass in that day That there will be no light; The lights will diminish. It shall be one day Which is known to the LORD Neither day nor night. But at evening time it shall happen That it will be light. Jesus described this Day of the Second Coming, known only to the Father: Matthew 24:36—But of that day and hour no one knows, not even the angels of heaven, but My Father only. Mark 13:32—But of that day and hour no one knows, not even the angels in heaven, nor the Son, but only the Father. Thus, the phrase "in that day" in Zechariah 13:2 has reference to what Jesus did on Calvary-but follows through to the end of the Christian Age! Therefore, if 'the unclean spirit" has reference to demonic spirits (more on that soon), it likely means that the unclean spirits will be continually removed from the land up till the time of the Second Coming. In other words, far from teaching that they 'were" removed when Jesus died on the cross, the passage is saying that they will continue to be removed from the land, beginning with His death and ending with His Second Coming! It is a process that will span the entire Christian Age. Second, notice the controversy over the phrase "the unclean spirit." There is a great deal of curiosity over the meaning of this particular phrase. Some believe that the phrase has reference to "sin," while others believe it references demonic spirits....The interpretation of "unclean spirit" as the general notion of sin is acknowledged in some of the ancient Jewish rabbinical commentators.34 However, with either interpretation, you have the same problem: the death of Christ did not bring a full end to sin, nor did His death at Calvary automatically force all demons out of the world (cf. Ephesians 6:12). Since demonic activity continued after the death of Jesus on the cross, and we are assured that in the New Testament it will continue throughout the end of the Christian Age (more on that soon), then whatever the "unclean spirit' is, it will continue throughout the end of the Christian Age. That is why interpreting Zechariah 13:1-2 in such a way that says demonic spirits were cast out of the Earth on the day Jesus died will not work. It will run into the same problems: The phrase "unclean spirit" may reference either the power of sin or demonic spirits: The phrase "in that day" stretches out the time frame between Jesus' death at Calvary all the way to the time of the Second Coming. For further confirmation of this point, notice that the passage also says that idols and false prophets will be cast "from the land" in "that day." When Jesus died on the cross, did that day immediately bring about the expulsion of all idols and false prophets from the world (cf. 2 Peter 2:1-2; 1 Corinthians 10:16-21)? To ask is to answer."*

(Timothy Packer, The Church of Christ Versus Ancient Powers of Darkness in Rural America, 189-203 (Kindle Edition): Ancient Words Press)

We need to realize that there are many demonic forces in the world today, and that these forces may operate through the plight of drug abuse. This is made evident in the Bible through two different ways.

## Familiar Spirits

The first way that demons may gain a foothold in a person is through what is referred to in the Bible as familiar spirits.

Throughout the Old Testament, we are told about creatures called "familiar spirits" (the Hebrew word *ob*).

What are familiar spirits?

To answer that, we must notice several things.

To begin with, let's notice all of the passages where the "familiar spirits" are mentioned.

---

*Leviticus 20:6—And the person who turns to mediums and familiar spirits, to prostitute himself with them, I will set My face against that person and cut him off from his people.*

*Leviticus 20:27-'A man or a woman who is a medium, or who has familiar spirits, shall surely be put to death; they shall stone them with stones. Their blood shall be upon them.' "*

*Deuteronomy 18:10-11—There shall not be found among you anyone who makes his son or his daughter pass through the fire, or one who practices witchcraft, or a soothsayer, or one who interprets omens, or a sorcerer, or one who conjures spells, or a medium, or a spiritist, or one who calls up the dead.*

*1 Samuel 28:3—Now Samuel had died, and all Israel had lamented for him and buried him in Ramah, in his own city. And Saul had put the mediums and the spiritists out of the land.*

*1 Samuel 28:7-9—Then Saul said to his servants, "Find me a woman who is a medium, that I may go to her and inquire of her." And his servants said to him, "In fact, there is a woman who is a medium at En Dor." So Saul disguised himself and put on other clothes, and he went, and two men with him; and they came to the woman by night. And he said, "Please conduct a síance for me, and bring up for me the one I shall name to you." Then the woman said to him, "Look, you know what Saul has done, how he has cut off the mediums and the spiritists from the land. Why then do you lay a snare for my life, to cause me to die?"*

*2 Kings 21:6—Also he made his son pass through the fire, practiced soothsaying, used witchcraft, and consulted spiritists and mediums. He did much evil in the sight of the LORD, to provoke Him to anger.*

*2 Kings 23:24—Moreover Josiah put away those who consulted mediums and spiritists, the household gods and idols, all the abominations that were seen in the land of Judah and in Jerusalem, that he might perform the words of the law which were written in the book that Hilkiah the priest found in the house of the LORD.*

*1 Chronicles 10:13—So Saul died for his unfaithfulness which he had committed against the LORD, because he did not keep the word of the LORD, and also because he consulted a medium for guidance.*

*2 Chronicles 33:6—Also he caused his sons to pass through the fire in the Valley of the Son of Hinnom; he practiced soothsaying, used witchcraft and sorcery, and consulted mediums and spiritists. He did much evil in the sight of the LORD, to provoke Him to anger.*

*Job 32:19—Indeed my belly is like wine that has no vent; It is ready to burst like new wineskins.*

*Isaiah 8:19—And when they say to you, "Seek those who are mediums and wizards, who whisper and mutter," should not a people seek their God? Should they seek the dead on behalf of the living?*

*Isaiah 19:3—The spirit of Egypt will fail in its midst; I will destroy their counsel, And they will consult the idols and the charmers, The mediums and the sorcerers.*

*Isaiah 29:4—You shall be brought down, You shall speak out of the ground; Your speech shall be low, out of the dust; Your voice shall be like a medium's, out of the ground; And your speech shall whisper out of the dust.*

---

First, let's notice the clues from these passages that "familiar spirits" are somehow connected with "the dead."

Nearly all of these passages connect "familiar spirits" with the dead. The most obvious example of this is in 1 Samuel 28, where Saul goes and consults a medium who raises up the "familiar spirit" of Samuel from the realm of Hades. Some deny that this medium was able to accomplish this: however, all of the passages that discuss mediums point out that they had the ability to summon the dead!

Since there is a clear connection between "mediums" and the spirits of the "dead," then it is clear that a "familiar spirit" had some connection with a deceased human being. We see this clearly again in Isaiah's passage and his use of Hebrew poetry to express his point:

---

*Isaiah 8:19—And when they say to you, "Seek those who are mediums and wizards, who whisper and mutter," should not a people seek their God? Should they seek the dead on behalf of the living?*

---

God is pointing out that the people were going to mediums for guidance, and not coming to Him. Then the Prophet shows us that going to a "medium" was the same as going to "the dead."

Second, a familiar spirit also had a connection at times with a spirit that was "familiar" to not only a person, but to a family. Indeed, the idea of a "familiar spirit" could include a spirit that had been passed down generationally within a family.

Scholar Merrill Unger points out:

*"The term "familiar" is applied to the foreboding demon,2 it would appear, because it was regarded by the English translators as a servant ("famulus"), belonging to the family ("familiaris"), who was on intimate terms with, and might readily be summoned by, the one possessing it. The significance of the Hebrew term is disputed. It is not impossible that it might be related to the Arabic root awaba ("to return"), with reference to the spirit who periodically comes back."" (Merrill F. Unger, Biblical Demonology: A Study of Spiritual Forces at Work Today, 144-145 (Kindle Edition): Grand Rapids, MI; Kregel Publications)*

So a familiar spirit could also have reference to a spirit that had been somehow handed down within a family line.

Kurt Koch points out:

> *"When a possessed person dies, the demon goes out and tries to enter another member of the family. Relatives of possessed persons are often themselves psychic, and so open to invasion by evil spirits. Sometimes a possessed person cannot die until the demon which has been inhabiting him has found another home. If one of these spirits succeeds in gaining possession of a grandchild, a certain family tradition is set up. A hypnotist who hypnotizes such a person back beyond his birth is in fact making contact with these family spirits, and it is from them that the knowledge about the ancestors is gained. This all sounds like an absurd construction. Even real Christians who have no experience of spirit possession, find it incredible and impossible to understand. But anyone, who has spent years counseling those who have come under occult influence, is familiar with such experiences. The fact that unbelieving, unregenerate psychiatrists, hypnotists, parapsychologists, and modernist theologians scoff at it does not invalidate the truth. It is significant that in various English translations of the Bible the term familiar spirits is used in Old Testament references to sorcery. Although this expression in its natural sense means intimate, well-known known spirits, it could also be taken in the original, literal sense of the word to mean spirits of the family. There are some families which are ruled for many years, even centuries, by such spirits. The evil spirits enjoy deceiving and misleading men and women. The "prenatal hypnotists" are without exception to be counted among their victims." (Kurt E. Koch, Occult ABC: Exposing Occult Practices and Ideologies, 311-320 (Kindle Edition); Grand Rapids, MI; Kregel Publications)*

Heiser goes into greater detail about the connection between familiar spirits and familial connections:

> *"3. "Spirits" ('ôb; plural: 'ōbôt, also 'ōbĕrîm [" those who have passed over"]) Some of the terminology for these fearful spirits derives from place names. For example, the geographical area that includes Oboth and Abarim in the Transjordan (Num 21:10–11; 33:43–48) was associated with ancient cults of the dead. These two place names mean, respectively, "spirits of the dead" and "those who have passed over [to the Netherworld]." 32 The Hebrew root '-b-r, behind the name Abarim, means "to cross over [from one side to another]," so the Qal participle 'ōbĕrîm means "those who cross over." Spronk notes that this participle "seems to have a special meaning in the context of the cult of the dead, denoting the spirits of the dead crossing the border between the land of the living and the world of the dead." 33 The Ugaritic parallels make this association clearly. The Ugaritic cognate of 'ōbĕrîm is 'brm found in KTU2 1.22 i: 15. In the Ugaritic text KTU2 1.22 describing a necromantic session, the king invokes the spirits of the dead (Rephaim) and celebrates a feast, probably the New Year Festival, with them. It is told that they came over traveling by horse-drawn chariots. As they are taking part in the meal served for them, they are explicitly called "those who came over." 34 The geographical associations with 'ōbĕrîm are evident in Ezekiel 39:11, which indicates the "Valley of the Travelers ['ōbĕrîm]" is "east of the sea" (ESV). According to Spronk, the sea "is probably the Dead Sea. So it was part of Transjordan. This is a region which shows many traces of ancient cults of the dead, such as the megalithic monuments called dolmens and place names referring to the dead and the netherworld, viz. Obot, Peor, and Abarim." 35 The Hebrew term "Oboth" ('ōbôt) likewise has an otherworldly overtone and is associated with the spirits*

*of the dead and those who worked to communicate with those departed spirits. Tropper explains that 'ôb is now more commonly understood to refer to the spirits of the dead, deriving the meaning from the Arabic cognate 'âba, "return." 36 Other possible etymologies suggest interpreting 'ôb "as 'hostile' (a derivation of the root 'yb 'to be an enemy'); or as 'ancestral.' "37 According to Tropper, those who argue for the meaning "ancestral" assume an etymological connection between 'ôb and 'āb "father, ancestor". The meaning "ancestral spirit" for 'ōb is based on a number of considerations. In the ancient Orient, necromancy was part of the Cult of the Ancestors. This essentially involved the invocation and interrogation of the dead patriarch from whom a family could seek advice and assistance. Several times in the OT, the Heb term 'ābôt "fathers", similar to 'ōbôt, designates dead ancestors. 38". (Michael S. Heiser, Demons: What the Bible Really Says About the Powers of Darkness, 15-16 (Kindle Edition): Bellingham, WA: Lexham Press)*

One young man that I worked with explained to me how his family had passed on a "familiar spirit" to him when a relative had died. Some of his kin were gathered at a funeral home where the deceased's body was being prepared, and they set him down beside the corpse. (At this time, he was a very young man, perhaps six or seven years old). He remembers-and others in his family have verified to him over the years -that as they performed the ceremony, "something" passed from the body of his deceased family member into him.

From that time forward, this "familiar spirit" has been with him. He said that it provided comfort for him in difficult and depressing days, but when the true Jesus was mentioned with any kind of seriousness or reverence, the spirit became infuriated. Indeed, it had been trying to convince the young man for most of

his life that he was antichrist! (I have seen these same lies per-
petrated by demonic spirits several times in my ministry).

Third, a "familiar spirit" could be termed such because it attempted to repeat the same cycle in the afflicted person as it
had in victims of the past.

People have often noticed that certain patterns seem to repeat
within families. Now of course, some of this may be due to genetics and environment (Genesis 3:17-19; 1 Corinthians 15:33).
However, a third possibility is the influence of familiar spirits.
Indeed, a "familiar spirit" may be termed such for this very reason!

> *"If you go to a doctor for a checkup, and it is your initial
> visit, you will likely be given a health questionnaire to fill
> out. The doctor wants to know what diseases, illnesses and
> vulnerabilities exist in your family history. Did your parents
> have diabetes? Has anyone had a heart attack? Is there a
> history of high blood pressure? Doctors do this because
> they know the propensity for these physical weaknesses to
> be passed on through the generations, right? Well, the
> same phenomenon is true in the realm of the spirit. If some-
> one in your family opened the door to the demonic through
> an iniquity, then demons can enter through that opening
> and travel down the family line. Even if you have never
> taken part in the particular sin that let the demons in, they
> can affect you and your children. This explains why we
> sometimes struggle in certain areas and cannot break free,
> or our children cannot break free, and we have no clue why.
> We simply cannot figure out if we did something to allow
> these things or to cause these things to happen. In many
> cases we are struggling with demonic personalities that
> have been living in our families for generations. These are
> also called "familiar spirits." They seem familiar, like an*

*unquestioned part of the family line, because they have been within the genealogy for years. Typical examples are spirits of unforgiveness, resentment, poverty, inferiority, judgment, condemnation, adultery, divorce, alcoholism, lust, lying, hate, anger, selfishness, doubt. Almost any type of demon can enter this way." (Rabbi K.A. Schneider, Self-Deliverance: How to Gain Victory over the Powers of Darkness, 315-324 (Kindle Edition); Grand Rapids, Michigan; Chosen Books)*

It is also important to realize here that the ones condemned in the Old Testament for "having" familiar spirits were actually the ones who were involved in willful sin by conjuring, communicating, and collaborating with these forces. Some people were just the victims of these vicious creatures, and were not therefore subject to the penalties described in these Scriptures.

Many claim that all such demonic activity is explained away by medicine and environment. These may account for some of the maladies that people experience (as noted above), but certainly not all of them.

Dr. Kenneth McAll was a physician who witnessed amazing examples of influence from familiar spirits in his mission work among the diseased and ravaged in China. Being skeptical that such spiritual and supernatural events occur in our day and age, he decided to become a psychiatrist.

What did he learn?

*"When patients come to me, often after enduring years of unsuccessful medical and psychiatric treatment, they can be in a highly unreceptive state of mind, unwilling to co-operate and reluctant to trust yet another doctor. It is essential first to establish their medical history, to check previous diagnoses and confirm that all the obvious necessary*

*medical tests have been carried out: nothing is taken for granted. When a mutual feeling of trust has been established, the patients are usually able to unburden themselves of the 'secrets' that have been the source of their illnesses. Many emotional problems have their roots in a purely biochemical imbalance which requires medication, and this can be remedied easily enough when once identified, although it is not always easy to discover. But many deep emotional hurts need a different sort of therapy and the supportive love of a Christian community. We cannot ignore any means by which the full healing of an individual can be achieved. An increasing number of the patients sent to me admitted that they suffered from the presence of 'spirits' or the intrusion of 'voices' from another world which were apparent and audible only to themselves and which psychiatry dismissed as madness. This was reminiscent of the traditional Chinese superstitions about good and evil spirits that I had encountered so many times when I lived in the Far East. Gradually, I realized that the spirits and the voices were real and also that there was a distinction between them. Some seemed to be evil and often came as a result of occult practices, while others seemed to be neutral, harmless voices begging for help. Sometimes the patient could identify the voices as belonging to a recently dead relative but often there was no known connection in the patient's mind. Who were these unbidden, unquiet spirits? Why and how could they hold living people in bondage? With careful and often painful analysis of the histories of my patients, by listening to them as they began to trust me, and by bringing them to trust God in the firm belief that he would lovingly listen to them and always forgive them, we were able to piece together the answer...It is essential to make a differential diagnosis in each case and to classify the possession syndrome into one or more of the defined categories. The bondage of the living to the living is the most obvious to diagnose. The bondage of the living to the dead, whether to ancestors, to those not related, to stillborn, aborted or miscarried babies, or to those who once inhabited a particular place now occupied by the living, can present considerable difficulties in diagnosis. The bondage of the living to occult control is, perhaps, the most dangerous evil to unravel. Deliverance is no one-step miracle pill to be swallowed on impulse for an instant cure. It is, rather, a long course of treatment, sometimes painful, to be followed conscientiously and trustingly until a cure is effected, although often the final moment of release can happen suddenly and dramatically. First, it is necessary to cut the known bond to the controlling person, alive or dead, then to forgive wholeheartedly, finally, to transfer control to Jesus Christ, making any essential environmental changes to support these steps." (Kenneth McAll, Healing the Family Tree (SPCK Classics Book 0), 5-7 (Kindle Edition); London, England; Society For Promoting Christian Knowledge)*

Familiar spirits are real, and so are the generational curses which they can bring. These all suggests a powerful connection between addicts. You see, many addicts find themselves embroiled in their struggle with generational habits. As such, there may very well be a connection between a drug addict's struggles and generational spirits.

Another powerful example of the connections between drug abuse and demonic roots comes from a particular word used in the New Testament, the Greek word pharmakeia.

---

*Revelation 9:20-21—But the rest of mankind, who were not killed by these plagues, did not repent of the works of their hands, that they should not worship demons, and idols of gold, silver, brass, stone, and wood, which can neither see nor hear nor walk. And they did not repent of their murders or their sorceries or their sexual immorality or their thefts.*

There is a footnote attached to the word "sorceries" in the NKJV of the Bible (my preferred and standard translation).

It reads "NU-Text and M-Text read *drugs.*" (The "NU Text" and the "M Text" refer to different text types of the Greek New Testament).

The word pharmakeia is very interesting. The root of this word is the basis for our English words "pharmacy" and "pharmaceutical." It is used only a couple of other times in the New Testament.

In describing the "works of the flesh" which will cause a person to be lost unless he repents, Paul mentions:

*Galatians 5:20-idolatry, SORCERY (PHARMAKEIA), hatred, contentions, jealousies, outbursts of wrath, selfish ambitions, dissensions, heresies,*

Later in the Book of Revelation, John also writes:

*Revelation 18:23—The light of a lamp shall not shine in you anymore, and the voice of bridegroom and bride shall not be heard in you anymore. For your merchants were the great men of the earth, for by your SORCERY (PHARMAKEIA) all the nations were deceived.*

So, in the New Testament there is some kind of connection between "drug abuse" and "sorcery."

Several Greek resources help us to better understand what Paul is talking about with this word "pharmakeia." By examining how the word was used in the first century among the Greeks, we will be able to better comprehend the application of this word in our day and age.

One excellent authority has this for us:

> "(Pαρμαχε(α, `sorcery', the use of cραεμαχα, `drugs', as in black magic, to do harm to others. In itself the word is as neutral as `pharmacy', its English derivative, meaning the dispensing of drugs for medical purposes. But it acquired two pejorative senses: the use of drugs to poison people and (as here) the use of drugs in witchcraft. In Ex. 7:11 cpap.taxo(is used of the `sorcerers' (Heb. mekass'pim) at Pharaoh's court. Apart from its present occurrence, the only occurrences of cραεμαxsia in the NT are in Rev. 9:21; 18:23 (cf. cραρμαxov, Rev. 9:21, and (ραρμαxos, Rev. 21:8; 22:15)." (F.F. Bruce, The New International Greek Testament Commentary: The Epistle To The Galatians-A Commentary On The Greek Text, 4449 (Kindle Edition); Grand Rapids, Michigan; William B. Eerdmans Publishing Company)

So from this we see that the word "pharmakeia" had clear references to the abuse of drugs. In fact, originally the word was a fairly benign term, referring to the good use of drugs. Over time, it came to describe the abuse of drugs, and then finally to the abuse of drugs in the way that witches and wizards made "potions" (hence, the translation as "sorcery"). Therefore, we can see that the word definitely at least carried with it the idea of any drug abuse, which could include occult practices. So, as Barclay has written:

*"Witchcraft: this literally means the use of drugs. It can mean the healing use of drugs by a doctor; but it can also mean poisoning, and it came to be especially connected with the use of drugs for sorcery, of which the ancient world was full." (William Barclay, The New Daily Study Bible: The Letters To The Galatians And Ephesians, 56 (Kindle Edition); Louisville, KY; Westminster John Knox Press)*

Another scholarly work informs us still further about "pharmakeia:"

*"Witchcraft (pharmakeia). At the root of this word is pharmakon, literally "drug," from which we derive our English word "pharmacy." In classical Greek pharmakeia referred to the use of drugs whether for medicinal or more sinister purposes, e.g., poisoning. In the New Testament, however, it is invariably associated with the occult, both here in Galatians and in Revelation, where it occurs twice (Rev 9:21; 18:23). English translations usually render pharmakeia as "witchcraft" (KJV, NIV) or "sorcery" (RSV, NEB). These words correctly convey the idea of black magic and demonic control, but they miss the more basic meaning of drug use. In New Testament times pharmakeia in fact denoted the use of drugs with occult properties for a variety of purposes including, especially, abortion. As J. T. Noonan has written, "Paul's usage here cannot be restricted to abortion, but the term he chose is comprehensive enough to include the use of abortifacient drugs." 86 In the early church both infanticide, often effected through the exposure of newborn babies to the harsh elements, and abortion, commonly brought about by the use of drugs, were regarded as murderous acts. Both are flagrant violations of Jesus' command to "love your neighbor as yourself." (Timothy George, The New American Commentary: Volume*

*Thirty-Galatians, 9724-9733 (Kindle Edition); Nashville, TN: B&H Publishing Group)*

## Conclusion

There are thus several possible roots that may lead to and influence a person in the world of drug addiction. We will now turn our attention to ministry.

The grace of the Lord Jesus Christ, and the love of God, and the communion of the Holy Spirit, be with you all. Amen.

# Chapter Two

# MOBILIZING THE LOCAL CHURCH FOR SUBSTANCE ABUSE MINISTRY

One of the great truths about the church that Jesus built is that it was designed to be an army of ministers reaching out to those in need. As Christians, we are the body of Christ. He is the Head, and we are the members of His body, carrying out His will and instructions in the world of man. Several passages of Scripture make this clear.

---

*1 Corinthians 12:12-27—For as the body is one and has many members, but all the members of that one body, being many, are one body, so also is Christ. For by one Spirit we were all baptized into one body—whether Jews or Greeks, whether slaves or free—and have all been made to drink into one Spirit. For in fact the body is not one member but many. If the foot should say, "Because I am not a hand, I am not of the body," is it therefore not of the body? And if the ear should say, "Because I am not an eye, I am not of the body," is it therefore not of the body? If the whole body were an eye, where would be the hearing? If the whole were hearing, where would be the smelling? But now God has set the members, each one of them, in the body just as He pleased. And if they were all one member, where would the body be? But now indeed there are many members, yet one body. And the eye cannot say to the hand, "I have no need of you"; nor again the head to the feet, "I have no need of you." No, much rather, those members of the body which seem to be weaker are necessary. And those members of the body which we think to be less honorable, on these we bestow greater honor; and our unpresentable parts have greater modesty, but our presentable parts have no need. But God composed the body, having given greater honor to that part which lacks it, that there should be no schism in the body, but that the members should have the same care for one another. And if one member suffers, all the members suffer with it; or if one member is honored, all the members rejoice with it. Now you are the body of Christ, and members individually.*

*Ephesians 1:22-23—And He put all things under His feet, and gave Him to be head over all things to the church, which is His body, the fullness of Him who fills all in all.*

---

Two of the most important works of the church are evangelism and edification. Evangelism has reference to preaching and teaching the Word of God to the lost and baptizing them into Christ. Jesus said:

---

*Matthew 28:19-20—Go therefore and make disciples of all the nations, baptizing them in the name of the Father and of the Son and of the Holy Spirit, teaching them to observe all things that I have commanded you; and lo, I am with you always, even to the end of the age." Amen.*

---

Cottrell has pointed out the significance of that phrase "in the name of" regarding baptism.

*"What this means can be more precisely explained when we understand how the expression "into the name" was used in New Testament times. Many feel that Jesus probably spoke the Aramaic language; thus the phrase should be understood in its Semitic sense. The basic Semitic equivalent had a quite general meaning, viz., "with respect to or*

*with regard to." In Rabbinic usage, though, it commonly had the more specific final sense. In this sense an action done "in the name" of something was done for a certain end or intention relating to it. Thus Jesus commissioned us to baptize people for a specific purpose relating to the Trinity, or into a specific relationship with the Trinity. 1 The precise nature of this relationship can be learned from the usage of the Greek phrase chosen by Matthew (and approved by the Holy Spirit via inspiration) to translate whatever Semitic original may have preceded it. The phrase is "eis to onoma," which was a technical term used in the world of Greek business and commerce. It was used to indicate the entry of a sum of money or an item of property into the account bearing the name of its owner. 2 Its use in Matthew 28:19 indicates that the purpose of baptism is to unite us with the Triune God in an ownership relation; we become his property in a special, intimate way. 3 As M.J. Harris says, since the phrase denotes transference of ownership, in Matthew 28:19 it means that "the person being baptized passes into the possession of the Triune God." 4". (Jack Cottrell, Baptism: A Biblical Study, 162-175 (Kindle Edition); Joplin, Missouri; College Press Publishing Company)*

This work of the church in evangelism is extremely important. However, the work goes beyond this! We are also called upon to work to "edify" or "build up" the church of Christ where we are located. Paul wrote about the importance of each member of the church doing what it could to minister and help the church grow. Every Christian has talents and abilities which he may use to help the local church grow.

---

*Ephesians 4:11-16—And He Himself gave some to be apostles, some prophets, some evangelists, and some pastors and teachers, for the equipping of the saints for the work of ministry, for the edifying of the body of Christ, till we all come to the unity of the faith and of the knowledge of the Son of God, to a perfect man, to the measure of the stature of the fullness of Christ; that we should no longer be children, tossed to and fro and carried about with every wind of doctrine, by the trickery of men, in the cunning craftiness of deceitful plotting, but, speaking the truth in love, may grow up in all things into Him who is the head—Christ—. from whom the whole body, joined and knit together by what every joint supplies, according to the effective working by which every part does its share, causes growth of the body for the edifying of itself in love.*

The works of evangelism and edification may involve outreach to addicts and their families.

## Get Organized

In God's plan for the church, every congregation where men are qualified should have elders put into place.

*Acts 11:30—This they also did, and sent it to the elders by the hands of Barnabas and Saul.*

*Acts 14:23—So when they had appointed elders in every church, and prayed with fasting, they commended them to the Lord in whom they had believed.*

*Acts 15:4—And when they had come to Jerusalem, they were received by the church and the apostles and the elders; and they reported all things that God had done with them.*

*Acts 20:17—From Miletus he sent to Ephesus and called for*

*the elders of the church.*

---

Several words are used in the New Testament to describe the ministry of elders. Each of these words demonstrates to us what kind of work is involved in the work of an eldership, and can help us especially in understanding the importance of outreach to addicts as we are discussing.

> *"There are three nouns in the Greek New Testament that are descriptive of the character and ministry of elders.*
>
> *• Presbuteros, translated "presbyter" or "elder." This word refers to an older man, one advanced in life, a senior. Although the word itself carries no official meaning, it exhibits the dignity of the ministry of elders.*
>
> *• Episkopos, translated "overseer," later in the second century to be called "bishop," is defined as "a man charged with the duty of seeing that things to be done by others are done rightly, any curator, guardian, or superintendent." In the New Testament the term is used of elders, denoting the watchful care they are to exercise (Acts 20:17-31)....*
>
> *• Poimein. Properly translated "shepherd" throughout the New Testament, it is translated but once by the word "pastor" (Ephesians 4:11). 3 The verb form poimaino is analogously used of elders who "shepherd the church" as a flock (Acts 20:28)....In the Greco-Roman society, in which Paul lived and wrote, the age of an elder was viewed to begin on or about one's 40th year....An elder must possess maturity that only adequate time and experience can provide....The three Greek words presbuteros, episkopos, poimein, from which we translate, elder or presbyter, overseer or bishop, and shepherd or pastor, all refer to the same*

*ministry group of men. This becomes apparent in light of the following:*

*• Acts 20:17-35. This passage uses a form of each of the three Greek words in reference to elders. Paul calls for the "elders (presbuteroi) of the church" at Ephesus (v. 17). When they arrive, he addresses them (vv. 18-35) and charges them to "take heed to yourselves and to all the flock, among which the Holy Spirit has made you overseers (episkopous)" (v. 28). Note that elders are addressed as overseers. Paul continues, saying to the elders, that they are "to shepherd (poimainein) the church of God" (v. 28). Elders, whom Paul calls "overseers," are instructed to "shepherd" the church. All three words are used in refer-ence to the Ephesian elders. The New Testament makes no distinction among elders, presbyters, overseers, bishops, pastors and shepherds. They are the same group of men addressed from the vantage points of their age (elders) and ministry performance (overseers that shepherd the church). The terms "shepherd" or "pastor," and "overseer" or "bishop," are not to be viewed as titles, but terms that express their biblical job description.*

*• Titus 1:5-7. In setting forth the qualifications of each el-der, Paul says he must be "blameless... for a bishop must be blameless, as a steward of God" (vv. 6-7). Paul tells us that elders are the bishops (overseers) of the local churches.*

*• 1 Peter 5:1-2. Once again all three words are used in reference to elders: "The elders (presbuterous) who are among you I exhort,... Shepherd (poimanate) the flock of God which is among you, serving as overseers*

*(episkopountes)." Peter agrees with Paul that elders, shep-*
*herds and overseers refer to the same ministry group.*

*• Preachers are not pastors. The New Testament does not*
*refer to its evangelists as pastors. The one verse in the Eng-*
*lish New Testament where the word poimein is translated*
*"pastor" rather than "shepherd" makes a very clear distinc-*
*tion between evangelists, who are preachers, and pastors:*
*"And He Himself gave some to be apostles, some prophets,*
*some evangelists, and some pastors and teachers" (Ephe-*
*sians 4:11). The ministries of pastor (shepherd) and*
*preacher are clearly stated here to be distinct. Although*
*preachers may also serve as elders (1 Peter 5:1) and while*
*elders may also minister as preachers (1 Timothy 5:17), we*
*cannot properly equate pastors (shepherds) with preach-*
*ers." (Ed Wharton, The Church Of Christ: The Distinctive Na-*
*ture Of The Church Of Christ, 1144-1197 (Kindle Edition);*
*Nashville, TN; Gospel Advocate Company).*

The Bible teaches that if men are not qualified to be elders, the
local evangelist should help especially to help the church grow
until elders are appointed.

---

*Titus 1:5—For this reason I left you in Crete, that you should*
*set in order the things that are lacking, and appoint elders*
*in every city as I commanded you...*

---

The things that evangelists are to "set in order" in the local
church are clearly outlined here for us in the Book of Titus.

*"What are the "things lacking" that need to be "set in or-*
*der"? The compound "set in order" implies that it has been*
*done up to a certain point before Paul left, but more was*
*needed. Titus is to supply and give a finishing touch to these*

*things. We surely may suppose that what is included in the remainder of Titus specifically names some of the things high on the agenda. (1) Appoint elders in every city, ka-tastēsēs kata polin presburterous. 'Ordain' is too strong a translation, and has a technical meaning. What Titus is to do is arrange for the selection and see that it is properly carried out. Per Titus 1:6ff, when Paul was on Crete, he had stated the qualification of elders. He now repeats them. There is no satisfactory evidence that the elders were im-posed on the churches without the consent of the individual congregations (Huther, Meyer's Commentary on the New Testatment, p.292). The work was city by city, and elders (plural) were to be appointed in every city (singular). There were 100 cities on the island. It seems Christianity has spread widely on the island. These 'shepherds, guardians, overseers' were needed because of the presence of false teachers in the area, whose doctrines would ruin the churches if not opposed. If we may add what is learned in Ephesians 4:11ff about the need for such offices in the church, it is that the saints may be equipped for service. (2) Conduct among church members, chapter 2. Another thing needing attention was the conduct of older men, younger men, older women, younger women, slaves. Titus was also to emphasize the basis of all Christian conduct (verses 11-15). (3) Conduct of church members in the world, chapter 3. The nature, reason, and encouragement of proper con-duct are stressed. This is part of an evangelist's job."* (Gareth Reese, New Testament Epistles: 1 & 2 Timothy Ti-tus: A Critical And Exegetical Comemntary, 6675-6688 (Kin-dle Edition): Moberly, Missouri: Scripture Exposition Books LLC)

Any outreach of the church needs to be organized. There is a need to have a plan in place before the outreach begins. It is helpful if the members can take an inventory of individual abilities and resources that volunteers could devote to this work.

Are there members of the church with a background in counseling or psychiatry? Members who have formal education in social work would be a tremendous advantage in this type of ministry.

Could there be some who have experience with working with addicts? This could involve formal work, or perhaps personal history.

Are there members of your church family who may have history with drug abuse personally or in a family setting? Sometimes addicts and families of addicts may be ideal in reaching out to other addicts. (We will have more to say about this later).

It would be prudent to get everyone on the same page and organized as you are preparing for this good work.

## Establish Your Goals

What are the goals that you are wanting to accomplish as you move forward in this ministry?

Here are some biblical goals that should be at the forefront of this type of work.

1. *Proclaim The Word Of God In Love*. This is one of the most important goals for every outreach that we are involved in as the church of God. We are here to be teachers and preachers of the Word of God (Matthew 28:19-20), with the commission to get that Message to every creature in all the world (Mark 16:15-16). We are here for the work of winning souls to Jesus, and of rescuing them from the snare of the devil (2 Timothy 2:24-26).

2. *Do What We Can To Help Addicts Find Sobriety.* One of the goals of the Christian life is to live "soberly, righteousness, and godly in this present age" (Titus 2:11-12). Addicts are those who have become ensnared in a terrible bondage and who will need our help to encourage them in their pursuit of sobriety. Each congregation must determine for itself the most expedient ways to help the addict reach this goal. Is the local church able and willing to spend financial resources in getting the addict into a drug rehab? Are you able to help them find housing if the need arises? Will you help them with food, clothing, and shelter? Each of these concerns (and others) will be addressed in more detail later. For now, start with a basic plan of what your capabilities are in this ministry.

3. *Encourage The Families Of Addicts.* Another important work of the church in this respect is in ministering to the families of addicts (Romans 15:14). Wives, children, mothers, fathers, and grandparents are all examples of family members who will need continual support and encouragement. Again, it is importnat to assess your congregational strengths and abilities to help the families of the addicts with whom you are ministering to. If the addict is in active addiction, odds are good that he is not able to hold down secular employment. The family may need help with food, clothing, shelter, bills, and transportation. There may very well be needed help with court costs, legal fees, as well as emotional and spiritual encouragement.

4. *Meetings.* One of the goals of this ministry should be regular meetings where addicts and others may get together in order to talk about their struggles, find strength, and pray together (and have others pray for and with them). Usually, these meetings are weekly

(although some congregations are able to do biweekly meetings, or even meetings with greater frequency). There are many great curricula that may be implemented in this work.

As you can see, it is very important for this work and ministry to be organized as far as possible.

## Mobilizing The Church For This Particular Ministry And Outreach

There are many ways that members of the church may be involved in ministry towards addicts. Here are some practical suggestions.

### Ask Members To Help With Food And Refreshments For The Support Meetings.

The Lord Jesus often ate with those to whom He ministered.

*Matthew 9:11—And when the Pharisees saw it, they said to His disciples, "Why does your Teacher eat with tax collectors and sinners?"*

*Luke 5:30—And their scribes and the Pharisees complained against His disciples, saying, "Why do You eat and drink with tax collectors and sinners?"*

*Luke 7:36—Then one of the Pharisees asked Him to eat with him. And He went to the Pharisee's house, and sat down to eat.*

*Luke 11:37—And as He spoke, a certain Pharisee asked Him to dine with him. So He went in and sat down to eat.*

After His resurrection from the dead, we read of how Jesus invited His Apostles to eat with Him.

---

*Luke 24:30—Now it came to pass, as He sat at the table with them, that He took bread, blessed and broke it, and gave it to them.*

*Luke 24:37-43—But they were terrified and frightened, and supposed they had seen a spirit. And He said to them, "Why are you troubled? And why do doubts arise in your hearts? Behold My hands and My feet, that it is I Myself. Handle Me and see, for a spirit does not have flesh and bones as you see I have." When He had said this, He showed them His hands and His feet. But while they still did not believe for joy, and marveled, He said to them, "Have you any food here?" So they gave Him a piece of a broiled fish and some honeycomb. And He took it and ate in their presence.*

---

We are even told that Jesus made food for His Apostles!

---

*John 21:1-13—After these things Jesus showed Himself again to the disciples at the Sea of Tiberias, and in this way He showed Himself: Simon Peter, Thomas called the Twin, Nathanael of Cana in Galilee, the sons of Zebedee, and two others of His disciples were together. Simon Peter said to them, "I am going fishing." They said to him, "We are going with you also." They went out and immediately got into the boat, and that night they caught nothing. But when the morning had now come, Jesus stood on the shore; yet the disciples did not know that it was Jesus. Then Jesus said to them, "Children, have you any food?" They answered Him, "No.". And He said to them, "Cast the net on the right side of the boat, and you will find some." So they cast, and now they were not able to draw it in because of the multitude of fish. Therefore that disciple whom Jesus loved said to Peter, "It is the Lord!" Now when Simon Peter heard that it was the Lord, he put on his outer garment (for he had removed it), and plunged into the sea. But the other disciples came in the little boat (for they were not far from land, but about two hundred cubits), dragging the net with fish. Then, as soon as they had come to land, they saw a fire of coals there, and fish laid on it, and bread. Jesus said to them, "Bring some of the fish which you have just caught." Simon Peter went up and dragged the net to land, full of large fish, one hundred and fifty-three; and although there were so many, the net was not broken. Jesus said to them, "Come and eat breakfast." Yet none of the disciples dared ask Him, "Who are You?"—knowing that it was the Lord. Jesus then came and took the bread and gave it to them, and likewise the fish.*

---

The original Greek vocabulary of this passage suggests that the Apostles were actually planning on leaving Christ and the ministry and return to their old occupations of being fishermen. Jesus appears to them and invites them to share a meal. The words of Wiersbe here are very enlightening:

> *"How loving of Jesus to feed Peter before He dealt with his spiritual needs. He gave Peter opportunity to dry off, get warm, satisfy his hunger, and enjoy personal fellowship. This is a good example for us to follow as we care for God's people. Certainly the spiritual is more important than the physical, but caring for the physical can prepare the way for spiritual ministry. Our Lord does not so emphasize "the soul" that He neglects the body." (Warren W. Wiersbe, The BE Series Bundle: The Gospels: Be Loyal, Be Diligent, Be Compassionate, Be Courageous, Be Alive, and Be Transformed, 15964-15965 (Kindle Edition): David C Cook)*

Fellowship over meals is a fantastic way to bond together and encourage each other. Furthermore, it is likely that members of your congregation will be very interested in utilizing their gifts for this type of outreach.

## Help With Clothes And Other Needs

Some addicts are in such terrible shape that they have pawned off their clothes and other personal belongings for money to get their next fix. As such, they may be in need of personal items (clothes, socks, shoes, underwear, pants, shorts, etc.). Several of the women that I have worked with over the years are very proficient in ministering to addicts with their God-given abilities to sew, crochet, make blankets, toboggans, etc. This reminds me of Tabitha in the New Testament:

*Acts 9:36-39—At Joppa there was a certain disciple named Tabitha, which is translated Dorcas. This woman was full of good works and charitable deeds which she did. But it happened in those days that she became sick and died. When they had washed her, they laid her in an upper room. And since Lydda was near Joppa, and the disciples had heard that Peter was there, they sent two men to him, imploring him not to delay in coming to them. Then Peter arose and went with them. When he had come, they brought him to the upper room. And all the widows stood by him weeping, showing the tunics and garments which Dorcas had made while she was with them.*

Remember: one of the goals of this type of outreach is to encourage all of the members to utilize whatever talents that they possess so that they may contribute and help.

## Becoming Familiar With Federal State And Local Resources (Including Drug Rehabs)

There are usually many local, state, and federal resources available to help addicts in finding their sobriety. We have precedent from the New Testament of how the Apostles would take advantage of their rights as citizens of their countries in order to promote the Gospel.

---

*Acts 16:35-39—And when it was day, the magistrates sent the officers, saying, "Let those men go." So the keeper of the prison reported these words to Paul, saying, "The magistrates have sent to let you go. Now therefore depart, and go in peace." But Paul said to them, "They have beaten us openly, uncondemned Romans, and have thrown us into prison. And now do they put us out secretly? No indeed! Let them come themselves and get us out." And the officers told these words to the magistrates, and they were afraid when they heard that they were Romans. Then they came and pleaded with them and brought them out, and asked them to depart from the city.*

*Acts 22:25-30—And as they bound him with thongs, Paul said to the centurion who stood by, "Is it lawful for you to scourge a man who is a Roman, and uncondemned?" When the centurion heard that, he went and told the commander, saying, "Take care what you do, for this man is a Roman." Then the commander came and said to him, "Tell me, are you a Roman?" He said, "Yes." The commander answered, "With a large sum I obtained this citizenship." And Paul said, "But I was born a citizen." Then immediately those who were about to examine him withdrew from him; and the commander was also afraid after he found out that he was a Roman, and because he had bound him. The next day, because he wanted to know for certain why he was accused by the Jews, he released him from his bonds, and commanded the chief priests and all their council to appear, and brought Paul down and set him before them.*

*Acts 25:7-12—When he had come, the Jews who had come down from Jerusalem stood about and laid many serious complaints against Paul, which they could not prove, while he answered for himself, "Neither against the law of the Jews, nor against the temple, nor against Caesar have I offended in anything at all." But Festus, wanting to do the Jews a favor, answered Paul and said, "Are you willing to go up to Jerusalem and there be judged before me concerning these things?" So Paul said, "I stand at Caesar's judgment seat, where I ought to be judged. To the Jews I have done no wrong, as you very well know. For if I am an offender, or have committed anything deserving of death, I do not object to dying; but if there is nothing in these things of which these men accuse me, no one can deliver me to them. I appeal to Caesar." Then Festus, when he had conferred with the council, answered, "You have appealed to Caesar? To Caesar you shall go!"*

Please notice in all of these passages that Paul used his rights as a citizen to give him advantage in promoting the Gospel.

*"After consultation with his advisers, Festus accepts the appeal to Caesar. Paul will go to Rome. These advisers were known as the consilium (συμβούλιον, symboulion; Schneider 1982:360; Tajra 1989:148–49; 4 Macc. 17:17; Josephus, Ant. 16.6.2 §163). Paul's appeal to Caesar is known as the provocatio, an appeal of a citizen for Caesar's judgment before a judgment has been rendered (BAGD 294 §2aβ; BDAG 373; Reese 1975). 1 Originally, this was the right of appeal to have the people, not a ruling official, decide a case. By the first century, the appeal was to have the*

*highest official make the decision (Conzelmann 1987:203–4). The case is extra ordinem (outside the order or code of law), which means that there is some freedom in how it is being handled. This secular use of provocatio (a calling upon) is a nice parallel to "calling upon the name of the Lord" in other texts in Acts (2:21, rendered invocatio in the Vulgate). This type of appeal is one of the oldest Roman ancient rights, dating back to 509 BC. 2 Bruce (1990:488–89) details this arrangement and also discusses how such an appeal made sense before the great persecutions of AD 64–65. Paul probably suspects a problem here in the Jewish proposal to return to Jerusalem and in how Festus might respond because of politics, something that might be confirmed in verses 19–20. So Paul makes a legal maneuver around Festus, who allows the move and takes himself out of the line of fire because it does fit Roman custom. Suetonius notes the procedure by which Nero would hear such a case (Nero 15.1; Eckey 2000:537). The judgment would not be rendered on the same day as the trial and would be given in writing. Acts, however, never brings us as far as this point. Numerous issues regarding Paul's appeal to Caesar are discussed among scholars: whether this right is limited to Roman citizens and capital cases, whether it can be made during a trial instead of after, and whether, once made, it prevents release (Garnsey 1966, who opts for appeals only after a trial). Paul is exercising his right not to be tried before an incompetent tribunal (Fitzmyer 1998:745). The final movement to Rome can now proceed (Acts 19:21; 23:11). The Caesar here is Nero, whose early reign, advised by Seneca and Afranius Burrus, enjoyed a relatively tranquil period (Suetonius, Nero 9–10) before, however, attaining a different kind of infamous notoriety. In sum, this exchange with Festus is a short outline of events, much like the scene with Felix, except that Paul's appeal to Caesar serves as protection for Paul the Roman citizen. Once again God's sovereignty has protected Paul through the means of the state's law. And once again Paul's key point of appeal, as he is tried, is that he has done nothing against the state, something that Festus recognizes is true. There is also irony here. Even though Festus senses Paul's innocence, he cannot release him because of Paul's appeal to Caesar. But he also is not sure what to write to Caesar, given the circumstances. In a sense, Paul sends himself to Rome through his own actions in appealing Roman law. It is not clear whether Paul's appeal is done for apologetic purposes, to argue that Christianity should be recognized by Rome, or because Paul desires to share the gospel in Rome. Against the former idea is that nowhere is there an indication that Paul expects justice in Rome (Jervell 1998:582, also n. 297). The sometimes critical portrait of Roman justice is also against this. But Roman justice is better than the expectation Paul would have with the Jewish leadership. So he seeks Rome's protection while telling the Romans that there is nothing to fear from him in terms of disturbing the peace. If there is an apologetic to Rome, here it is indirect. Paul's greater concern is to take the gospel to Rome, and this appeal is an easy way to do so. Paul has a sense of his priorities as a servant of the gospel. Again we see how sometimes God's plan works in unusual ways, ways where our own actions can move the plan forward. Luke's concern is to show that this new faith of the Way is rooted in God's ancient promises, is committed to hope, and is not a public threat to peace for anyone." (Darrell L. Bock, Acts (Baker Exegetical Commentary on the New Testament), 1062-1064 (Kindle Edition): Grand Rapids, MI: Baker Academic)*

As Paul utilized his rights as a Roman citizen in the effort of promoting the Gospel, so we as Christians may utilize our national rights for the same purpose. It would be prudent to have someone in your congregation reach out to the local, state, and federal officials to learn what funding and resources may be available for your outreach.

## The Need For Apologetics

There is a great need for ministers to be familiar with Apologetics (or "defenses") in studying and working with addicts. The Apostle Peter tells us about this:

---

*1 Peter 3:15—But sanctify the Lord God in your hearts, and always be ready to give a defense to everyone who asks you a reason for the hope that is in you, with meekness and fear;*

---

The word "defense" speaks to us about making a rational defense of the Christian faith.

*"The word was often used of the argument for the defense in a court of law, and though the word may have the idea of a judicial interrogation in which one is called to answer for the manner in which he has exercised his responsibility (Beare), the word can also mean an informal explanation or defense of one's position. The word would aptly describe giving an answer to the skeptical, abusive, or derisive inquiries of ill-disposed neighbors (Kelly) (Cleon Rogers II and III, The New Linguistic And Exegetical Key To The Greek New Testament, 575; Grand Rapids, Michigan, Zondervan Publishing House)."*

Throughout the Book of Acts, we see how Paul and the other early Christians worked in defending the faith. As I have written elsewhere:

*"God has declared: Isaiah 1:18—Come now, and let us reason together," Says the LORD, "Though your sins are like scarlet, They shall be as white as snow; Though they are red like crimson, They shall be as wool. Notice how God calls upon people to "reason" together. This reminds me of what the Apostle Paul said about "rationality." When he was presenting a defense of Christianity, Paul was accused of being "mad" by the Jewish high priest Festus (Acts 26:24). Paul responded: Acts 26:25—But he said, "I am not mad, most noble Festus, but speak the words of truth and reason. The word translated as "reason" in the NKJV is the Greek sophrosunē, which has an interesting meaning of that which is logical and rational.[ 2] Paul wants us to understand that Christianity is not based upon "insanity," but rather on "sober truth." This is especially interesting when we consider that throughout the New Testament, the Apostles and early Christians were seen as those who often "reasoned" with their unbelieving neighbors. Acts 17:2—Then Paul, as his custom was, went in to them, and for three Sabbaths reasoned with them from the Scriptures, Acts 17:17—Therefore he reasoned in the synagogue with the Jews and with the Gentile worshipers, and in the marketplace daily with those who happened to be there. Acts 18:4—And he reasoned in the synagogue every Sabbath, and persuaded both Jews and Greeks. Acts 18:19—And he came to Ephesus, and left them there; but he himself entered the synagogue and reasoned with the Jews. Acts 19:8-9—And he went into the synagogue and spoke boldly for three months, reasoning and persuading concerning the things of the kingdom of God. But when some were hardened and did not believe, but spoke evil of the Way before the multitude, he departed from them and withdrew the disciples, reasoning daily in the school of Tyrannus. Acts 24:12—And they neither found me in the temple disputing with anyone nor inciting the crowd, either in the*

*synagogues or in the city. Acts 24:25—Now as he reasoned about righteousness, self-control, and the judgment to come, Felix was afraid and answered, "Go away for now; when I have a convenient time I will call for you." The word translated in these passages is dialegomai, and Mounce reminds us about the important implications of this word for every Christian: "If we are to emulate Paul's preaching and teaching, we must do much more than just talk. dialegomai involves preaching and teaching that harnesses reason and logic into a defensive and positive exposition of God's Word to persuade and edify." (William D. Mounce (General Editor, Mounce's Complete Expository Dictionary of Old and New Testament Words, 1103 (Kindle Edition); Grand Rapids, Michigan; Zondervan) This shows us that the Christian is to be prepared to show logical and rational evidences to his friends and neighbors." (Mark Tabata, Old Apologetics For A New Age: Volume One: The Existence of God, 5-7 (Kindle Edition): Charleston, AR: Cobb Publishing)*

Many addicts come from a background of agnostic, atheistic, or pagan mindset. (An agnostic is one who claims that we can't know if God exists, while an atheist is one who makes the bold claim, "I know that God does not exist.") Many addicts embrace a blend of paganism and satanism. Add to this the many "conspiracy theories" against the Bible that are so common in our day and age, and we can easily and readily see why we need to arm ourselves with Christian Apologetics. As such, it will be wise for members of your outreach ministry to begin grounding themselves in these Christian defenses, which usually focus on evidence for the existence of God, the Divine inspiration of the Bible, and the Deity (Godhood) of Jesus Christ. At the end of this book, I will include several helpful types of Apologetics material.

## Confidentiality And Addiction

This is a topic that can become very difficult very fast.

Addicts generally have a rough time opening up to others. One possible reason for this is because they have committed crimes while in the madness of addiction and they are concerned that the ones who are trying to help them will turn them in. As such, we must be careful in taking steps to protect their confidences while at the same time doing whatever we can to uphold the laws of God and of man. Hopefully, the addict will be able to get sober and then begin to make amends to those whom he has wronged when such is expedient.

There are of course examples and guidelines from Scripture in dealing with situations like this, which I would encourage you to carefully consider.

---

*Exodus 2:11-14—Now it came to pass in those days, when Moses was grown, that he went out to his brethren and looked at their burdens. And he saw an Egyptian beating a Hebrew, one of his brethren. So he looked this way and that way, and when he saw no one, he killed the Egyptian and hid him in the sand. And when he went out the second day, behold, two Hebrew men were fighting, and he said to the one who did the wrong, "Why are you striking your companion?" Then he said, "Who made you a prince and a judge over us? Do you intend to kill me as you killed the Egyptian?" So Moses feared and said, "Surely this thing is known!"*

*Exodus 23:2—You shall not follow a crowd to do evil; nor shall you testify in a dispute so as to turn aside after many to pervert justice.*

*Leviticus 19:15-18—You shall do no injustice in judgment.*

> *You shall not be partial to the poor, nor honor the person of*
> *the mighty. In righteousness you shall judge your neighbor.*
> *You shall not go about as a talebearer among your people;*
> *nor shall you take a stand against the life of your neighbor: I*
> *am the LORD. 'You shall not hate your brother in your heart.*
> *You shall surely rebuke your neighbor, and not bear sin be-*
> *cause of him. You shall not take vengeance, nor bear any*
> *grudge against the children of your people, but you shall*
> *love your neighbor as yourself: I am the LORD.*

Remember what Paul declared:

> *Acts 25:11—For if I am an offender, or have committed any-*
> *thing deserving of death, I do not object to dying; but if*
> *there is nothing in these things of which these men accuse*
> *me, no one can deliver me to them. I appeal to Caesar."*

The Apostle acknowledged that if he had committed crimes, he was willing to pay the price. When we work with addicts, we do our best to help them achieve sobriety so that they can make amends to those whom they have wronged. Being addicted to drugs is no excuse for breaking the law, and is not a "get out of jail free" card. However, our goal is to help the addicts get back on their feet and stand with them as they begin to salvage their lives as best they are able. As Christians we are messengers of God, not executioners. The only times in my life when I have felt compelled to break confidences were in situations where another person's life was in jeopardy.

Let me also suggest that in your meetings, you not have police officers present. While some would no doubt be faithful and hold confidences, others wouldn't. Having law enforcement present during group meetings could also hinder addicts from seeking help and desiring to attain sobriety.

Others will have a difficult time in meetings because they are afraid that their personal secrets will become the focus of malicious gossip. Sadly, I have seen this happen. Some addicts turn to drug abuse because they themselves were in some way physically, sexually, or emotionally abused. As such, make it a priority that whatever addicts open up and reveal about themselves and their struggles will be kept in the strictest confidence.

## Take Precautions

It is also very important to take precautions as much as possible. Some addicts will take advantage of kindness in others, seeing such as weakness that may be exploited for their personal gain. Therefore, it will be wise to take precautions. Here are a few suggestions.

1.   Do Not Be Alone With Addicts Or Their Children. As Christians, we must do what we can to safeguard the personal integrity of the workers. All it takes is one person making a rumor of something inappropriate and your ministry can be devastated. Always have another person with you in your ministry.

2.   Consider Self-Defense. Jesus teaches us that there is a time and a place for personal safety.

---

*Luke 22:36—Then He said to them, "But now, he who has a money bag, let him take it, and likewise a knapsack; and he who has no sword, let him sell his garment and buy one."*

---

Of particular interest is the meaning of this particular word translated as "sword." In his fascinating book on difficult verses of the Bible, Ron Rhodes has written: "Jesus advised the disciples to buy a sword (Luke 22:36). Here the sword (Greek: maxairan ) is a dagger or short sword that belonged to the Jewish traveler's equipment as protection against robbers and wild animals. A plain reading of the passage would seem to indicate that Jesus approved of self- defense." (Ron Rhodes, *Commonly Misunderstood Bible Verses: Clear Explanations For The Difficult Passages,* 200 (Kindle Edition); Eugene, Oregon; Harvest House Publishers). There is a time to defend yourself and others. I have carried a firearm with me over the years, as well as other weapons (tasers, pepper spray, etc.).

3. Be Aware That Your Meetings May Be Used By Some Addicts For Nefarious Purposes. Sadly, this is a very real concern in this type of ministry. You must do what you can to safeguard your church and your meeting assembly. Pay attention for any suspicious signs. Perhaps consider equipping your church building with security cameras. Several times in my ministry I have worked with addicts who left contraband in vehicles and meeting houses. Perhaps they did not mean to do so, or perhaps they did. Either way, do what you can to safeguard yourselves and others.

---

*Matthew 10:16—Behold, I send you out as sheep in the midst of wolves. Therefore be wise as serpents and harmless as doves. Be compassionate, but also be wary.*

---

4. Limit What Personal Information That You Share With Addicts. I mean here be careful of sharing your personal information whether in regards to your own sins, your own past encounters and experiences. Also included in this is the need to take precautions about sharing member's phone numbers and personal addresses.

In the next chapter, we will begin examining how we may go about providing help for the addict's physical condition.

The grace of the Lord Jesus Christ, and the love of God, and the communion of the Holy Spirit, be with you all. Amen.

# Chapter Three

# MINISTERING TO THE NEEDS OF THE ADDICT

In this chapter, we will discuss some of the ways that we may minister to addicts based on the outline provided above: physically, environmentally, traumatically, and spiritually.

## Ministering To The Physical Needs Of Addicts

One of the ways that drugs work on a person is in and through their bodies. The physical body of a human being may quickly be hijacked by the illicit substances that a person abuses. This is powerfully illustrated in a groundbreaking and truly horrifying book called Dopesick. The author (an investigate journalist) uncovered how several leading drug companies and pharmaceutical businesses began to pour oxycodone into several small towns and states in America.

> *"Contacted by the same Richmond reporter, a spokesman for Purdue Pharma declined to discuss the illicit use of the company's drug. So it happened that in the early 2000s Debbie Honaker, a happily married twenty-seven-year-old mother from the town of Lebanon, two counties to the east of Van Zee, recovered from a fairly routine gallbladder surgery with a thirty-day prescription of "Oxy tens," followed by another script at her postsurgery checkup for another month's supply, this time for Oxy forties. When she called to complain that her incision was still hurting, the surgeon gave her a third prescription, for 7.5-milligram Percocet, designed to quell her "breakthrough pain," with instructions to take it not "as needed for pain" but as frequently as every two hours—concurrent with the twelve-hour Oxys. To remind her to take the Percocet, she was supposed to*

*set an alarm for the middle of the night. "The doctor didn't force me to take them," Honaker said. "But they're like a high-standard person, someone you're supposed to trust and believe in. My husband and I both understood that I was supposed to take the pills every two hours." They have discussed that defining moment a lot in the intervening years. They've wondered aloud what might have happened had her gallbladder not given out at the same time the factories and mines were laying off and shutting down. She might not have visited a neighbor, a well-known pill abuser, for advice on what to do when the pain wouldn't subside. "If you snort 'em up your nose, they hit you better," her neighbor told her. She might not have found herself doubled over and dopesick the day her prescriptions ran out. "You're throwing up. You have diarrhea. You ache so bad and you're so irritable that you can't stand to be touched. Your legs shake so bad you can't sleep. You're as ill as one hornet could ever be," she recalled. "And believe me, you'll do anything to make that pain go away." She might not have later turned, in the throes of withdrawal, to her sixty-year-old neighbor, Margie, one of the growing legions of laid-off workers in town. Or suggested that, given Margie's bad hip from decades of standing on hard factory floors, she should go visit the town's so-called pain doctor and ask him to "write you"—parlance for coaxing a prescription out of a doctor by making the pain seem more debilitating than it really is. She might not have driven Margie to the appointment, then coached her on what to say. "She didn't want to do it," Honaker recalled. "Margie would say, 'God knows I wouldn't be doing this if I didn't have to choose between paying a bill or going to the doctor to get the medicines I really need,'" for diabetes and high blood pressure. Within the span of three months, Honaker had mastered the classic drug-seeking emergency-room trick, beginning with an impassioned complaint about kidney stone pain.*

*"I'd say, 'My back's killing me,' and [in the ER bathroom] I'd pierce my finger, then put a drop of blood into my urine sample," she recalled. She'd leave with a prescription for Percocet. She was a full-blown opioid addict when she resorted to stealing the money her husband set aside for paying the electric bill and spending it at the office of a well-known Lebanon doctor who began most of her visits to him with the question "What do you want?" The Board of Medicine suspended Dr. Dwight Bailey's license to practice medicine in 2014 for excessive prescribing and poor record keeping, noting that five patients had died from drug overdoses while under his care—but that was more than a decade after Honaker first came through his doors. Honaker went on to steal painkillers from her husband's elderly grandmother. She bought pills from people who paid one dollar for their OxyContin prescriptions using their Medicaid cards." (Beth Macy, Dopesick: Dealers, Doctors, and the Drug Company that Addicted America, 40-42 (Kindle Edition): New York, NY: Little, Brown and Company Hachette Book Group)*

Please notice some of the physical symptoms that an addict will go through when in active withdrawal. Some substances are worse to come off of than others, but with about all of them there are physical symptoms. I have personally sat at the bedside of addicts who were withdrawing from heroin, cocaine and alcohol. The withdrawals are truly horrifying to behold. Another author describes it well:

*"Like viruses, addictive substances are foreign toxins that enter the body and alter its natural functions to propagate their continued use. Like viruses, addictive substances use our DNA (through epigenetics) to promote their continued use. The result is the specific syndrome of signs and symptoms that we call addiction. As with other diseases,*

*addiction causes physiological and structural changes to the body. An overwhelming body of research evidence has shown that addiction involves physical changes in DNA and other molecular structures and functions in brain cells, and changes in the connections and activities of brain circuits (if you're not sure what exactly that means, don't worry— you'll be an expert by the time you finish this book). These are real changes that can be seen on MRI scans and under the microscope. As well, addictive substances trigger the brain's immune system, resulting in harmful inflammation, which also happens with viral infections. As such, addiction is demonstrably a physical disease that causes disruptive physical changes in the body, not at all unlike how viruses cause disease." (Andrew Proulx M.D., What Happened To Me???: Why People Become Addicted --- our brain, genetics, and psychology in addiction and recovery, 38 (Kindle Edition): Recovery Polio Publishing)*

The body may become dependent on drugs, which is another reason why medical treatment will be needed.

Here are some practical suggestions to help you as you set up your outreach ministry to addicts.

## Understand That The Bible Encourages People To Seek Medical Help When Genuinely Needed

Over the years, I have worked with some folks who believe that seeking medical help is a bad idea: that if we really trusted God, we would not need doctors and medicines. Some have even gone so far to tell me that going to a doctor is sinful!

However, the Bible teaches the exact opposite.

*"In the figurative account of the evil case of Judah and Israel because of their backsliding (Jer 30:13), the prophet says they have had no rephu'ah, or "healing medicines." Later on (Jer 46:11), when pronouncing the futility of the contest of Neco against Nebuchadrezzar, Jeremiah compares Egypt to an incurably sick woman going up to Gilead to take balm as a medicine, without any benefit. In Ezekiel's vision of the trees of life, the leaves are said (the King James Version) to be for medicine, the Revised Version (British and American) reads "healing," thereby assimilating the language to that in Re 22:2, "leaves of the tree.... for the healing of the nations" (compare Eze 47:12). Very few specific remedies are mentioned in the Bible. "Balm of Gilead" is said to be an anodyne (Jer 8:22; compare Jer 51:8). The love-fruits, "mandrakes" (Ge 30:14) and "caperberry" (Ec 12:5 margin), myrrh, anise, rue, cummin, the "oil and wine" of the Good Samaritan, soap and sodic carbonate ("natron," called by mistake "nitre") as cleansers, and Hezekiah's "fig poultice" nearly exhaust the catalogue. In the Apocrypha we have the heart, liver and gall of Tobit's fish (Tobit 6:7). In the Egyptian pharmacopoeia are the names of many plants which cannot be identified, but most of the remedies used by them were dietetic, such as honey, milk, meal, oil, vinegar, wine. The Babylonian medicines, as far as they can be identified, are similar. In the Mishna we have references to wormwood, poppy, hemlock, aconite and other drugs. The apothecary mentioned in the King James Version (Ex 30:25, etc.) was a maker of perfumes, not of medicines. Among the fellahin many common plants are used as folk-remedies, but they put most confidence in amulets or charms, which are worn by most Palestinian peasants to ward off or to heal diseases." (Alexander Macalister, "Medicine," in James Orr, The International Standard Bible Encyclopedia, 117347-117366 (Kindle Edition); Osnova)*

Again:

> *"Medical care in biblical times frequently employed the use of different kinds of salves and ointments. Olive oil was used widely, either alone or as an ingredient in ointments. The use of oil for the treatment of wounds is mentioned in Isa. 1:6 and Luke 10:34. Oil also became a symbol of medicine, and its use was coupled with prayer for the ill (Mark 6:13; James 5:14). Herbs and various products obtained from many different plants were among the most popular of ancient medicines. These were applied to the body as a poultice, or, in many cases, taken by mouth. Frankincense and myrrh—gum resins obtained from trees—were commonly used to treat a variety of diseases, although their main use was in perfumes and incense. Wine was commonly thought to have medicinal value. One of its uses was to alleviate pain and discomfort. Wine, mixed with gall and myrrh, was offered to Jesus prior to His crucifixion, but He refused to drink it (Matt. 27:34; Mark 15:23). Wine also was used to sooth stomach and intestinal disorders (1 Tim. 5:23) and to treat a variety of other physical problems. Beer was also widely used as an ingredient in several medicines, especially by the Babylonians....When Leah suffered a temporary period of sterility, she sent her son, Reuben, to the field to obtain mandrakes. Her barren sister, Rachel, also asked for some of the mandrakes (Gen. 30:9-24). The root of the mandrake was widely used in the ancient world to promote conception, although there is no reason to believe it was truly effective. It was also used as a narcotic." (Kenneth Eakins, "Diseases," in Holman Illustrated Bible Dictionary, 14729-14755 (Kindle Edition); Nashville, TN: Holman Reference)*

The writer of Proverbs teaches us about the value of alcohol as a remedy for those who are suffering (physically and mentally):

*Proverbs 31:6-8 Give strong drink to him who is perishing, And wine to those who are bitter of heart. Let him drink and forget his poverty, And remember his misery no more. Open your mouth for the speechless, In the cause of all who are appointed to die.*

I believe these words from the apocryphal book Wisdom Of Sirach are helpful here:

*Sirach 38:1-2, 4-8, 12-15—"Honor the physician with the honor due him, according to your need of him, for the Lord created him; for healing comes from the Most High, and he will receive a gift from the king... The Lord created medicines from the earth, and a sensible man will not despise them. Was not water made sweet with a tree in order that his power might be known? And he gave skill to men that he might be glorified in his marvelous works. By them he heals and takes away pain; the pharmacist makes of them a compound. His works will never be finished; and from him health is upon the face of the earth... And give the physician his place, for the Lord created him; let him not leave you, for there is need of him. There is a time when success lies in the hands of physicians, for they too will pray to the Lord that he should grant them success in diagnosis and in healing, for the sake of preserving life. He who sins before his Maker, may he fall into the care of a physician."*

One thing that I have noticed that helps addicts when used properly is a drug called Suboxone.

*"Sold under the brand name Narcan or Evzio, naloxone is a fast-acting drug that, when administered during an overdose, blocks the effects of opioids on the brain and restores breathing within two to three minutes of administration.*

*Approved by the FDA in 1971, naloxone has been used safely and effectively for over 4 decades in ambulances and emergency rooms across America. In America and around the world, naloxone distribution programs are currently training potential overdose witnesses to correctly recognize an overdose and administer the drug, greatly reducing the risk of accidental death. The CDC has recognized co-prescribed naloxone in their 2016 guidelines as an effort to reduce death in high risk pain populations that include advanced age, chronic disease and doses that exceed 50 morphine milli-equivalents (MME) and/ or co-medication with benzodiazepines…. "Why do you need naloxone? Why does America need naloxone? 52,404 people died of drug overdose in 2015 and we are tracking for 70,000. Naloxone could have saved 63% of them It's all about the death curve. You need American Narcan because you cannot change enough laws or educate enough doctors to change the death curve. The death curve is also very likely worse than what is reported. You need American Narcan because lawmakers still just don't get it. You need American Narcan because your doctor doesn't get it. Heroin is below the radar of state appointed bureaucrats and law makers. Despite comprising a smaller user population, there were more treatment admissions to publicly funded facilities for heroin than for any other drug. Abstinence based therapy and Community Health Centers still have not wrapped their head around the death curve. I walk amoung people weekly that debate whether or not they should support community naloxone. It's all about the death curve. Every publically funded facility for heroin treatment or opioid use disorder should be a hub for the distribution or prescribing of naloxone." (William Morrone, American Narcan: Naloxone & Heroin-Fentanyl associated mortality (American Narcotics Book 2), 9-11 (Kindle Edition); Morrone & Morrone)*

Hopefully, you will be able to help addicts by getting them into a proper facility and clinic.

## Contact Local Hospitals And Rehabilitation Units

It would be wise to have one of your members contact the local hospitals and rehabilitation unites. In Kentucky, the preeminent addiction recovery program is run by ARC (Addiction Recovery Care). I have worked with several ARC facilities over the years in helping addicts get into treatment. Sometimes these rehabs can be difficult for the addict, and often the ARC facilities will require an addict to go through a detox at a local hospital before being admitted. However, these steps are absolutely necessary for an addict to get help.

Often, health insurance will cover these treatment plans and costs. However, I have also seen where health insurance doesn't cover treatment. This is one reason why it is so important to gather as much information as possible for treatment options for the addicts that you minister to. Some places may also require a copay arrangement, so it would again be wise to set up a financial budget for situations like this which may arise.

When the addict goes into treatment, it would be wise to keep his location secret from family or friends who may be enablers or who may bring contraband into a facility. I have witnessed this where family members and spouses were blackmailed into bringing drugs into federal institutions and rehabs. Some family and friends genuinely love their relative who struggles with addiction, and may simply not know how to tell them "no." Others no doubt don't care for the addict. In any case, it would be wise and prudent to keep location and treatment time information to yourselves as much as possible. Usually, rehabs will have guidelines to help guide you in the process.

## Physical And Material Needs

Addicts that you work with may have need for other physical needs (groceries, help with bills, clothes, etc.). One of the responsibilities that we have as Christians is to help those in need as much as we are able to and when such is truly expedient.

*Galatians 6:10—Therefore, as we have opportunity, let us do good to all, especially to those who are of the household of faith.*

In rehab, the addict will also likely be taught basic life skills that he may not have learned, or which he may have learned and lost due to his chemical dependency. When he gets out of rehab, he will hopefully have a plan in place to help him continue in his new life and sobriety. There is a good chance that he will be in the Suboxone clinic.

## Ministering To The Environmental Needs Of The Addict

Environment is one of the most crucial elements in the continued sobriety of the addict. The Bible reminds us time after time about the dangers of bad influences. It reminds us time after time that we need to be willing to cut off influences that will lead us to sin, while at the same time cultivating good relationships that will encourage us in our walk.

One of my favorite examples of this comes from the story of Simon Peter.

*Mark 14:54—But Peter followed Him at a distance, right into the courtyard of the high priest. And he sat with the servants and warmed himself at the fire.*

Sometimes comfort can be a good thing.

But other times, comfort isn't necessarily a good thing.

Or to be more precise, the things that adjoin comfort can be bad for us.

Case in point: Peter warming himself at the fire.

He had seen Christ arrested, and had fled.

---

*Mark 14:50—Then they all forsook Him and fled.*

---

Then he had gone and followed Jesus at a distance, eventually deciding to warm himself at the fire.

Look what happens next:

---

*Mark 14:66-72—Now as Peter was below in the courtyard, one of the servant girls of the high priest came. And when she saw Peter warming himself, she looked at him and said, "You also were with Jesus of Nazareth." But he denied it, saying, "I neither know nor understand what you are saying." And he went out on the porch, and a rooster crowed. And the servant girl saw him again, and began to say to those who stood by, "This is one of them." But he denied it again. And a little later those who stood by said to Peter again, "Surely you are one of them; for you are a Galilean, and your speech shows it." Then he began to curse and swear, "I do not know this Man of whom you speak!" A second time the rooster crowed. Then Peter called to mind the word that Jesus had said to him, "Before the rooster crows twice, you will deny Me three times." And when he thought about it, he wept.*

---

Look what happens: the fire that was meant to comfort Peter became a fire that tormented him.

We often choose our companions, and the comforts which they can afford to us. If we surround ourselves with those who are not followers of the Lord Jesus, then we will find ourselves in a place where it is easy to deny Him.

Really, this passage teaches us about the progressive nature of sin. The comfort of the fire that Peter enjoyed was such that it became easier to deny Christ time after time. There is a progressive nature here to sin that we need to pick up on. Throughout the Bible, sin is depicted as leaven. As you know, leaven is an agent which continually grows and expands. That is how sin is: it is something which (if left untreated) will expand until it corrupts everything. That is why Paul reminds us:

> *1 Corinthians 5:6—Your glorying is not good. Do you not know that a little leaven leavens the whole lump?*
>
> *Galatians 5:9—A little leaven leavens the whole lump.*

Notice something interesting about the context here.

> *"Very probably it was this. The Roman night was divided into four watches from 6 pm to 6 am. At the end of the third watch, at 3 am, the guard was changed. When the guard was changed there was a bugle call which was called the gallicinium, which is the Latin for the cock-crow. Most likely what happened was that as Peter spoke his third denial, the clear note of the bugle call rang out over the silent city, and Peter heard it. He remembered and his heart broke. Make no mistake—Peter fell to a temptation which would have come only to a man of fantastic courage. It ill*

*becomes the more prudent and safety-seeking among us to criticize Peter for falling to a temptation which would never, in the same circumstances, have come to them at all. Everyone has a breaking point. Peter reached his here, but 999 men out of every 1,000 would have reached theirs long before. We would do well to be amazed at Peter's courage rather than to be shocked at his fall. But there is another thing. There is only one source from which this story could have come—and that is Peter himself. We saw in the introduction that Mark's gospel is the preaching material of Peter. That is to say, over and over again Peter must have told the story of his own denial. 'That is what I did,' he must have said, 'and this amazing Jesus never stopped loving me.'" (William Barclay, The Gospel of Mark (The New Daily Study Bible), 477 (Kindle Edition): Edinburgh, England; Saint Andrews Press)*

Scripture abounds with warnings to us about who we choose as our companions.

---

*Proverbs 13:20—He who walks with wise men will be wise, But the companion of fools will be destroyed.*

*1 Corinthians 15:33—Do not be deceived: "Evil company corrupts good habits."*

---

Bad friendships can lead us into all kinds of trouble and mischief. The addict you minister to needs to learn this lesson-and sometimes it can be a very difficult lesson to learn.

## Establish Good Friendships

The challenge for the church is to create an environment where the recovering addict can build a new life with new and encouraging friends. We were not made to be an island to our-selves: we were created for fellowship. The Psalmist said that the action of God creating the universe and mankind was a direct result of His love.

---

*Psalm 136:1-9—Oh, give thanks to the LORD, for He is good! For His mercy endures forever. Oh, give thanks to the God of gods! For His mercy endures forever. Oh, give thanks to the Lord of lords! For His mercy endures forever: To Him who alone does great wonders, For His mercy endures forever; To Him who by wisdom made the heavens, For His mercy endures forever; To Him who laid out the earth above the waters, For His mercy endures forever; To Him who made great lights, For His mercy endures forever—. The sun to rule by day, For His mercy endures forever; The moon and stars to rule by night, For His mercy endures forever.*

---

We were not created because God "needed" anything from us. We were made as an act of loving grace. One author reminds us of this fact in a powerful illustration about the Trinity:

*"God's first gracious act toward humanity was not the Exodus nor the Cross, it was Creation. When God created, he acted freely and without compulsion. Humanity did not deserve to be created; it had no inherent right to exist. Neither was there some need which God had to satisfy through creation. God was not compelled by some inner necessity to create in order to preserve his own mental health. Creation was an act of unmerited love which arose freely out of God's will. God is praised in Revelation 4:11 because he created all things by his will. Creation was God's free decision and determined by his own will. But why does God seek a communion of love with creatures? Is God a solitary figure who needs to create in order to have fellowship with*

*others? Does God need company? The Christian doctrine of Trinity, which is the triune nature of God's life, answers these questions. In the light of God's revelation in Christ, we understand more about God's creative intent than is revealed in Genesis 1. While the doctrine of "Trinity" (however that word may be defined, and it has variant meanings) seems remote, speculative and cumbersome to some, it is helpful in understanding God's purpose in creating the cosmos. 2 One does not have to be an astute theologian to recognize the impact that Trinitarian theology can have on understanding God's creative act. Indeed, Scripture reveals that creation was a Trinitarian act of God. God the Father is the fountainhead of creation; he is the source and origin of everything that exists. Everything in the universe originated with him; it was "from" him (Rom. 11:36; 1 Cor. 8:6). Yet, the Son is the instrument of creation. He is the means by which the Father created (John 1:1-3; 1 Cor. 8:6). The Father created nothing without the agency of the Son. The Spirit, as the breath of life, is God's dynamic presence which energizes life in the world (Job 26:13; 33:4; Psalm 33:6; 104:30). The Spirit was present at creation, and was the power by which life invaded what was lifeless (Gen. 1:2; 2:7). Creation, therefore, is from God the Father through the agency of the Son by the power of the Spirit. The one God, then, performed the mighty work of creation as a community just as that same God performs the mighty work of redemption as a triune community (cf. Eph. 2:18; 1 Pet. 1:2). Both creation and redemption are the work of the triune community. The doctrine of the Trinity teaches that the divine reality is a community of loving fellowship between the Father, Son and Spirit. It is a community of holy love. This communion of love explains why God created the cosmos. Even before the cosmos existed, there existed a community of love between the Father, Son and Spirit. Jesus prayed that his disciples might see the glory the Father had given him, and the Father gave him this glory because he loved him "before the foundation of the world" (John 17:24). This text provides a glimpse into the common life of the Father and Son before the act of creation. Before the cosmos existed, there existed a community of shared love (agape) between the Father and the Son. The high priestly prayer of John 17 also points us to the redemptive love of God which flows from the love the Father has for the Son. Jesus promised his Father that he would continue to make the Father known to his disciples "so that the love with which you have loved me may be in them" (John 17:26). The intent of redemption is to bring the fallen world into the orbit of God's agape fellowship where just as the Father dwells in the Son and the Son in the Father, so God's people may dwell in them and they in God (John 17:21). God has acted in Christ Jesus in order that we might have fellowship with him. God's intent is that our fellowship might be with the Father and the Son (1 John 1:3). If the intent of redemption is modeled after creation, then the intent of creation is clear. God intended to create a people to share his loving community; to have fellowship with God through the sharing of his love. Creation is an expression of grace and love which engages his people in the fellowship of the Spirit (2 Cor. 13:14). But this fellowship was not created by a solitary, lonely God. Before the creation of the world, God existed as a community, not as a solitary being. God did not create because he needed fellowship, since he already enjoyed fellowship through the triune communion of the Father, Son and Spirit. This fellowship was not created by God, as though at some point in time God became a fellowship. Rather, it is who God is. God is a community of love because God is agape (1 John 4:8). Consequently, God did not need to turn to anything outside of himself in order to experience loving fellowship and community. This was experienced in the mutual indwelling of God's Trinitarian fellowship. The grace of God was expressed in the act of creation. The gracious act of creation, an act of agape love, is God's decision to share what he already possessed. It was not to gain something he lacked. Rather, God decided to share his own loving fellowship within the triune community with others. This is an astounding but wondrous thought. God, without compulsion, decided to share his holy communion with those whom he created. God created out of the overflow of his love. It flows from the inner-Trinitarian love which decided to share itself with others. God decided to express his love by creating us. Just as God so loved the world that he gave his Son, he also so loved that he created a world with which to share his love. God's love, by his free decision, is self-giving and other-centered so that it seeks to share the joy of the divine communion with others. The best analogy for understanding this act of God—as limited as it is—is a couple's decision to have children. Why do couples decide to have children? Certainly, in a fallen world, there are less than pure motives. But in the purest sense, why do couples decide to have children? While there is a certain biological drive inherent in the human psyche, there is also the yearning to share our love. In the best of motives, couples decide to have children in order to share their love with another. When a couple decides to have a child, the couple has, in the best of circumstances, made a selfless decision. They have decided to share something that they could have kept to themselves. The love which exists between a husband and wife is a communion unsurpassed in human relations. When children are born into that loving communion, the children share something they did not create. The parents give something they were not compelled to share. Children, and we wish it were true in every instance, are born out of the loving communion between parents. They share their love with another. When the Trinitarian community decided to create, they decided to share something they already enjoyed for the benefit of another. We humans did not create that fellowship, but it is offered to us in love. God created out of his love. He did not create in order to receive (as if he needed anything outside of himself), but he created to give and consequently experience the joy of communion with others. Thus, the act of creation is an act of grace, an act of selfless love." (John Mark Hicks, Come to the Table: Revisioning the Lord's Supper, 70-120 (Kindle Edition): Abilene, TX: Leafwood Publishers)*

Let's notice some practical suggestions about ministering to the environmental needs of the addict.

## Help Them Build Their Relationship With God

In God's Presence is fullness of joy (Psalm 16:11), and He wants the addict to come to Him for redemption. That is what the Gospel is all about (1 Corinthians 15:1-8; 1 Timothy 1:15). One way that you can help the ones you minister to is by encouraging them to be present in the worship assemblies of the church. Not only is this a command from God (Hebrews 10:24-26), but there are other great benefits and blessings of this. It is in the worship assembly especially that we are filled with the Holy Spirit (Ephesians 5:18-19). This will be a great encouragement to everyone involved. However, if the addict is a baptized believer, I would encourage you to take your time in encouraging the addict to take part in any public or leadership capacity in the worship service. Often, addicts need time to build (or rebuild) their self-esteem.

## Support Meetings

Also, it will be good to encourage the addict to attend any group meetings whenever possible. Hopefully, these types of meetings will become a part of your outreach ministry. Typically, here is how a regular meeting is organized.

- Opening Prayer

- Each person introduces himself by his first name and shares anything that he would like about struggles that he is facing.

- Selected Scripture may be shared after this (I highly recommend Psalms).

- Usually any other things may be shared at this point (songs, books, movie thoughts, etc.)

- Break For Refreshment

- Curriculum Study And Discussion.

Typically in the meetings that I have conducted over the years, we use the curriculum put out by New Life Behavior. Their program is called Christians Against Substance Abuse (CASA). This is not only popular and effective in small group meetings, but also in jail and prison ministries.

It is also encouraging to keep track of important calendar dates for the addicts to whom you minister. Usually I would try to keep track of Day One, First Month, Third Month, Sixth Month, Ninth Month, and One Year. As each date approaches, try to arrange a small celebration with a cake and maybe some kind of token or gift.

## **Ministering To The Traumatic Needs Of The Addict**

As noted above, many addicts turn to drugs due to traumatic

experiences which they have undergone throughout their life. Sometimes these experiences may be difficult for an addict to discuss, so I always encourage patience and gentleness when working with addicts along these lines. Let's notice some practical suggestions.

## Utilize The Gifts Of Professionals As Much As Possible

There is a great blessing in the body of Christ today in that we have many Christians who have formal education, training, and experience in the healing arts. Indeed, there is an amazing connection between psychiatry and the Bible!

> *"OUR MODERN WORD "PSYCHIATRY" COMES FROM THE TWO Greek words Ψυχή (psyche) and ιατρεία (iatreia): psyche-iatreia. The word "psyche" really means the person, and is variously translated as "breath," "soul," "mind," "reason," and the like. The word iatreia means "treatment," "healing," "restoring," and the like. So, put the two words together and we have "the healing of the mind," or, as David might have said, "the restoring of the soul." The word can mean medical treatment, or the treatment by a physician, but that is only one of its meanings, and I feel that the science of psychiatry is not to be limited to the medical profession. Often the minister is a psychiatrist, because he deals not only with the minds of people but also with their souls. In fact, the very essence of religion is to adjust the mind and soul of man, and we have long ago learned, as in this book I quote Augustine as saying, "My soul is restless until it finds its rest in Thee, O God." Healing means bringing the person into a right relationship with the physical, mental and spiritual laws of God. The physician is a minister of God. All true scientific research is merely an organized effort to learn the laws of God and how they operate. The teacher is also a minister of God. The teacher*

*seeks to train the mind, to seek truth and know truth when it is found. A mind which thinks error is a sick mind. So a teacher is practicing part of the great science of psychiatry. Beyond our bodies and minds are our souls. The minister is concerned with man's soul; he believes that if his soul is sick the man is sick, indeed. And only God can heal the soul. So, the first and most important psychiatry must be God's psychiatry, the essence of which I find contained in the four best known passages of The Bible: The Twenty-Third Psalm, The Ten Commandments, The Lord's Prayer, and The Beatitudes." (Charles L. Allen, God's Psychiatry: Healing for Your Troubled Heart, 5-6 (Kindle Edition); Grand Rapids, MI; Baker Books)*

Sadly, some modern day psychiatry has been greatly influenced by Darwinian evolution, with the result being that many people see mankind simply as an animal. The result of this is the belief that spiritual problems are actually physical problems, with completely chemical solutions.

*"Until the last fifty years or so, Western culture strongly reflected the core Judeo-Christian conviction that God created the human race and put us all here on this beautiful globe we call Earth, and that we, alone among all creatures, were given the ability—and destiny—to choose between good and evil. That was then. Today's cultural elite, including those in the healing arts, basically no longer think of man in spiritual terms, of morality, character, self-understanding, repentance, and forgiveness. Rather, most of today's experts look at man and see a soulless animal whose behavior problems are mostly genetic or organic in origin and, in any event, usually manageable with drugs. The truth is, most pill-dispensing mental health practitioners don't really understand why people experience clinical depression or other "mental illnesses." Go search WebMD*

*and five or ten other websites on, let's say, postpartum de-
pression (or any other syndrome). You'll be stunned at the
lack of real substance with regard to what causes it. Instead, you'll see statements like "The causes haven't been
pinpointed yet," along with reams of authoritative-sound-
ing data on symptoms and predisposing factors and what
drugs to take and how valuable it is to have a support
group and what vitamins help in recovery and so on." (David Kupelian, How Evil Works: Understanding and Over-
coming the Destructive Forces That Are Transforming
America, 104 (Kindle Edition); New York, N.Y.; Threshold
Editions)*

Please do not misunderstand me here. There is a definite place
for medicine in treating all kinds of physical maladies. I personally use medicines to help me with medical problems of all kinds.
That isn't the point I am making though. Sometimes there are
spiritual roots to our problems, and those spiritual issues must
be treated just as physical issues must be. What is needed in the
modern world (just like in the world of the Bible) is a recognition
of the need to treat both spiritual and physical issues.

If you are blessed to have a member of your outreach ministry
who holds to the Bible worldview and who is willing to utilize
his/her talents in this type of capacity, then by all means grate-
fully and humbly accept the help offered.

## Emphasize How The Teachings Of Jesus Can Bring Spiritual Healing

Jesus teaches us that there is great value that may be found in
His teachings. This value is not only on eternal salvation, but also
in finding personal fulfillment and healing in this life.

*Matthew 11:28-30—Come to Me, all you who labor and are*

*heavy laden, and I will give you rest. Take My yoke upon you and learn from Me, for I am gentle and lowly in heart, and you will find rest for your souls. For My yoke is easy and My burden is light."*

Through the years, many have pointed out the profound power in Jesus' teachings in bringing "rest for the weary."

For example:

*"For a specific illustration, I believe the following to be true: If you were to take the sum total of all the authoritative articles ever written by the most qualified of psychologists and psychiatrists on the subject of mental hygiene—if you were to combine them, and refine them, and cleave out the excess verbage—if you were to take the whole of the meat and none of the parsley, and if you were to have these un-adulterated bits of pure scientific knowledge concisely ex-pressed by the most capable of living poets, you would have an awkward and incomplete summation of the Ser-mon on the Mount. And it would suffer immeasurably through comparison. For nearly two thousand years the Christian world has been holding in its hands the complete answer to its restless and fruitless yearnings. And it might almost as well have been holding a slab of Egyptian hiero-glyphics before the discovery of the Rosetta Stone. Here, and in other great religious teachings of the world, rests the blueprint for successful human life, with optimum men-tal health and contentment. But there are, unfortunately, many self-avowed atheists and many agnostics who refuse to listen." (Dr. James T. Fisher and Lowell S. Hawley, A Few Buttons Missing: The Case Book of a Psychiatrist, 3267-3275 (Kindle Edition); Muriwai Books)*

Again:

*"Jesus understood people. We know this because he is the most influential person in all of history. Entire cultures have been shaped, and countless individual lives transformed, as a result of his three-year itinerant ministry two thousand years ago. As a psychologist, I am fascinated with the question of why his teachings were so powerful. After years of study, I have found that a psychological understanding of the teachings of Jesus helps us see why his words had such an impact upon his followers. Using our best psychological theories today, I believe we can see how Jesus's psychologically brilliant grasp of people made them want to listen to him….My study of contemporary psychoanalytic theories has allowed me to understand the teachings of Jesus in a different light that has enriched my life and the lives of my patients. Rather than finding the teachings of Jesus contradicted by these new psychological developments, I have found them illuminated as profound psychological insights that I had not understood before….I believe a number of spiritual principles in the teachings of Jesus can benefit us in our attempts to live psychologically healthy lives. I will be giving examples of how these spiritual principles apply to the lives of people today. The examples I use have been taken from the lives of people I have worked with, known, or read about." (Mark W. Baker, Jesus, the Greatest Therapist Who Ever Lived, 242-284 (Kindle Edition); New York, NY; HarperCollins Publishers Inc.)*

And again:

*"A student at a California university told me that his psychology professor had said in class that "all he has to do is pick up the Bible and read portions of Christ's teaching to many of his patients. That's all the counseling they need.""* (Josh & Sean McDowell, More Than a Carpenter, 550-553

*(Kindle Edition); Carol Stream, IL; Tyndale House Publish-
ers)*

Encourage the addict to learn and meditate on the Word of God.

## Bummer Lambs

I also emphasize that even though God begins the healing process in this life, it will not be fully completed until the Second
Coming. Christianity is not a band-aid: the Lord works in us and
through us in ways that we may not fully realize, and sometimes
that healing work will not be completed before we die.

One author powerfully illustrates this.

> *"The LORD is close to the brokenhearted and saves those
> who are crushed in spirit.—PSALM 34:18 I started out on
> this journey with the best intentions in the world—to love
> and serve God—but somehow, somewhere, I took a wrong
> turn and got lost. I found my way but in the process was
> left broken. I grew up in Scotland with sheep all around me,
> field after field of white wool and incessant crying echoing
> throughout pastures. Of all the lessons I have learned from
> these defenseless, gentle animals, the most profound is the
> most painful. Every now and then, a ewe will give birth to
> a lamb and immediately reject it. Sometimes the lamb is
> rejected because it is one of twins and the mother doesn't
> have enough milk or she is old and, frankly, quite tired of
> the whole business. If the lamb is returned to the ewe, the
> mother may even kick the poor animal away. They call
> those lambs "bummer lambs." Unless the shepherd inter-
> venes, that lamb will die. So the shepherd will take that lit-
> tle lost one into his home and hand-feed it from a bottle
> and keep it warm by the fire. He will wrap it up with soft
> blankets and hold it to his chest so the bummer will hear a*

*heartbeat. When the lamb is strong, the shepherd will place it back in the field with the rest of the flock. "Off you go now, you can do this, I'm right here." The most beautiful sight to see is when the shepherd approaches his flock in the morning and calls out to them, "Sheep, sheep, sheep!" The first to run to him are the bummer lambs because they know his voice. It's not that they are more loved; it's just that they believe it. I am so grateful that Christ calls Himself the Good Shepherd. He calls his own sheep by name and leads them out. After he has gathered his own flock, he walks ahead of them, and they follow him because they know his voice. (John 10:3–4 NLT) I am a bummer lamb. Chances are you are too. I've come to accept the fact that I'll be broken as long as I'm on this earth. I used to think that at some point God would fix me and my testimony would be a great story for other people. I don't think that will be true anymore. And I'm at peace. I think most of us will carry with us the reminders of being broken. We bear scars from a painful divorce, the loss of a loved one, the grip of addiction, the negative report from the doctor. Oh, God will help and strengthen us in the process. We will learn a lot more. And we'll have a greater understanding and empathy for each other because of it. But until we see Jesus face-to-face, we'll be broken. But this is no longer the bad news; it's the best news! We don't need to waste our time continually pointing out what's wrong with us or what's wrong with our lives or what happened to us that's plain wrong; we can spend our time on earth concentrating on what's gloriously perfect about Christ and sharing that revolutionary news with the world. We can dare to believe Him. We can dare to immerse ourselves in His love. We can dare to stay so close to Him that we never forget the sound of His gentle voice." (Shelia Walsh, Loved Back to Life: How I Found the Courage to Live Free, 207-208 (Kindle Edition); Nashville, TN; Nelson Books)*

Even though the healing process begins in this life, it is not completed until the Lord returns for us or we go to meet Him in the vail.

## Ministering To The Spiritual Needs Of The Addict

We need to also consider ways to minister to the spiritual needs of the addict. These needs may be very general, or very specific. For example, it is possible that the addict has simply had no background of any kind from a spiritual point of view. Many of the addicts that I work with were not raised in church or in any kind of Christian education whatsoever. Sometimes these came from homes that were very troubled, with abuse, neglect, and chaos the main theme of the family. Some were raised in homes where drug dealing was a family business, passed on from grandparents, to parents, etc.

We must be careful not to look down upon families in these situations. Many simply do not know better, having never been raised any differently. The Book of Genesis reminds us that nearly every family since the Fall in the Garden of Eden has been dysfunctional in one way or another.

> *"Genesis is filled with human drama that touches and helps every one of us on a personal level. For example, every family in Genesis is what we today would call dysfunctional. I regard this as a divine gift. If your family is dysfunctional, the fact that all the families in Genesis are dysfunctional should provide you with some solace. I think the Bible is telling us that family dysfunction is a normal—though not necessarily inevitable—part of the human condition. Indeed, all of Genesis is a statement of how troubled the human condition is. The rest of the Bible, especially the next four books, provides solutions to the troubled human*

*condition. To put it in medical terms, Genesis describes the patient's (the human being's) pathology, and the books that follow offer the wisdom and moral instruction neces-sary to cure the patient." (Dennis Prager, The Rational Bi-ble: Genesis, 15-16 (Kindle Edition): Washington, D.C.: Reg-nery Faith)*

Sometimes addicts spiritual needs will be very specific. Many have been involved in pagan religions and philosophies, and this means that we need to be willing to do whatever we can to help them find their way out of this darkness and into the light of Christ (Philippians 2:14-15).

## Confronting Demonic Strongholds

As we noticed earlier, there is a great deal of evidence which shows us that demons are alive and at work on our planet, and they are intent on our destruction. Let's notice two Scriptures which make this abundantly clear.

*Ephesians 6:12—For we do not wrestle against flesh and blood, but against principalities, against powers, against the rulers of the darkness of this age, against spiritual hosts of wickedness in the heavenly places.*

*Colossians 1:16—For by Him all things were created that are in heaven and that are on earth, visible and invisible, whether thrones or dominions or principalities or powers. All things were created through Him and for Him.*

In these passages, Paul uses phrases that were well-known in his day and age to refer to the angelic and demonic powers. Arnold documents for us:

*"An important question we face is whether Paul depended primarily on the Jewish demonology of his time or on an understanding of evil spirits rooted more in pagan popular belief. It is not adequate to say Paul derived his terms for evil spirits exclusively from the Old Testament, although quite a few of the words he used appear in the Greek Old Testament (the LXX, or Septuagint). While the terms "Satan" and "devil" are common in the Old Testament, the name "Belial" never appears (see 2 Cor 6:15). Whereas the word translated "powers" (dynameis) is quite frequent in the Greek Old Testament, Paul's most common expressions for the powers, archai and exousiai, are never used.' Most scholars believe Paul's vocabulary for the powers reflects the Jewish demonology of his own day. All of the terms Paul used for the powers can be found in Jewish documents of the Greco-Roman period. The Judaism of Paul's time had a highly developed angelology, as evidenced by the following citations from Jewish documents that contain many of the same terms used by Paul: And he [God] will summon all the forces [dynameis] of the heavens, and all the holy ones above, and the forces of the Lord-the cherubim, seraphim, ophanim, all the angels of governance [archai], the Elect One, and the other forces [exousiai] on earth and over the water. (1 Enoch 61:10)2 And I saw there [in the seventh heaven] an exceptionally great light, and all the fiery armies of the great archangels, and the incorporeal forces [dynameis] and the dominions [kyriotetesJ and the origins [archaiJ and the authorities [exousiaiJ, the cherubim and the seraphim and the many-eyed thrones [thronoi]. (2 Enoch 20:1)' There with him [God] are the thrones [thronoi]) and authorities [exousiai]; there praises to God are offered eternally. (Testament of Levi 3:8) While all three texts refer to the angelic hierarchy surrounding God's throne, the Jews believed the same hierarchy existed in the kingdom of evil. Furthermore, many of these terms were*

*commonly used to refer to various ranks of human leaders in governmental positions of authority. The angelic kingdom was widely believed to be structured in an analogous way to earthly political kingdoms. Although Paul used many terms for the angelic powers known to Judaism, this does not mean that what he had to say about the powers of darkness would have been incomprehensible to the non Jew. While "principalities" (archai) and "authorities" (exousiai) seem to be uniquely Jewish expressions for the unseen realm, many of the other words he used were also used by Gentiles to refer to the world of spirits and invisible powers. Words like "powers" (dynameis), "dominions" (kyriotetes), "thrones" (thronoi), "angels" (angeloi), "world rulers" (kosmokratores), "demons" (daimonia), "elemental spirits" (stoicheia) and "rulers" (archontes) were known and used by pagans, as evidenced in their magical and astrological texts.""* (Clinton E. Arnold, Powers of Darkness: Principalities & Powers in Paul's Letters, 89-91 (Kindle Edition): Grand Rapids, MI: Baker Books)

We also see reference to these beings in the book known as the Testament Of Solomon, which was a second century B.C. Work that both Jesus (Matthew 12:24-37) and Paul (Ephesians 6:12) show familiarity with.

*Testament Of Solomon 114. I therefore, having heard this, glorified the Lord God, and again I questioned the demon, saying: "Tell me how you can ascend into heaven, being demons, and amidst the stars and holy angels intermingle." And he answered: "Just as things are fulfilled in heaven, so also on Earth (are fulfilled) the types of all of them. For there are principalities, authorities, world-rulers, and we demons fly about in the air; and we hear the voices of the heavenly beings, and survey all the powers. And as having no basis on which (Translated by F. C. Conybeare-Revised*

*English and partial translation by Jeremy Kapp, The Testament Of Solomon, 94-98 (Kindle Edition))*

The only difference between this quotation and the one in Ephesians 6:12 is that the word "demons" (Testament Of Solomon) is used in place of "spiritual hosts of wickedness in the heavenly places" (Ephesians). This could suggest that by Paul's day, the phrase "spiritual hosts of wickedness in the heavenly places" was used interchangeably with the word "demons."

Please observe that Paul makes it evident that these demonic powers will continue on throughout the Christian Age. While many claim that demonic forces were thrust into Hell when Jesus died on the Cross, the Bible is adamant that these powers are still here and at work in our world. Indeed, addicts have a special vulnerability to these forces. We have already discussed the connections between addiction and familiar spirits, as well as the Jewish belief that drug abuse opened up a person to become more susceptible to demonic forces. What you may not be aware of is that often, occultists will curse certain drugs and bind demonic spirits to them in order to try and afflict the ones who abuse those drugs. In my ministry, I have encountered several examples where this took place.

## What To Do In These Situations

There are many things that the Bible teaches us regarding these matters of spiritual warfare. Here are a few practical suggestions.

### Acknowledge That Demons Exist

If the Bible is the Word of God, and if the Bible teaches that demons exist, then demons exist. The Bible is the Word of God (multiple evidences of this will be provided in the Appendix section of this book), and the Bible teaches that demons exist (Ephesians 6:12). Therefore, demons exist.

Not only does the Bible teach that demonic forces exist, but so do many who have studied the matter from a secular point of view. For example:

> *"Until the day I met Jersey I did not believe in the devil. Or, to be perfectly precise, up until three hours after I had met her I was 99 + percent sure that the devil did not exist. In-deed, I was using Jersey as part of a strategy to prove the devil's nonexistence as scientifically as possible—to myself. Only my experiment began to backfire the minute I heard Jersey say about her demons, "I feel sorry for them; they're really rather weak and pathetic creatures." When I flew home after that first evaluation I was hardly converted to a belief in the devil; it was fifty-fifty at best. Still, what an extraordinary movement of the mind! From antagonistic to neutral within the course of a single day—certainly enough to keep on investigating. Three months later, after Terry and I had confronted Jersey, exposing a flagrantly evil per-sonality, and after I'd talked to Malachi and had time to digest the experience, I suppose I had been converted. I was now 95 percent sure, enough to command an exorcism to be performed, even though I knew that my own profession might well seek my excommunication. Two months later, on the eve of the exorcism, having heard Jersey scream at me while simultaneously smiling, my certainty that she was demonically possessed was 99 percent. Four days later it was 100 percent. Total. I would never again doubt the ex-istence of Satan. Beccah's exorcism did not increase my certainty of the devil's existence; there is no place to go be-yond total certainty. All I can say is that it was so confus-ing—that Beccah/Lucifer toyed with us so viciously—I'm not sure I could have survived it without my total certainty.*

*As a psychiatrist, I had been converted by Jersey's case alone, from a belief that the devil did not exist to a belief— a certainty—that the devil does exist and probably demons (under the control of the devil) as well. By the devil, I mean a spirit that is powerful (it may be many places at the same time and manifest itself in a variety of distinctly paranormal ways), thoroughly malevolent (its only motivation seemed to be the destruction of human beings or the entire human race), deceitful and vain, capable of taking up a kind of residence within the mind, brain, soul, or body of susceptible and willing human beings—a spirit that had various names (among them Lucifer and Satan), that was real and did exist. I have attempted to tell the stories of Jersey and Beccah with the greatest possible scientific thoroughness. I have left out no significant detail. Consequently, you and I have exactly the same database to work from. But I do not think it likely at this point in time that we would arrive at the same conclusions. So I was converted to a belief in the devil....In summary, it is my hope that you will envision that matters of possession and exorcism, of demons and deliverance, constitute a proper field of scientific inquiry. Specifically, I wish that you will join me in proposing that "demonology" be made an incipient subspecialty of psychiatry and psychology." (M. Scott Peck, M.D., Glimpses of the Devil: A Psychiatrist's Personal Accounts of Possession, Exorcism, and Redemption, 237-239 (Kindle Edition); New York, N.Y.; Free Press)*

Again:

*"Initial medical and religious reaction in many quarters to the draft—from both well-informed academics and doctors as well as from experienced exorcists—has been gratifyingly positive. Readers may be surprised to learn that many physician colleagues of mine—around the world—agree*

*with my findings, though they may be reluctant to speak out so openly—with some notable exceptions. For instance, a Harvard faculty psychiatrist has called this book "especially compelling... unquestionably by a world expert whose academic rigor is impeccable and whose personal integrity is above reproach." A prominent professor of neurology found the manuscript "most striking... by a witness who is completely trustworthy and one of the smartest persons I have ever met." A leading American exorcist describes it as "extremely helpful coming as the book does from America's 'go-to' medical expert on the subject of diabolic attacks.... Whenever I need help, I go to him. He's so respected in the field." Demonic Foes relates unmistakable cases of demonic possession and other diabolic attacks that I directly encountered over the past twenty-five years. I did not originally volunteer to consult upon these cases; rather, I responded to requests from religious leaders for my professional opinion. And I overcame my hesitation about writing this book only after securing the permission of the afflicted men and women I agreed to help." (Richard Gallagher, Demonic Foes: My Twenty-Five Years as a Psychiatrist Investigating Possessions, Diabolic Attacks, and the Paranormal, 1-2 (Kindle Edition); New York, NY; Harper-Collins Publishers, Inc.)*

## Acknowledge That Not All Issues Are Demonic

The Bible makes it clear that sometimes physical illnesses have a non-spiritual cause.

For example:

*Matthew 4:23-24—And Jesus went about all Galilee, teaching in their synagogues, preaching the gospel of the kingdom, and healing all kinds of sickness and all kinds of disease among the people. Then His fame went throughout all Syria; and they brought to Him all sick people who were afflicted with various diseases and torments, and those who were demon-possessed, epileptics, and paralytics; and He healed them.*

Please notice how the people brought to Jesus those who were "afflicted with various diseases and torments," AND "those who were demon-possessed, epileptics, and paralytics." The Bible is clear that not all medical problems are a result of a demonic affliction.

## Acknowledge That Demons May Also Work Through Physical Ailments

We are again reminded that demons may work in various ways through physical symptoms.

*Isaiah 61:3—To console those who mourn in Zion, To give them beauty for ashes, The oil of joy for mourning, The garment of praise for the spirit of heaviness; That they may be called trees of righteousness, The planting of the LORD, that He may be glorified."*

*Matthew 9:32-33—As they went out, behold, they brought to Him a man, mute and demon-possessed. 33. And when the demon was cast out, the mute spoke. And the multitudes marveled, saying, "It was never seen like this in Israel!"*

*Matthew 12:22—Then one was brought to Him who was demon-possessed, blind and mute; and He healed him, so that the blind and mute man both spoke and saw.*

*Mark 9:17—Then one of the crowd answered and said,
"Teacher, I brought You my son, who has a mute spirit.*

*Luke 11:14—And He was casting out a demon, and it was
mute. So it was, when the demon had gone out, that the
mute spoke; and the multitudes marveled.*

*Luke 13:11-16—And behold, there was a woman who had a
spirit of infirmity eighteen years, and was bent over and
could in no way raise herself up. But when Jesus saw her, He
called her to Him and said to her, "Woman, you are loosed
from your infirmity." And He laid His hands on her, and immediately she was made straight, and glorified God. But the
ruler of the synagogue answered with indignation, because
Jesus had healed on the Sabbath; and he said to the crowd,
"There are six days on which men ought to work; therefore
come and be healed on them, and not on the Sabbath day."
The Lord then answered him and said, "Hypocrite! Does not
each one of you on the Sabbath loose his ox or donkey from
the stall, and lead it away to water it? So ought not this
woman, being a daughter of Abraham, whom Satan has
bound—think of it—for eighteen years, be loosed from this
bond on the Sabbath?"*

*Acts 16:16—Now it happened, as we went to prayer, that a
certain slave girl possessed with a spirit of divination met
us, who brought her masters much profit by fortune-telling.*

---

All of these verses teach us about some of the physical ailments
which demons can cause.

## The Gospel Is The Key In Spiritual Warfare

Paul makes it clear that the way to defeat demonic forces is
through the preaching and teaching of the Gospel. In Colossians,

Paul says that our victory occurs when we are baptized into Christ Jesus:

---

*Colossians 2:11-15—In Him you were also circumcised with the circumcision made without hands, by putting off the body of the sins of the flesh, by the circumcision of Christ, buried with Him in baptism, in which you also were raised with Him through faith in the working of God, who raised Him from the dead. And you, being dead in your trespasses and the uncircumcision of your flesh, He has made alive together with Him, having forgiven you all trespasses, having wiped out the handwriting of requirements that was against us, which was contrary to us. And He has taken it out of the way, having nailed it to the cross. Having disarmed principalities and powers, He made a public spectacle of them, triumphing over them in it.*

---

The Apostle here ties together where we are "raised together" and granted the victory...in and through the act of baptism! This is a powerful rebuke to those religious teachers who reject the act of baptism as part of God's plan of salvation. Indeed, please notice that Paul here in Colossians tells us that it is through this Gospel that we are granted access to the Cross, which provides victory over the principalities and powers!

What are the principalities and powers here in context?

*"Rather, we should suppose a hierarchy of heavenly powers-"thrones" superior to "lordships," and so on (see particularly Lightfoot 151-52). The "thrones" are assuredly to be located in heaven (cf. Dan. 7:9; Rev. 4:4; though cf. Wis. 7:8), not least because the word is used for heavenly beings in Testament of Levi 3:8 (in the seventh heaven, with "authorities"); 2 Enoch 20:1; and Apocalypse of Elijah 1:10-11.*

*Likewise the "dominions" (xvptotirltiES) are almost cer-
tainly to be taken as referring to heavenly powers, in the
light of Eph. 1:20-21 (also I Enoch 61:10 and 2 Enoch 20:1;
F. Schroger, EDNT 2.332). But the same must be true of the
"principalities" (apxai) and "authorities" (~4ovaiat) in the
light of 2:10 and 15, not to mention the other New Testament parallels (I Cor. 15:24; Eph. 1:21 again; 3:10; 6:12; see
also on 2:10). The fact that all four terms thus refer only to
the invisible, heavenly realm23 and the repeated emphasis
on Christ's supremacy and triumph over the "principalities
and powers" in 2:10 and 15 do therefore strengthen the
likelihood that the two lines were inserted by the author(s)
of the letter, sacrificing the balance of the hymn in order to
add a further reference to Christ's superiority over all beings in heaven as well as on earth." (James D.G. Dunn, The
Epistles to the Colossians and to Philemon (The New International Greek Testament Commentary), 1291-1300 (Kindle Edition): Grand Rapids, MI: William B. Eerdmans Publishing Company)*

The Gospel has the power to free a person from the slavery of
these beings. When the Lord commissioned Paul to preach the
Word of God, He told him:

---

*Acts 26:17-18- I will deliver you from the Jewish people, as
well as from the Gentiles, to whom I now send you, to open
their eyes, in order to turn them from darkness to light, and
from the power of Satan to God, that they may receive forgiveness of sins and an inheritance among those who are
sanctified by faith in Me.'*

---

## Obey The Gospel

It could be that the addict has some sin in his heart and life that is allowing those demonic forces to gain a foothold. If the addict is willing as a believer in Jesus Christ to repent of his sin and be baptized into Christ, then through the cross those powers will be defeated (as noted from the passage from Colossians referenced above).

However, the addict must be willing to be diligent in the fight against these powers, because they will try to gain access again.

---

*Ephesians 4:26-27—BE ANGRY, AND DO NOT SIN": do not let the sun go down on your wrath, nor give place to the devil.*

---

That phrase "nor give place to the devil" reminds us that children of God may again bring themselves under demonic oppression through willful sin that is unrepented of.

*"Although it is possible to take this term in the metaphorical sense of "chance" or "opportunity," 13 it is best interpreted according to its spatial significance of "place." 14 This is in accord with the fact that spatial language abounds in this letter, especially as illustrated by Paul's frequent use of the language of "filling" (πληρόω/ πλήρωμα; 3:19; 4:10; 5:18) and indwelling (2:22; 3:17). It is also significant that the term "place" is used elsewhere in the NT to refer to the inhabiting place of an evil spirit. Luke records Jesus as saying, "When an evil spirit comes out of a man, it goes through arid places (τόπων) seeking rest and does not find it. Then it says, 'I will return to the house I left' " (Luke 11:24). A similar usage is found in the Apocalypse: "And there was war in heaven. Michael and his angels fought against the dragon, and the dragon and his angels fought back. But he was not strong enough, and they lost their place (τόπος) in heaven" (Rev 12:7–8). First-century*

*Judaism saw anger as a magnet that attracted the working of an evil spirit: "Anger and falsehood together are a double-edged evil, and work together to perturb the reason. And when the soul is continually perturbed, the Lord withdraws from it and Beliar rules it" (T. Dan 4:7; see also 5:1). In fact, the same work speaks of a "spirit of anger" that attacks the people of God (T. Dan 1:8; 2:1, 4). The earliest allusions to Eph 4:27 interpret "place" spatially and speak of anger and sinful practices as making one susceptible to the work of a demonic spirit (see Herm. Mand. 5.1.3; 12.5.1–4; Origen, Princ. 2.3.4). Paul presents "the devil" as a powerful being that needs to be resisted (6:11). He is the same entity that Paul referred to earlier as "the ruler of the realm of the air, the spirit who is now powerfully working in the sons of disobedience" (2:2). The early Christians also knew him as Satan (Rev 12:9; 20:2). As ruler of a realm of spirits, it is unlikely that he is personally assailing every Christian, but is assigning his spirit emissaries to do this work. By allowing anger to fester and grow, believers can surrender space to a demonic intruder. This is how Origen understood this passage. He warned believers that by thinking intently about and following the wrong inclinations of the soul, "these assents summon the devil to enter our souls" (citing Judas as an example; John 13:2, 27). 15 Similarly, Ambrosiaster notes, "An angry mind will necessarily think evil thoughts, as the devil desires. If the devil finds a mind ready for evil and slipping toward it, he deceives the person who was created for life. The thought, you see, is human. But the devil completes it." 16 Calvin notes, "I have no doubt that Paul was warning us to beware lest Satan should take possession of our minds, like an enemy-occupied fortress, and do whatever he pleases." 17 Similarly, Robinson warned that persisting anger "gives immediate opportunity for the entry of an evil spirit." 18 This does not mean that believers forfeit their new identity in*

*Christ; Paul presents this new creation and new identity as a firmly established fact. It does mean that the Holy Spirit is grieved (4:30) and that the demonic spirit has a new ability to exploit the believer. O'Brien is probably correct in observing that this warning not only provides a motivation for controlling anger, but is equally applicable to any behavior that is characteristic of the old self. 19 The implication of this would be that unchecked sinful behavior will eventually yield a place to the enemy to further his goals of stunting the sanctifying work of God." (Clinton Arnold, Ephesians: Exegetical Commentary On The New Testament, 512-514 (Kindle Edition): Grand Rapids, MI: Zondervan).*

## Prayer And Fasting

Jesus Himself teaches us that we must be willing to pray and fast for those under demonic oppression.

---

*Mark 9:29—So He said to them, "This kind can come out by nothing but prayer and fasting."*

---

Any kind of fast should be approved by a medical professional.

## Be Prepared For Relapse

Addicts need to be reminded that sometimes we all fall short. I cannot tell you how many addicts I have worked with over the years who have given up on the fight for sobriety because they succumbed to temptation. Every Christian needs to be reminded (and to remind others) that the Christian life is a series of battles. We will win some: we will lose some. Yet with Jesus, we have won (and are winning) the war. Welch provides this important lesson for us to remember:

*"After detection and, if necessary, detoxification, the work begins. Many families, friends, and churches err at this point. Sin, slavery, and idolatry do not go away overnight. There is a Christian myth that change is an event rather than a process; that it is more like a light switch that is turned on than a battle that must be engaged. For some reason, we tend to think—wrongly—that immediate liberation from the slavery of addiction is more glamorous than the gradual process of taking a little bit of land at a time. Such expectations have implicitly encouraged addicts to tell great, though fabricated, stories of liberation instead of simply being honest about their struggles, and finding in that honesty something highly praiseworthy. We must remember that for everyone, the Christian life is an ongoing battle. It is a daily process of mortifying the flesh. We must "encourage one another daily, as long as it is called Today, so that none of you may be hardened by sin's deceitfulness" (Heb. 3:13). To our shame, Alcoholics Anonymous has a better understanding of the need for daily exhortation than the church." (Edward T. Welch, Addictions: A Banquet In The Grave-Finding Hope In The Power Of The Gospel, 112 (Kindle Edition); Glenside, PA; The Christian Counseling And Educational Foundation)*

Remind the struggling addict of Scriptures like these:

---

*Psalm 103:11-14—For as the heavens are high above the earth, So great is His mercy toward those who fear Him; As far as the east is from the west, So far has He removed our transgressions from us. As a father pities his children, So the LORD pities those who fear Him. For He knows our frame; He remembers that we are dust.*

*Psalm 130:3-4—If You, LORD, should mark iniquities, O Lord, who could stand? But there is forgiveness with You,*

*That You may be feared.*

*Micah 7:18—Who is a God like You, Pardoning iniquity And passing over the transgression of the remnant of His heritage? He does not retain His anger forever, Because He delights in mercy.*

*Hebrews 4:15-16—For we do not have a High Priest who cannot sympathize with our weaknesses, but was in all points tempted as we are, yet without sin. Let us therefore come boldly to the throne of grace, that we may obtain mercy and find grace to help in time of need.*

*1 John 1:9—If we confess our sins, He is faithful and just to forgive us our sins and to cleanse us from all unrighteousness.*

---

May the Lord bless you richly in your efforts to reach out and encourage addicts on their path to sobriety.

The grace of the Lord Jesus Christ, and the love of God, and the communion of the Holy Spirit, be with you all. Amen.

# COMMON QUESTIONS AND ANSWERS

In this final chapter, we are going to spend some time reviewing various questions that come up when working with addicts. Some of these questions are difficult to answer, and as such some of my suggestions will come from years of Bible study and experiences with individuals and families. Please keep this in mind as we proceed.

## Question: What Role Should Alcoholic Anonymous (AA) And Narcotics Anonymous (NA) Have In Our Outreach To Addicts?

Answer: I recommend using some of the resources from AA and NA with caution.

We would be foolish to ignore the role that these groups have in helping addicts in recovery over the years. Throughout my ministry, I have known many who struggle with various addictions that were helped by the material and programs offered by AA and NA. Some of their philosophy is extremely helpful and rooted in Scripture. This is especially true of the Twelve Steps:

> "Here are the steps we took, which are suggested as a program of recovery: We admitted we were powerless over alcohol—that our lives had become unmanageable. Came to believe that a Power greater than ourselves could restore us to sanity. Made a decision to turn our will and our lives over to the care of God as we understood Him. Made a searching and fearless moral inventory of ourselves. Admitted to God, to ourselves, and to another human being the exact nature of our wrongs. Were entirely ready to have God remove all these defects of character. Humbly asked

*Him to remove our shortcomings. Made a list of all persons we had harmed, and became willing to make amends to them all. Made direct amends to such people wherever possible, except when to do so would injure them or others. Continued to take personal inventory and when we were wrong promptly admitted it. Sought through prayer and meditation to improve our conscious contact with God as we understood Him, praying only for knowledge of His will for us and the power to carry that out. Having had a spiritual awakening as the result of these steps, we tried to carry this message to alcoholics, and to practice these principles in all our affairs." (Alcoholics Anonymous World Service Inc., Alcoholics Anonymous, Fourth Edition: The Official "Big Book" From Alcoholic Anonymous, 31-32 (Kindle Edition): New York, NY: Alcoholics Anonymous World Service, Inc).*

Let's take a look at each of the steps, and compare them with some Scriptures which go along with them. We will then notice some concerns that have been raised about the twelve steps, and some things to beware of regarding AA and NA.

| Twelve Steps | Holy Scripture |
|---|---|
| "We admitted we were powerless over alcohol—that our lives had become unmanageable." | Romans 7:14-25—For we know that the law is spiritual, but I am carnal, sold under sin. For what I am doing, I do not understand. For what I will to do, that I do not practice; but what I hate, that I do. If, then, I do what I will not to do, I agree with the law that *it is* good. But now, *it is* no longer I who do it, but sin that dwells in me. For I know that in me (that is, in my flesh) nothing good dwells; for to will is present with me, but *how* to perform what is good I do not find. For the good that I will *to do,* I do not do; but the evil I will not *to do,* that I practice. Now if I do what I will not *to do,* it is no longer I who do it, but sin that dwells in me. I find then a law, that evil is present with me, the one who wills to do good. For I delight in the law of God according to the inward man. But I see another law in my members, warring against the law of my mind, and bringing me into captivity to the law of sin which is in my members. O wretched man that I am! Who will deliver me from this body of death? I thank God—through Jesus Christ our Lord! So then, with the mind I myself serve the law of God, but with the flesh the law of sin. |

| "Came to believe that a Power greater than ourselves could restore us to sanity." | Isaiah 55:6-11—Seek the LORD while He may be found, Call upon Him while He is near. Let the wicked forsake his way, And the unrighteous man his thoughts; Let him return to the LORD, And He will have mercy on him; And to our God, For He will abundantly pardon. "For My thoughts *are* not your thoughts, Nor *are* your ways My ways," says the LORD. "For *as* the heavens are higher than the earth, So are My ways higher than your ways, And My thoughts than your thoughts. "For as the rain comes down, and the snow from heaven, And do not return there, But water the earth, And make it bring forth and bud, That it may give seed to the sower And bread to the eater, So shall My word be that goes forth from My mouth; It shall not return to Me void, But it shall accomplish what I please, And it shall prosper *in the thing* for which I sent it. |
| "Made a decision to turn our will and our lives over to the care of God as we understood Him." | Matthew 11:28-30—Come to Me, all *you* who labor and are heavy laden, and I will give you rest. Take My yoke upon you and learn from Me, for I am gentle and lowly in heart, and you will find rest for your souls. For My yoke *is* easy and My burden is light." |

| | |
|---|---|
| "Made a searching and fearless moral inventory of ourselves." | Psalm 119:59—I thought about my ways, And turned my feet to Your testimonies.<br><br>Psalm 139:23-24—Search me, O God, and know my heart; Try me, and know my anxieties; 24 And see if there is any wicked way in me, And lead me in the way everlasting. |
| "Admitted to God, to ourselves, and to another human being the exact nature of our wrongs." | Psalm 51:3-4—For I acknowledge my transgressions, And my sin *is* always before me. Against You, You only, have I sinned, And done *this* evil in Your sight—That You may be found just when You speak, *And* blameless when You judge.<br><br>Galatians 6:1-2—Brethren, if a man is overtaken in any trespass, you who *are* spiritual restore such a one in a spirit of gentleness, considering yourself lest you also be tempted. Bear one another's burdens, and so fulfill the law of Christ. |
| "Were entirely ready to have God remove all these defects of character." | Romans 8:12-13 — Therefore, brethren, we are debtors—not to the flesh, to live according to the flesh. For if you live according to the flesh you will die; but if by the Spirit you put to death the deeds of the body, you will live.<br><br>2 Corinthians 7:1 — Therefore, |

| | having these promises, beloved, let us cleanse ourselves from all filthiness of the flesh and spirit, perfecting holiness in the fear of God. |
|---|---|
| "Humbly asked Him to remove our shortcomings." | James 4:7-10—Therefore submit to God. Resist the devil and he will flee from you. Draw near to God and He will draw near to you. Cleanse *your* hands, *you* sinners; and purify *your* hearts, *you* double-minded. Lament and mourn and weep! Let your laughter be turned to mourning and *your* joy to gloom. Humble yourselves in the sight of the Lord, and He will lift you up. |
| "Made a list of all persons we had harmed, and became willing to make amends to them all." | Matthew 5:23-24—Therefore if you bring your gift to the altar, and there remember that your brother has something against you, leave your gift there before the altar, and go your way. First be reconciled to your brother, and then come and offer your gift. |
| "Made direct amends to such people wherever possible, except when to do so would injure them or others." | Ephesians 4:28—Let him who stole steal no longer, but rather let him labor, working with *his* hands what is good, that he may have something to give him who has need.<br><br>Philemon 1:10-16—I appeal to you for my son Onesimus, whom |

| | |
|---|---|
| | I have begotten *while* in my chains, who once was unprofitable to you, but now is profitable to you and to me. I am sending him back. You therefore receive him, that is, my own heart, whom I wished to keep with me, that on your behalf he might minister to me in my chains for the gospel. But without your consent I wanted to do nothing, that your good deed might not be by compulsion, as it were, but voluntary. For perhaps he departed for a while for this *purpose,* that you might receive him forever, no longer as a slave but more than a slave—a beloved brother, especially to me but how much more to you, both in the flesh and in the Lord. |
| "Continued to take personal inventory and when we were wrong promptly admitted it." | 2 Corinthians 13:5—Examine yourselves *as to* whether you are in the faith. Test yourselves. Do you not know yourselves, that Jesus Christ is in you?—unless indeed you are disqualified. |
| "Sought through prayer and meditation to improve our conscious contact with God as we understood Him, praying only for knowledge of His will for us and the power to carry that out." | Jeremiah 33:3—Call to Me, and I will answer you, and show you great and mighty things, which you do not know.'<br><br>Matthew 7:7-11—Ask, and it will be given to you; seek, and you will find; knock, and it will be opened to you. For everyone who |

| | |
|---|---|
| | asks receives, and he who seeks finds, and to him who knocks it will be opened. Or what man is there among you who, if his son asks for bread, will give him a stone? Or if he asks for a fish, will he give him a serpent? If you then, being evil, know how to give good gifts to your children, how much more will your Father who is in heaven give good things to those who ask Him! |
| "Having had a spiritual awakening as the result of these steps, we tried to carry this message to alcoholics, and to practice these principles in all our affairs." | Daniel 12:3—Those who are wise shall shine Like the brightness of the firmament, And those who turn many to righteousness Like the stars forever and ever.<br><br>Matthew 28:19-20—Go therefore and make disciples of all the nations, baptizing them in the name of the Father and of the Son and of the Holy Spirit, teaching them to observe all things that I have commanded you; and lo, I am with you always, *even* to the end of the age." Amen. |

As we see, there are many ways that the twelve steps are rooted in the Bible and Scriptural principles. However, there are some serious concerns with some of these that you may want to carefully consider in your preparations for an outreach to addicts.

The first one deals with the subject of acknowledging God "as you understand him." Several addicts that I have worked with over the years have told me that their acceptance of AA and NA was such that a belief in any kind of god was sufficient for their acceptance into these programs. As such, several that I have worked with over the years have been committed pagans and Satanists.

David L. Simmons was a firm believer in the "A.A." (Alcoholics Anonymous) program. He spent years in A.A., sponsored many people, and was a firm believer in the "Big Book" (i.e., the primary text of A.A.). He did not believe in the God of the Bible, but instead prayed to nature as a form of pantheistic religion. Then, his eyes were gradually opened as he studied the New Testament and listened to a preacher out of Tennessee. He began to realize one of the greatest deceptions of A.A.: "god as you conceive him."

Well, look what Simmons writes:

> *"We find these same thoughts from Bill W: "Those having religious affiliations will find nothing here disturbing to their beliefs or ceremonies. There is no friction among us over such matters." Whatever god you serve or spiritual path you are on, bring those convictions to AA because there are many paths to God, or so they say. The essential thought is that whatever god you choose to believe in, that path to that god is right for you. This line of reasoning is more evident in another text by Bill W. in which he writes, "We took AA's Twelve Steps over to the largest Buddhist monastery in this province. We showed them to the priest at the head of it. After he had finished looking over the Twelve Steps, the monk said, 'Why, these are fine! Since we as Buddhists don't understand god just as you do, it might be slightly more acceptable if you inserted the word "good" in your steps instead of "God." Nevertheless, you say in these steps that it is God, as you understand Him. That*

*clears up the point for us. Yes, AA's Twelve Steps will cer-*
*tainly be accepted by the Buddhists around here.'" The am-*
*biguity of the AA steps allows a Buddhist priest to readily*
*accept them. If you're just an AA member, then this proba-*
*bly doesn't mean a whole lot to you. If you're an AA mem-*
*ber who also professes to be a Christian, then this should*
*greatly concern you. AA's errant message originated with*
*Bill W., whose "writing and speaking would be character-*
*ized by a continuing refusal to introduce Christian doctrine*
*to AA." Bill W. and several of his followers also had a dis-*
*turbing ritual of trying to contact the spirits of the dead.*
*The Bible repeatedly warns against this practice (Leviticus*
*19:31, 20:6, 27, Deuteronomy 18:10, 11), yet Bill's conten-*
*tion was that "the mystery could, and should, be removed*
*from mysticism ... benefits of mysticism could be available*
*to everyone ... The Wilsons and the Smiths don't seem to*
*have seen any conflict between their belief in God and a*
*curiosity about the world of the spirits. When the Smiths*
*were visiting the Wilsons ... they joined Bill and Lois in the*
*séances ..." (David L. Simmons, Christianity and Alcoholics*
*Anonymous: Competing or Compatible?: A.A. Weighed and*
*Measured Through the Scales of Scripture, 17-18 (Kindle*
*Edition); Bloomington, IN; WestBow Press)*

Dave Hunt, another researcher, has noted:

*"AA's 12—Step program (and the others patterned after it)*
*opens the door to the occult by introducing members to a*
*generic "god." Step 2 says, "Came to believe that a Power*
*greater than ourselves could restore us to sanity." Step 3*
*continues, "Made a decision to turn our will and our lives*
*over to God as we [Hindu, Buddhist, Christian, Mormon,*
*Catholic, agnostic, et al.] understood Him." As in Masonry,*
*any false god will do. Obviously, a willingness to submit to*
*and trust in Al Gore's Higher Power "by whatever name"*

*provides Satan and his minions with a perfect front for their influence and activity. Satan is not an atheist. He knows that God exists and he wants to take His place and to be worshiped by mankind. To that end, he encourages belief in a "higher power" in order to turn men from the true God to himself. Satan knows that all people have a sense of alienation from God and that the Holy Spirit is wooing mankind to Himself. What better way for Satan to prevent such reconciliation with the true God through Christ than to effect a pseudo-reconciliation with a counterfeit higher power?" (Dave Hunt, Occult Invasion: The Subtle Seduction of the World and Church, 6047-6056 (Kindle Edition); Bend, OR; The Berean Call)*

While this type of approach within AA and NA is acceptable for those who adhere to the religions of the world, Christians know from the Word of God that there are dangerous spiritual forces at work in and through the other gods and goddesses. When a person in these programs is encouraged to reach out to god "as you conceive him," they are being encouraged to open the doorway to demonic forces. This is dangerous, and we are reminded about the numerous Scriptures which tell us to stay away from these other gods and goddesses.

For example:

---

*Exodus 20:3—You shall have no other gods before Me.*

*Deuteronomy 6:14—You shall not go after other gods, the gods of the peoples who are all around you;*

*Deuteronomy 8:19—Then it shall be, if you by any means forget the LORD your God, and follow other gods, and serve them and worship them, I testify against you this day that you shall surely perish.*

*Psalm 81:9—There shall be no foreign god among you; Nor shall you worship any foreign god.*

*1 Corinthians 8:5-6—For even if there are so-called gods, whether in heaven or on earth (as there are many gods and many lords), yet for us there is one God, the Father, of whom are all things, and we for Him; and one Lord Jesus Christ, through whom are all things, and through whom we live.*

*1 Corinthians 10:19-20—What am I saying then? That an idol is anything, or what is offered to idols is anything? Rather, that the things which the Gentiles sacrifice they sacrifice to demons and not to God, and I do not want you to have fellowship with demons.*

---

There are many other Scriptures which document the reality and wicked nature of these spirits who often portray themselves as benevolent helpers of mankind. However, the Bible identifies them clearly as fallen angels and demons (Psalm 82:1,6; 96:4-5; 97:7).

As such, I strongly suggest using these twelve steps when they are in harmony with the Word of God. I would encourage you to make it clear to those that you minister to that there is only one true (eternal) God, and that He is the only Source for hope and salvation (John 14:6).

Another issue you will find with the twelve steps is the idea of addiction being a "disease." This is based on the fact that there are different and competing ideas of the word "disease." For example, some people will say that the word "disease" has the idea of some kind of genetic or physical illness that afflicts a person, making it inevitable that the person would begin to drink or abuse drugs. In this viewpoint, "disease" is equivalent to something inevitable which afflicts a person, making it impossible for them to resist abusing drugs. Others use the word "disease" as something which afflicts a person after they begin to abuse drugs, and is a result of their genetic and ancestral background.

If drug abuse really is a physical disease, then there should be no accountability held for the person who suffers from such, for it is inevitable that he abuse the drugs. We know that a person under the influence of drugs, however, is accountable for the actions that he takes under said influence. This implies that we know intuitively that there is some measure of accountability and that drug abuse is not "merely" a physical disease. Indeed, our definition of the word "disease" is extremely important. One researcher writes:

> *"What Are Real Diseases? Most of this book deals with what it means to regard addiction as a disease. But if we are to distinguish between addiction and other diseases, then we first need to understand what have been called diseases historically and how these differ from what are being called diseases today. To do so, let us review three generations of diseases—physical ailments, mental disorders, and addictions. The first generation of diseases consists of disorders known through their physical manifestations, like malaria, tuberculosis, cancer, and AIDS. The era of medical understanding that these diseases ushered in began with the discovery of specific microbes that cause particular diseases and for which preventive inoculations—and eventually antibodies—were developed. These maladies are the ones we can unreservedly call diseases without clouding the issue. This first generation of diseases differs fundamentally from what were later called diseases in that the former are defined by their measurable physical effects. They are clearly connected to the functioning of the body,*

*and our concern is with the damage the disease does to the body. The second generation of diseases are the so-called mental illnesses (now referred to as emotional disorders). They are not defined in the same way as the first genera-tion. Emotional disorders are apparent to us not because of what we measure in people's bodies but because of the feelings, thoughts, and behaviors that they produce in peo-ple, which we can only know from what the sufferers say and do. We do not diagnose emotional disorders from a brain scan; if a person cannot tell reality from fantasy, we call the person mentally ill, no matter what the person's EEG says. The third generation of diseases—addictions—strays still farther from the model of physical disorder to which the name disease was first applied by modern medi-cine. That is, unlike a mental illness such as schizophrenia, which is indicated by disordered thinking and feelings, ad-dictive disorders are known by the behaviors they describe. We call a person a drug addict who consumes drugs com-pulsively or excessively and whose life is devoted to seeking out these substances. If an addicted smoker gives up smok-ing or if an habituated coffee drinker decides to drink coffee only after Sunday dinner, then each ceases to be addicted. We cannot tell whether a person is addicted or will be ad-dicted in the absence of the ongoing behavior—the person with a hypothetical alcoholic predisposition (say, one who has an alcoholic parent or whose face flushes when drink-ing) but who drinks occasionally and moderately is not an alcoholic. In order to clarify the differences between third-generation and first-generation diseases, we often have to overcome shifting definitions that have been changed solely for the purpose of obscuring crucial differences be-tween problems like cancer and addiction. After a time, we seem not to recognize how our views have been manipu-lated by such gerrymandered disease criteria. For example, by claiming that alcoholics are alcoholics even if they haven't drunk for fifteen years, alcoholism is made to seem less tied to drinking behavior and more like cancer. Sometimes it seems necessary to remind ourselves of the obvious: that a person does not get over cancer by stopping a single behavior or even by changing a whole life-style, but the sole and essential indicator for successful remission of alcoholism is that the person ceases to drink. Addictions involve appetites and behaviors. While a connection can be traced between individual and cultural beliefs and first-and second-generation diseases, this connection is most pronounced for addictions. Behaviors and appetites are addictions only in particular cultural contexts—obviously, obesity matters only where people have enough to eat and think it is important to be thin. Symptoms like loss-of-control drinking depend completely on cultural and personal meanings, and we will explore in subsequent chapters how cultural groups that don't understand how people can lose control of their drinking are almost immune to alcoholism. What is most important, however, is not how cultural beliefs affect addictions but how our defining of addictions as diseases affects our views of ourselves as individuals and as a society." (Stanton Peele, Diseasing of America: How We Allowed Recovery Zealots and the Treatment Industry to Convince Us We Are Out of Control, 16-17 (Kindle Edition): New York, NY: Lexington Books)*

Peele goes on later to describe the nature of addiction:

*"People seek specific, essential human experiences from their addictive involvement, no matter whether it is drinking, eating, smoking, loving, shopping, or gambling. People can come to depend on such an involvement for these experiences until—in the extreme—the involvement is totally consuming and potentially destructive. Addiction can occasionally veer into total abandonment, as well as periodic*

*excesses and loss of control. Nonetheless, even in cases where addicts die from their excesses, an addiction must be understood as a human response that is motivated by the addict's desires and principles. All addictions accomplish something for the addict. They are ways of coping with feelings and situations with which addicts cannot otherwise cope. What is wrong with disease theories as science is that they are tautologies; they avoid the work of understanding why people drink or smoke in favor of simply declaring these activities to be addictions, as in the statement "he drinks so much because he's an alcoholic." Addicts seek experiences that satisfy needs they cannot otherwise fulfill. Any addiction involves three components—the person, the situation or environment, and the addictive involvement or experience (see Table 1). In addition to the individual, the situation, and the experience, we also need to consider the overall cultural and social factors that affect addiction in our society." (Stanton Peele, Diseasing of America: How We Allowed Recovery Zealots and the Treatment Industry to Convince Us We Are Out of Control, 125-126 (Kindle Edition): New York, NY: Lexington Books)*

If a person is convinced that he will be unable to alter his behavior, then odds are that he will continue to live in and justify that behavior (no matter how terrible the consequences). In my life, I have worked with some addicts who believe in the "disease model" so strongly that they simply throw up their hands and ask, "Why try?" To me, this is one of the dangers of clinging too tightly to a disease model of addiction.

On the other hand, I can readily see the fact that our sin-warped world has caused a lot of damage to our bodies that God never intended. How strongly has the ravages of sin affected our physical bodies? Could there be some kind of genetic link to addiction?

The full answer to these questions are beyond me.

Personally, I believe that there are many roots of addiction. What is important to emphasize is that no matter the degree that a person holds to the "disease" model, it must not be so strong a conviction that the addict believes he is unable to alter his behavior. Not only does the Word of God teach that changing behavior is possible, but so also does the experience of tens of thousands of addicts who have been able (with the help of God through Jesus Christ) to accomplish just that.

As such, I strongly suggest that you be cautious in what level of AA and NA philosophy, literature, and programs you introduce into and rely on with your ministry outreach. While the 12 Steps are biblical in some ways, in others they are very unbiblical and can be extremely dangerous (from both a spiritual and practical standpoint).

## Question: How Far Do Addicts Need To Go In Making Amends To Those Whom They Have Wronged?

Answer: As far as is necessary to restore a relationship between themselves and the ones whom they have wronged.

Making amends is one of the greatest challenges that addicts will face, and for that reason they will greatly need your spiritual and emotional support. The principle of making amends is one that is relevant not only to addicts of course. Every Christian needs to understand the principles from God's Word for making amends to those that we have wronged (either in ignorance or intentionally).

It is right here that we need to make some important notes from a Bible point of view. The first is that making amends is a Bible principle that needs to be recognized and applied personally. Throughout the Old and New Testaments, God had taught the principle of making amends. One example comes from the Book of Leviticus.

---

*Leviticus 6:1-7—And the LORD spoke to Moses, saying: "If a person sins and commits a trespass against the LORD by lying to his neighbor about what was delivered to him for safekeeping, or about a pledge, or about a robbery, or if he has extorted from his neighbor, or if he has found what was lost and lies concerning it, and swears falsely—in any one of these things that a man may do in which he sins: then it shall be, because he has sinned and is guilty, that he shall restore what he has stolen, or the thing which he has extorted, or what was delivered to him for safekeeping, or the lost thing which he found, or all that about which he has sworn falsely. He shall restore its full value, add one-fifth more to it, and give it to whomever it belongs, on the day of his trespass offering. And he shall bring his trespass offering to the LORD, a ram without blemish from the flock, with your valuation, as a trespass offering, to the priest. So the priest shall make atonement for him before the LORD, and he shall be forgiven for any one of these things that he may have done in which he trespasses."*

---

This passage teaches us that forgiveness is offered by God to those who repent, even of what we would call "willful sin." Here is a man who intentionally deceives and defrauds his brother. Please carefully observe that there is forgiveness possible for such sin, conditioned upon repentance. I bring this up because many believe that only sins of ignorance may be forgiven by God. However, this passage (and many others may be cited) demonstrates that the Lord provides forgiveness for all sins that a person repents of. Michael Brown has some fascinating commentary on this passage.

> *"Before answering your objection, it's important that I clear up some misconceptions. First, as we have noted previously, Christians and Messianic Jews do not believe for a moment that sacrifices without out repentance and faith did anyone any good (see vol. 1, 1.11, and above, 3.8-3.9). Second, we do not believe that after every sin an Israelite had to go to the Temple in Jerusalem (or before that, to the Tabernacle) and offer a sacrifice. Every animal in the land fit for sacrifice would have been slaughtered within days if that were the case, and no one would have had time to do anything except offer sacrifices day and night. Normal life would completely cease if such an impossible scenario existed. Third, we do not believe that God's people can sin freely, then repent and bring a sacrifice, then sin freely again. Rather, as we pointed out in an earlier discussion, we agree with the Talmudic statement that "he who says, I will sin and repent, I will sin and repent, repentance is not vouchsafed to him" (m. Yoma 8:9, and see above, 3.8). As the psalmist expressed it, "If I had cherished sin in my heart, the Lord would not have listened" (Ps. 66:18). Fourth, we believe that for those who continue in willful and defiant sin, there is no forgiveness (we'll come back to this point shortly). What then was the purpose of sacrifices and offerings in Israel? We must remember that there were different kinds of sacrifices and different functions for those sacrifices in the religious life of our people. Some sacrifices, such as the burnt offerings (Hebrew, 'olah, also known as the whole offering or holocaust), were offered up as symbols of complete dedication and devotion to the Lord.220 Other sacrifices, such as the todah, were offered in thanksgiving to the Lord, while other sacrifices, such as the sin offering*

*(Hebrew, hatta't), were offered to remove ritual impurity (among other things), and still others, such as the fellowship (or peace) offerings (Hebrew, shelamirn), were offered in worshipful communion. As to differences between the sin and guilt offerings (hatta't and 'asham respectively), Hebrew professor George Buchanan Gray, lecturing in the 1920s, could state, "The precise distinction between the sin-offering and the guilt-or trespass-offering is not altogether clear, and has been much discussed." More recently, however, R. Laird Harris, a Christian biblical scholar and Hebraist, wrote: The difference between the sin offering and the guilt offering was in the nature of the sin. The former was for what might be called general sins; the latter for sins that injured other people or detracted from the sacred worship. The guilt offering thus involved not only a sacrifice but also restitution plus a fine of 20 percent (6:5 [5:24 in the Hebrew]). The sins for which the sin offering was prescribed are called "unintentional sins" (4:2), or those done "through ignorance" (iuv). The same expression is used in connection with the guilt offering (5:15). Or as expressed by Baruch Levine, a leading Jewish authority on atonement and sacrifice: Chapters 4 and 5 [of Leviticus] contain the laws governing expiatory sacrifices, the purpose of which is to secure atonement and forgiveness from God. These offerings are efficacious only when offenses are inadvertent or unwitting. They do not apply to defiant acts of premeditated crimes. Whenever an individual Israelite, a tribal leader, a priest, or even the chief priest, or the Israelite community at large is guilty of an inadvertent offense or of failing to do what the law requires, expiation through sacrifices is required. However, under certain circumstances, the 'asham could atone for intentional sins. As Levine noted: The offenses outlined here [in Lev. 5:20-26, or 6:1-7 in most English translations] were quite definitely intentional! A person misappropriated property or funds*

*entrusted to his safekeeping, or defrauded another, or failed to restore lost property he had located.... If, subsequently, , the accused came forth on his own and admitted to having lied under oath-thus assuming liability for the unrecovered property-he was given the opportunity to clear himself by making restitution and by paying a fine of 20 percent to the aggrieved party. Having lied under oath, he had also offended God and was obliged to offer an 'asham sacrifice in expiation.... God accepts the expiation even of one who swears falsely in His name because the guilty person is willing to make restitution to the victim of his crime. This observation alone shoots a hole in the anti-missionary teaching that only unintentional sins could be atoned for with blood sacrifices.*

*"But," you object, "that's hardly sufficient proof. If anything, all you've demonstrated is that for a very small number of specifically enumerated sins, one particular sacrifice brought atonement. What about all the other sins people commit? Where does the Torah say that sacrifices provided atonement?" The Torah says so explicitly in Leviticus 16, the most important atonement chapter in all of the Pentateuch, the chapter in which the rituals for the Day of Atonement are laid out. However, before turning o Leviticus 16, let me give you an important Talmudic perspective.. As noted by the Rabbinic scholar Solomon Schechter in his discussion of sacrifices and atonement, The continual offering was a communal offering, nor is there in the Bible ascribed to it any atoning power; but there is a marked tendency in Rabbinic literature to bestow on all sacrifices, even such as the burnt-offering offering and the peace-offering, some sort of atoning power for certain classes of sins, both of commission and omission, for which the Bible ascribes no sacrifice at all.*

*Thus, the rabbis went beyond the Torah in ascribing aton-ing power for all kinds of sins to all kinds of sacrifices. Again, we see how flawed the anti-missionary position ac-tually is, also exposing that in its zeal to counteract the claims of the New Testament, it will sometimes counteract the claims of Rabbinic Judaism too. And when we read Le-viticus 16, we see that the position is not flawed in a minor way. It is fatally flawed. Look carefully at these key verses: When Aaron has finished making atonement for the Most Holy Place, the Tent of Meeting and the altar, he shall bring forward the live goat [in English, this is commonly known as the "scapegoat"]. He is to lay both hands on the head of the live goat and confess over it all the wickedness and re-bellion of the Israelites-all their sins-and put them on the goat's head. He shall send the goat away into the desert in the care of a man appointed for the task. The goat will carry on itself all their sins to a solitary place; and the man shall release it in the desert. Leviticus 16:20-22*

*Notice carefully what the text says: The High Priest is to confess over the head of this goat "all the wickedness and rebellion of the Israelites-all their sins"-and "all" means "all." Notice also that the text specifically speaks of the "wickedness" (or "iniquity"; Hebrew, 'awon) and "rebel-lion" (Hebrew, pesha, meaning willful transgression) of the Israelites, not merely their unintentional sins. "But what do the rabbis say about this? What is written in the Talmud?" With regard to the kinds of sins atoned for by the sacrificial goats of Yom Kippur, the Talmud is even more explicit than the biblical text. Here are two different translations of m. Shevu'ot 1:6, a well-known known text in traditional Jewish law: A. And for a deliberate act of imparting uncleanness to the sanctuary and its Holy Things, a goat [whose blood is sprinkled] inside and the Day of Atonement effect atone-ment. B. And for all other transgressions which are in the*

*Torah-C. the minor or serious, deliberate or inadvertent, those done knowingly ingly or done unknowingly, violating a positive or a negative commandment, mandment, those punishable by extirpation [karet] and those punishable able by death at the hands of the court, D. the goat which is sent away [Lev. 16:21 ] effects atonement. And for uncleanness that occurs in the Temple and to its holy sacrifices rifices through wantonness, [the] goat whose blood is sprinkled within [the Holy of Holies on the Day of Atonement] and the Day of Atonement ment effect atonement, and for [all] other transgressions [spoken of] in the Law, light or grace, premeditated or inadvertent, aware or unaware, transgressions of positive commands or negative commands, sin whose penalty is excision or sins punishable by death imposed by the court, the scapegoat makes atonement."' As codified and explained by Maimonides almost one thousand years later (Laws of Repentance, 1:2): Since the goat sent [to Azazeil] atones for all of Israel, the High Priest confesses on it as the spokesman for all of Israel, as [Lev. 16:21] states: "He shall confess on it all the sins of the Children of Israel." The goat sent to Azazeil atones for all the transgressions in the Torah, the severe and the lighter [sins]; those violated intentionally and those transgressed inadvertently; those which [the transgressor] became conscious of and those which he was not conscious of. All are atoned for by the goat sent [to Azazeil]. This applies only if one repents. If one does not repent, the goat only atones for the light [sins]. Which are light sins and which are severe ones? Severe sins are those which are punishable by execution by the court or by premature death [karetJ. [The violation of] the other prohibitions that are not punishable able by premature death are considered light [sins].230 Here, then, is a perfectly clear statement from the most authoritative sources of traditional Judaism that the sacrifices offered and the ceremonies performed*

*on the Day of Atonement effected atonement for all kinds
of sins, intentional and unintentional, willful and inadvertent. The only question raised by the Rabbinic sources is to
what degree repentance was a necessary part of the equation, a question that all Messianic Jews would answer by
saying, "Repentance plays a vital part in the equation!"
(See below, 3.21.) In this context, Jacob Milgrom notes:
Even the annual purification rite for the sanctuary and nation requires that the high priest confess the deliberate sins
of the Israelites (Lev. 16:21), while the latter demonstrate
their penitence, not by coming to the Temple-from which
deliberate sinners are barred-but by fasting and other acts
of self-denial (Lev. 16:29; 23:27-32; Num. 29:7). Thus, con-
trition for involuntary sin and confession for deliberate sin
are indispensable to the atonement produced by the sacrificial system, and they differ in no way from the call to repentance formulated by the prophets.2 ' Returning to the
Talmudic discussion, I should also point out to you what the
Talmud says about the atoning power of the goat whose
blood is sprinkled inside the Most Holy Place. As we read
previously in m. Shevu'ot 1:6, "And for uncleanness that occurs in the Temple and to its holy sacrifices through wantonness, [the] goat whose blood is sprinkled within [the
Holy of Holies on the Day of Atonement] and the Day of
Atonement effect atonement." The Talmud explains this
with reference to Leviticus 16:15-16: He [i.e., the High
Priest] shall then slaughter the goat for the sin offering for
the people and take its blood behind the curtain and do
with it as he did with the bull's blood: He shall sprinkle it on
the atonement cover and in front of it. In this way he will
make atonement for the Most Holy Place because of the
uncleanness and rebellion of the Israelites, whatever their
sins have been. He is to do the same for the Tent of Meeting, which is among them in the midst of their uncleanness.
The rabbis (see b. Shevu'ot 2b; 6b-14a) comment*

*specifically on the words rebellion (transgressions in He-brew) and sins, explaining that "transgressions" refers to acts of rebellion-which are certainly intentional-while "sins" refers to inadvertent acts.232 And it is the goat whose blood is sprinkled in the Most Holy Place that effects atonement for the people, just as the blood of the bull of-fered up by the High Priest effects atonement for him (m. Shevu'ot 1:7, following Lev. 16:11, "Aaron shall bring the bull for his own sin offering to make atonement for himself and his household, and he is to slaughter the bull for his own sin offering."). Notice also that it is a sin offering that effects atonement for Aaron and the people of Israel, demonstrating that it is not only the guilt offering that ef-fects atonement for willful sins.-"' Let me also remind you of the prayer of Solomon offered up at the dedication of the Temple (1 Kings 8; 2 Chronicles 6), in which he asked God to forgive his sinning people when they turned to God in repentance and prayed toward the Temple. The Lord prom-ised that he would, in fact, forgive and restore-because of the sacrifices offered up in the Temple (see 2 Chron. 7:12-16, and the discussion above, 3.9)-and the text makes clear that inadvertent or unintentional sins were not the only things covered by Solomon's prayer. See, for example, I Kings 8:33-36, 46-50; 2 Chronicles 7:14, clearly referring to all kinds of sins and transgressions. We can also ask why many Orthodox Jews still practice the custom tom of kap-paros (or kapparot) on the eve of Yom Kippur (or Rosh Hashanah) if sacrifices only atoned for unintentional sins. Why then do they take a live fowl and wave it around their heads while confessing fessing that the fowl is their substi-tute and payment? As described by Rabbi Abraham Chill: A custom that has prevailed in many Jewish communities throughout the world for centuries and which was the cause of a great deal of controversy and apologetics is that of Kapparot, the expiatory offering. This ritual, which takes place during the night and early morning preceding Yom Kippur, involves taking a live white fowl, swinging it around one's head while reciting: "This is my atonement; this is my ransom; this is my substitute." As if saying: if on Yom Kippur it is decreed that I must die, then this fowl which will shortly be slaughtered should serve as my substitute."*

*"It's also fair to ask, What kinds of sins do Jews confess every year on Yom Kippur? The answer-known to all who have ever recited the prescribed prayers and confessions for that day-is that Jews confess to almost every imaginable sin on Yom Kippur, leaving almost no stone unturned. Yet, while the Temple was standing, those were the very sins for which atonement was sought through sacrifice, repentance, , and fasting. We could also ask, If prayer and repentance replace sacrifices according to Rabbinic teaching, what are they actually replacing if sacrifices were so ineffective?"' The answer is obvious: The sacrifices were anything but ineffective. How then should we understand Numbers 15:22-31 ? These verses seem to teach that sacrifices could be brought to atone for unintentional sins, but for willful, defiant sins no sacrifice was possible. The sinner's guilt would remain on him. Let's look at this passage, allowing some Jewish biblical scholars to explain its meaning: Now if you unintentionally fail to keep any of these commands the LORD gave Moses—any of the LORD's commands to you through him, from the day the LORD gave them and continuing through the generations to come— and if this is done unintentionally without the community being aware of it, then the whole community is to offer a young bull for a burnt offering as an aroma pleasing to the LORD, along with its prescribed grain offering and drink offering, and a male goat for a sin offering. The priest is to make atonement for the whole Israelite community, and they will be forgiven, for it was not intentional and they*

*have brought to the LORD for their wrong an offering made by fire and a sin offering. The whole Israelite community munity and the aliens living among them will be forgiven, because all the people were involved in the unintentional wrong. But if just one person sins unintentionally, he must bring a year-old female goat for a sin offering. The priest is to make atonement before the LORD for the one who erred by sinning unintentionally, and when atonement has been made for him, he will be forgiven. One and the same law applies to everyone who sins unintentionally, whether he is a native-born Israelite or an alien. But anyone who sins defiantly, whether native-born or alien, blasphemes the LORD, and that person must be cut off from his people. Because he has despised the LORD'S word and broken his commands, that person must surely be cut off; his guilt remains on him." Milgrom explains: The possibility of sacrificial atonement is explicitly denied to the individual who presumptuously violates God's law (Num. 15:30-31). This, however, does not mean, as many critics aver, that sacrificial atonement is possible only for involuntary wrongdoers. To cite but one exception, the askant offering is prescribed for that premeditated crime called by the rabbis asham gezelot (Lev. 5:20ff.; Num. 5:5-8). A more correct assertion, then, would be that the priestly system prohibits sacrificial atonement to the unrepentant sinner, for the one who "acts defiantly... it is the Lord he reviles" (Num. 15:30). This is an explicit postulate of post-biblical literature: "the hattat, the asham, and death do not atone except with repentance" (Tosef., Yoma 5:9; cf. Yoma 8:8).*

*"Or as expressed concisely by Rashi, "Only at the time when his iniquity is upon him shall he be cut off, meaning, as long as he has not repented" making reference to b. Sanhedrin 90b, where the Talmud mud explains that Numbers 15:31 leaves open the possibility that the sinner might still repent.*

*Thus, his guilt remains on him as long as he fails to repent. Interestingly, there is almost an exact New Testament parallel to this warning in Numbers 15:30-31, and it is found- not surprisingly-in in the Letter to the Hebrews: If we deliberately keep on sinning after we have received the knowledge edge of the truth, no sacrifice for sins is left, but only a fearful expectation of judgment and of raging fire that will consume the enemies of God. Anyone who rejected the law of Moses died without mercy on the testimony of two or three witnesses. How much more severely do you think a man deserves to be punished who has trampled the Son of God under foot, who has treated as an unholy thing the blood of the covenant that sanctified him, and who has insulted the Spirit of grace? For we know him who said, "It is mine to avenge; I will repay," and again, "The Lord will judge his people." It is a dreadful thing to fall into the hands of the living God. Hebrews 10:26-31 The point in both cases is clear: There is no sacrifice, no forgiveness, ness, no atonement for those who commit—and continue in—willful, defiant sin. If they don't turn back in repentance, nothing will atone for them. As noted by R. L. Harris with reference to Numbers 15:30-31, "Here the NIV has correctly caught the sense of the unpardonable sin-not one done intentionally, but one done 'defiantly,' i.e., in rebellion, sinning against light (cf. Matt. 12:31-32)."1'" The Hebrew image is quite clear: The sinner transgresses "with a high hand" (bevad ramah)-almost challenging God to punish him or hold him to account. But God is not one to be challenged! As Moses reminded the children of Israel, "Know therefore that the LORD your God is God; he is the faithful God, keeping his covenant of love to a thousand generations of those who love him and keep his commands. But those who hate him he will repay to their face by destruction; he will not be slow to repay to their face those who hate him" (Deut. 7:9-10). But for those who would repent and perform the required Temple service, abundant mercy and pardon was available (see vol. 1, 1.11, and below, 3.21). Looking back, then, at what we have seen so far, we can say categorically that sacrifices were not for unintentional sins only. The sacrifices on Yom Kippur argue against this position, specific sacrifices (the'asham and the hatta't) argue against it, other scriptural principles argue against it, the Talmud and Law Codes argue against it, the custom tom of kapparot argues against it, and the concept of repentance offered in conjunction with sacrifices argues against it. But there is something else we should look at briefly, namely, the Rabbinic view that through repentance, intentional sins, even quite deliberate sins, could be converted verted to unintentional sins, and thus covered through normal atonement rites. Dr. Rich Robinson, a research scholar for Jews for Jesus, has put together some important quotations on this subject. He observes that "according to the sages, repentance could turn an intentional sin into an unintentional sin and so be eligible for sacrifice," offering the following ancient and modern sources in support:*

*R. Simeon b. Lakish said: Great is repentance, which converts intentional sins into unintentional ones (b. Yoma 86b; this is the rendering of Milgrom; as rendered in the Soncino edition, it reads: Great is repentance, for because of it premeditated sins are accounted as errors). This literary image [of the "high hand"; Num. 15:30-31 ] is most apposite for the brazen sinner who commits his acts in open defiance of the Lord (cf. Job. 38:15). The essence of this sin is that it is committed mitted flauntingly. However, sins performed in secret, even deliberately, can be commuted to the status of inadvertencies by means of repentance." '... I submit that the repentance of the sinner, through his remorse... and confession....     reduces     his     intentional     sin     to     an*

*inadvertence, thereby rendering it eligible for sacrificial ex-
piation.2i"... The early rabbis... raise the question of how
the high priest's bull is capable of atoning for his deliberate
sins, and they reply, "Because he has confessed his brazen
and rebellious deeds it is as if they become as unintentional
ones before him" (Sipra, Ahare par. 2:4,6; cf. t. Yoma 2:1).
Thus it is clear that the Tannaites attribute to repentance-
strikingly, in a sacrificial ritual-the power to transform a
presumptuous sumptuous sin against God, punishable by
death, into an act of inadvertence, expiable by sacrifice.2"
Of course, there are other scholars who reject this Rabbinic
concept that intentional sins can be "converted" to unintentional sins through repentance, and I am not fully convinced of it myself.242 I only bring it up because it reflects
another problem (from a Rabbinic perspective) with the
anti-missionary position regarding sacrifice and atonement. In any case, I have presented clear, definite scriptural
evidence, supported ported by Rabbinic tradition as well,
that the sacrificial system instituted by God for the people
of Israel, joined, of course, with repentance, provided
atonement for intentional as well as any unintentional
sins." (Michael L. Brown, Answering Jewish Objections to
Jesus: Theological Objections Vol. 2, 126-136 (Kindle Edition): Grand Rapids, MI: Baker Book House)*

Please notice that according to this passage, a person needed to repent and make restitution to his brother for what had been stolen. He was also to add 1/5 of the value to the person who had been taken advantage of. The purpose of the restoration of what was stolen and the paying of interest was rooted in restoring the relationship. Jesus Himself makes this clear when He addressed the Pharisees of His day and age who so often neglected this Scripture:

*Matthew 5:23-24—Therefore if you bring your gift to the*

> *altar, and there remember that your brother has something against you, leave your gift there before the altar, and go your way. First be reconciled to your brother, and then come and offer your gift.*

The same principle is seen throughout the Bible.

As another example, consider Zacchaeus.

> *Luke 19:1-10—Then Jesus entered and passed through Jericho. Now behold, there was a man named Zacchaeus who was a chief tax collector, and he was rich. And he sought to see who Jesus was, but could not because of the crowd, for he was of short stature. So he ran ahead and climbed up into a sycamore tree to see Him, for He was going to pass that way. And when Jesus came to the place, He looked up and saw him, and said to him, "Zacchaeus, make haste and come down, for today I must stay at your house." So he made haste and came down, and received Him joyfully. But when they saw it, they all complained, saying, "He has gone to be a guest with a man who is a sinner." Then Zacchaeus stood and said to the Lord, "Look, Lord, I give half of my goods to the poor; and if I have taken anything from anyone by false accusation, I restore fourfold." And Jesus said to him, "Today salvation has come to this house, because he also is a son of Abraham; for the Son of Man has come to seek and to save that which was lost."*

Zacchaeus was willing to go beyond what the Law of Moses commanded and to restore fourfold to those whom he had wronged. Not only is he willing to make amends according to the Jewish Law, but he is even willing to be accountable to Roman law on these matters.

*"First, tax collectors are lumped together with sinners throughout the gospel (5:30; 7:34; 15:1; see Matt 5:46; 18:17; 21:31–32) and are assumed to need repentance (3:12–13) and mercy (18:13). Rabbinic texts further illustrate how tax collectors were regarded by others and why they were hated. It was not only their collaboration with the Romans but their notorious dishonesty that made them so despised. Had Zacchaeus been so generous, as Fitzmyer contends, why does the crowd harbor such antagonism toward him? He would be acclaimed rather than scorned. His affirmation is more likely a promise to bear the "fruits… of repentance" that John demanded of tax collectors and soldiers (3:8, 12–14), but it is far more. He will not merely desist from dishonest appraisals and extortion; he will repay all that he had defrauded to his victims, plus a self-levied penalty. Marshall contends: "The conditional clause is to be translated 'From whomsoever I have wrongfully exacted anything,' and thus does not put the fact of extortion in doubt, but rather its extent." 10 Zacchaeus accepts for himself the law imposed on rustlers who were compelled to make double restitution (if an animal was alive) or fourfold or fivefold restitution (if an animal died; Exod 22:1, 3–4; 2 Sam 12:6). 11 Horsley contends from inscriptional evidence that the fourfold recompense matches a Roman milieu. Zacchaeus was "offering to provide restitution in the same proportion as he would have been liable to under Roman law if he had been brought to court." 12 Second (in response to Fitzmyer), how could Zacchaeus regularly be giving half of his possessions to the poor and restoring fourfold any discovered extortion and still be rich? 13 It is more likely that Zacchaeus is enthusiastically announcing a change in his life's direction. He will now attend to the needs of the poor. Johnson acidly observes that Zacchaeus "clearly has not impoverished himself (half a bundle can still be a bundle)." 14 But he is not trying to keep half of his*

*goods for himself and get off with less than that demanded of the rich man in 18:22. Zacchaeus identifies two separate groups who will receive his wealth: the poor and the victims of extortion. The poor would have been less likely to carry goods through his customs house to be fleeced by his tax enterprise. Zacchaeus needs to retain the other half of his wealth if he is to make good on his commitment to restore fourfold to those he swindled. 15 The result is that when Jesus opens up his heart to him, Zacchaeus opens up his heart to the poor." David E. Garland, Clinton E. Arnold, Luke: Zondervan Exegetical Commentary On The New Testament, 17487-17507 (Kindle Edition): Grand Rapids, MI: Zondervan)*

Another final example of making amends comes from the Book of Philemon. A young slave named Onesimus had run off from his owner, a Christian named Philemon. Indications are that he stole some kind of money or property from Philemon. Later, he had met the Apostle Paul and been converted to Christ.

*"Such an appeal can only be made if the good faith can be demonstrated, should that be necessary. Onesimus had evidently wronged (i &xrlcev; the same verb as used in Col. 3:25) Philemon in some way not made explicit, or was financially in debt to Philemon (o$eiXct; cf. Matt. 18:28, 30, 34; Luke 7:41; 16:5, 7; again regularly in the papyri: MM s.v. 606kco). "If" presumably does not indicate that Paul was treating the matter lightly or that he had any uncertainty that Onesimus had told him the whole story. The letter itself attests to some serious breach between Philemon and Onesimus, and the immediately preceding expression of confidence in Onesimus as Paul's representative would prevent the "if" from being read as any kind of doubt regarding Onesimus's trustworthiness.. But it neatly serves the purpose of taking for granted Philemon's view that*

*Onesimus was guilty of serious misdemeanor, without wholly conceding that Philemon's judgment was entirely correct. The "if" has, indeed, the force of "whatever," the rhetorical effect being to underline the comprehensiveness of Paul's guarantee: "whatever wrong he has done or debt he has incurred curred...."34". (James D.G. Dunn, The Epistles to the Colossians and to Philemon (New International Greek Testament Commentary (NIGTC)), 4880-4886 (Kindle Edition): Grand Rapids, MI: William B. Eerdmans Publishing Company)*

What was Onesimus to do?

---

*Philemon 1:10-16—I appeal to you for my son Onesimus, whom I have begotten while in my chains, who once was unprofitable to you, but now is profitable to you and to me. I am sending him back. You therefore receive him, that is, my own heart, whom I wished to keep with me, that on your behalf he might minister to me in my chains for the gospel. But without your consent I wanted to do nothing, that your good deed might not be by compulsion, as it were, but voluntary. For perhaps he departed for a while for this purpose, that you might receive him forever, no longer as a slave but more than a slave—a beloved brother, especially to me but how much more to you, both in the flesh and in the Lord.*

---

Notice that Paul points out some great lessons here about the providential working of God. As one scholar has pointed out:

*"In addition to appealing to Philemon's human side (sympathy) and his spiritual side, Paul now brings God's providence into the discussion. Many times things happen and we don't know why. Is there some greater purpose being*

*served? Is God working things out in a specific way so that something else can happen later?*

*Sometimes the answer is "yes." Sometimes the answer is "no." God does not send out emails letting us know that He is working out specific situations so that later on something good will come. We will not know, this side of eternity, how much on this earth is God's providence. What greater good comes from stubbing my toe? Did God use that providentially? Not likely.*

*Philemon must have wondered why Onesimus ran away in the first place. This was likely something that was at the forefront of his mind whenever his slave's name was mentioned. Paul here renders all of that questioning meaningless. It does not matter what caused him to run away. Perhaps this was all part of God's plan. Had Onesimus not run away, he would never have come into contact with Paul. Had he not come into contact with Paul, he never would have become a Christian. Which is better: having a slave whose soul is lost or having a slave who runs away, but later returns as a Christian? The answer to the question is obvious. Now that Onesimus has returned as a Christian, Philemon will have no worries that this slave will run away again.*

*Look back in your life. What great influences in your life brought you to Christ? Would you have your spouse if not for certain events or people? What if you never met those people? What trying events made you a stronger person and better prepared for something later in life? Do you realize that some of these things may indeed be God working things out for your benefit? Have faith in God during the bad times, because you never know what great things He has in store for you in the future!" (Bradley Cobb, The Prodigal Slave: A Study of the Letter to Philemon (Cobb's Commentaries), 44-45 (Kindle Edition): Charleston, AR: Cobb Publishing)*

In all of these cases, we see that making restitution and amends was something that was an integral part of the process of repentance. Indeed, I am reminded of the famous Jewish scholar, Maimonides.

*"Moses Maimonides was a twelfth-century philosopher and scholar of Jewish law. He offers a powerful, game-changing path to healing and repair, which can be useful for everyone, regardless of background or belief system. Yes, he wrote and codified Jewish law intended for Jews living within the religious framework of the Torah and the Talmud, but the stages of repentance that he lays out in his masterwork, the Mishneh Torah—and the nuances of each stage—are clear and specific, and can illuminate many situations that to our contemporary American eyes may seem messy and impenetrable. Applying his lens to the challenges of today—even in ways he might not have dreamed of, or that he might consider novel or unorthodox—can illuminate, quickly and profoundly, questions about what to do in the wake of harm: how to deal with it, who is responsible and what that responsibility looks like, how far it extends, and what its limits are. After years of working with Maimonides' stages of repentance, I have become convinced that they make sense not only in our individual lives—as we make mistakes with our coworkers, friends, family, and intimate partners—but also on the communal, cultural, and even national level. Moses ben Maimon— commonly known as Maimonides—was born in Córdoba, in what's now Spain, around 1135 CE, under the Berber Muslim Almoravid Empire. When a different caliphate*

*conquered the area in 1148, the Jews living there became vulnerable to forced conversion, death, or exile. His family escaped, and Maimonides eventually settled in Egypt. By the time he got there, in 1168, he had already gained some acclaim through his authoritative commentary on the Mishnah—an ancient collection of Jewish laws compiled around 200 CE, the cornerstone text of Rabbinic Judaism known to Jews as the "Oral Torah." In Egypt, Maimonides first worked with his brother in an importing business and, after his brother's untimely death, returned to being a doctor, his former profession. Eventually he served as physician to the sultan Saladin. Around the same time, he began working on his magnum opus, the work that would define him and his legacy. The Mishneh Torah (along with his later philosophical treatise, The Guide for the Perplexed) came to be considered so important, his tombstone is engraved with the majestic epitaph: "From Moses [of the Bible] to Moses [ben Maimon], there was none like Moses." Maimonides—also known as Rambam, an acronym for Rabbi Moses ben Maimon—set out to write the Mishneh Torah in order to make it easier for Jews to follow Jewish law without having to study the Talmud—a complex, often winding, frequently unresolved discourse on the meaning of the Torah and the Mishnah. He assumed that scholars would still go deep into the Talmudic debates, but most people just needed the bottom line: what to do and how to do it. This was a brilliant step forward in the evolution of Judaism: clear, concise instructions, organized in a way entirely different from the Mishnah and the Talmud, taken primarily from the Talmud and other authoritative sources but also developed, in places, with Maimonides' own innovations and flourishes. (So yes, many of the ideas and even phrases I cite here with the opening "Maimonides says," are, in fact, Maimonides' rephrasing or even quoting of the Talmud itself. For simplicity's sake, I mostly stick with the text of the*

*Mishneh Torah. Those of you who care about chasing down sources—and you know who you are—can certainly do so with greater ease now that we live in the Great Golden Age of Sefaria.) 1 Many extraordinary things make up the Mishneh Torah; Maimonides' Laws of Repentance are among them. Here, as elsewhere, he takes ideas scattered all over the tradition and lays them out, sometimes with his own crucial additions, to give a clear, systematic guide for not only repairing harm but for becoming the kind of person who will not cause harm in the future. The Laws of Repentance are about amends, but also about transformation. According to Maimonides, a person doesn't just get to mess up, mumble, "Sorry," and get on with it. They're not entitled to forgiveness if they haven't done the work of repair. (And they're not necessarily entitled to forgiveness even if they have.) Another human being's suffering is not magically erased because the person who caused it says that they didn't mean to do it. This is true in our personal lives, and it's also true of politicians caught saying racist things, celebrities named as sexual abusers, human resources departments that cover up employee complaints, and governments perpetrating harm against individuals or groups. Fixing damage involves taking specific steps; there's a process. We can't ever undo what happened, but we can transform the situation and ourselves. But you can't cut corners.*

*Of course, it's hard. Owning up to the hurt you have caused someone else is difficult. And how much more so when an injury was not accidental, when you must admit that you knowingly lied to a loved one, let down someone in need, unfairly lashed out in anger, chose to be complicit in abuse, violated boundaries, or took other actions with real, painful implications. Owning the fact that we've done wrong is challenging—even threatening or scary—but it is the work we are obligated to do. Maimonides is very clear about what that work is meant to look like—and his clarity can help guide us. OK, so, some context: Jewish thinking on re-pentance comes originally from legal writing about Yom Kippur, the Day of Atonement. A long time ago, Yom Kippur was the day on which the High Priest purged the ancient Temple in Jerusalem of ritual impurity and made expiation for himself, his family, and the Israelite people—a clearing out of sin, a spiritual purification. 2 When the Second Tem-ple was destroyed by the Romans in 70 CE, the more per-sonal, sin-clearing aspect of the day became even stronger. The Mishnah—the ancient oral tradition mentioned ear-lier—notes that the atonement for interpersonal sins of-fered on Yom Kippur will not work until the person who did harm "appeases their friend." 3 The holy atonement reset button doesn't work until we've cleaned up our own mess. The Babylonian Talmud, which expounded on the Mishnah and was redacted around the fifth century CE, struggled to understand what it means to "appease" one's friend. What do you need to do? When? How? What are the limits to and obligations of this appeasement? As mentioned earlier, Maimonides' Laws of Repentance took many of the ques-tions and much of the thinking in the Mishnah, the Talmud, and elsewhere and synthesized them into distinct steps—a path to follow. In a moment, we'll get into the weeds of what those steps are, and in the chapters that follow, we'll apply them to a range of situations and types of harm, in-cluding those with deep historical roots. Occasionally it will make sense to translate Maimonides' thinking into our twenty-first-century context. Things that we now know to be true will bump up against the limits of his medieval-era thinking, and we'll discuss them as needed. (Do I wish Mai-monides could do repentance work for some of his writings about women, among other things? Sure. But that's out-side the scope of this book.) As noted in the introduction, Judaism doesn't emphasize forgiveness to the same degree that Christianity and secular American society do. Jewish law teaches that the person harmed is certainly not obligated to forgive a perpetrator who has not done the work of repentance. And even if repentance is wholehearted and demonstrable, if apologies have been offered and amends made, how and when forgiveness factors in is not always straightforward, as we'll see in Chapter Seven. Is forgiveness something the victim can choose to do at any point? Definitely. Can it sometimes be a useful part of the healing process? For sure. Is a victim obligated to forgive? Well, as we rabbis are fond of saying, that's a whole other conversation. It's worth mentioning that forgiveness isn't the same as reconciliation—returning to some sort of relationship that will continue into the future. Regardless, I want to spell out that, in Judaism, a person can do real, profound, comprehensive repentance work and even get right with God—experience atonement—even if their victim never forgives them. Repentance and forgiveness are separate processes. For the rabbis of the Mishnah and the Talmud, and for our guide Maimonides, forgiveness is much less important than the repair work that the person who caused harm is obligated to do. The Hebrew word that is often translated as "repentance" is tshuvah, which literally means "returning." In Modern Hebrew, a tshuvah is an answer to a question—you've gotten back to someone— but it also means "returning" in the sense of "I'll also need a return ticket for this bus ride." In a spiritual context, tshuvah is about coming back to where we are supposed to be, returning to the person we know we're capable of being— coming home, in humility and with intentionality, to behave as the person we'd like to believe we are. In order to see how Maimonides' ideas about repentance can help transform our own lives and personal relationships, the institutions of which we are a part, and our culture and country as a whole, we need to have a solid grasp on what those steps are. As we look at some complex and seemingly*

*intractable situations in the chapters to come, it will be cru-*
*cial to understand the basics of Maimonides' thinking, so*
*that we can apply it to today's challenges with flexibility*
*and ease. For the rest of this chapter, we'll do a deep dive*
*into his five steps of repentance and the ways they can po-*
*tentially effect not only repair and healing for those who*
*have been harmed, but also profound transformation for*
*the person who—intentionally or unintentionally—caused*
*that harm in the first place." (Danya Ruttenberg, On Re-*
*pentance and Repair: Making Amends in an Unapologetic*
*World, 21-26 (Kindle Edition): Boston, Massachusetts: Bea-*
*con Press)*

After spending years studying the Old Testament, Maimonides revealed the "Five Laws Of Repentance." He postulated that any type of activity called repentance that did not include these five components was not truly repentance. They are:

1). Naming And Owning Harm. This mainly has the idea of specifically naming the offense that was done, acknowledging the harm that was caused, and being willing to take accountability for it.

2). Starting To Change. This is the process of inner reformation that seeks to be and to do better. Maimonides points out that the true test of repentance is in finding yourself in the same situation in which you previously failed and seeing if you do better the next time around. This is really what happened with Joseph and his brothers (Genesis 42). After having sold him into slavery and telling their father that he was dead, Jospeh's brothers were going to be put to the test by Joseph to see if they had learned their lesson. Had they really changed?

*"Joseph was preparing to test his brothers to see if they had*
*remorse for what they had done to him. What sort of test*

*would demonstrate whether the brothers were repentant? A good answer is provided in the definition of repentance later written by Maimonides in his Code of Jewish Law: "What constitutes complete repentance? He who is confronted by the identical situation in which he transgressed and it lies within his power to commit the transgression again but he nevertheless abstains... out of repentance and not out of fear [of being caught].... [For example,] if he had relations with a woman forbidden to him and he is subsequently alone with her, still in the full throes of his passion for her and his virility unabated... If he abstains and does not sin, this is a true penitent." 1 Joseph's plan was to engineer a test placing his brothers in a situation similar to the one in which they betrayed him, a situation in which they could save themselves by abandoning their youngest brother, Benjamin to a life of slavery (see Genesis 44:10, 33). Would they protect Benjamin or themselves?" (Dennis Prager, The Rational Bible: Genesis, 607 (Kindle Edition): Washington, DC: Regnery Faith)*

3). Restitution And Accepting Consequence. As we have been discussing, this is where the rubber meets the road in the personal step work.

4). Apology. The apology is specific (not generic). An apology is not a statement of, "I did this, but...". This is not an apology! A true apology does not make excuses for bad behavior: it does not seek to lay accountability anywhere else but on the individual who has done the wrong. An apology will be a sincere and heartfelt expression of remorse.

5). Making Different Choices. Changed behavior is the greatest example of true repentance.

The addicts that you work with may come from a background of very grievous actions against others. Work with them and encourage them to make amends as they are able to. It is easy to be overwhelmed by the burden of guilt. Encourage the addict to seek God's forgiveness first (Acts 2:38), and then as part of his changed life try to make amends to the ones that he has harmed.

## Question: What Can Be Done To Support The Families Of Addicts That We Minister To?

Answer: Whatever your group is capable of providing.

There is a great need for Christians to be a group of support not only for addicts but for their families as well. Addicts rarely suffer alone: almost always there are family members and friends who suffer together with them. Part of being the body of Christ is being an encouragement to each other as we live in this world. Paul was proud of the fact that the church in Rome was composed of members who were able to be there to encourage and support each other.

---

*Romans 15:14—Now I myself am confident concerning you, my brethren, that you also are full of goodness, filled with all knowledge, able also to admonish one another.*

---

Paul said that the Romans were able to "admonish one another." The phrase used there had the meaning of caring for one another's needs in whatever context was under consideration.

*"And able also to admonish one another. Noutheteō can be translated "admonish, warn, or instruct."7 "What is denoted is the earnest attempt by words spoken (or written) to correct what is wrong in another, to encourage him to do what is right and to refrain from what is evil."8 It means "to direct (another) with brotherly feeling."9 Goodness*

*resulting from knowledge is a prerequisite for effective in-structing and admonishing.". (Gareth Reese, New Testament Epistles: Romans-A Critical And Exegetical Commentary, 22830-22833 (Kindle Edition): Moberly, Missouri: Scripture Exposition Texts)*

Here are some ways that your group can encourage the families and loved ones of addicts.

- Pray For Them And With Them.

- Visit Regularly.

- Encourage Them To Come To Church Services And Group Meetings.

- Take An Interest Especially In The Lives Of The Children.

- If The Addicts Are Incarcerated, Help With Visits.

Based on the capabilities of your ministry group, do whatever you are capable of doing to encourage the families and friends of addicts that you minister to.

## Question: What Are Some Practical Suggestions About Starting A Jail Ministry To Help Addicts?

Answer: Be wise as serpents, and harmless as doves.

There is a great need for ministry in jail, especially in reaching out to addicts. We are called to take the Gospel into all the world and to every creature (Mark 16:15-16). Jails and prisons provide ideal environments for the Word of God (Luke 8:11-15). With that in mind, here are some things to keep in mind.

1). Be prepared for meeting some incredible people. Some of the greatest people that I have met have been in jail ministry. Over the years, I have been blessed to know many who are truly seeking the Lord behind bars. We have a tendency to stereotype everyone in jail as "bad persons." Truth is, I have often met more "bad persons" in churches then I have in jail ministry. It has often been in churches that I have found people who are extremely self-righteous, entitled, backstabbing, sexually immoral, greedy, and dictator like. Keep in mind, I am well aware that I am a sinner saved by grace (1 Timothy 1:15). However, many of those that I have been blessed to work with in jail ministry are characterized as being "poor in spirit" (Matthew 5:3). They recognize that they are spiritually broken and in need of God's Presence and salvation. More to the point, you will meet many in jail ministry who come from some of the most diverse backgrounds. Prepare yourself for heart wrenching stories as you prepare yourself for this ministry.

2). Be prepared for those who are seeking to take advantage of your kindness. There are sadly those in our lives and ministries who will do whatever they can simply to gain some possible kind of advantage. As such, be on your guard for this type of situation. Years ago, I baptized several in a local jail ministry and the local officers were kindly willing to let me start a New Christian Class for those that I was baptizing. One day I was sitting with them in the officer's break room and one of the men started to weep about how sad he was that he was in jail while struggling with an addiction to certain drugs and pornography. I focused my attention on him and did what I could to encourage him. The next day when I came back to the jail for ministry, one of the deputies showed me a video of the break room where I was the day before. On the screen, as I was consoling the young man, the other inmates were breaking into the officers lockers and stealing their snacks and lunches! As you minister to those in jail ministry, be prepared for the ones that will take advantage.

3). Be mindful of your level of court participation. Inmates that you study with and work with in your drug ministry may want you to become actively involved in court cases. Over the years, my level of participation in these areas has been mainly limited to writing letters of recommendation to the judges and trying to help inmates get into drug rehabs. I would advise against going much further then this in drug ministry in jail.

4). Make sure that your ministry team recognizes the local jail laws and customs and do whatever you can to honor those as far as possible. You are in the jail as a courtesy of your local law enforcement officers. Remember this and treat the officers and their regulations with the utmost respect.

5). There will be times in jail ministry where God can work in the lives of addicts in unexpected and amazing ways, even years later. Many addicts (often due to their experiences with the spiritual world) recognize and appreciate these things. Let me share an example. Years ago, while in jail ministry, a fight broke out between two young men in our church service. One young man had allegedly stolen something from another young man before they were incarcerated. The deputies rushed in and tased the young men, but not before one of our elderly members had his lip split in the altercation. Fast forward about seventeen years. I was in jail ministry and was working with several addicts. They were asking questions of faith and one of the gentlemen spoke up and said that he would like to ask us about an alleged Bible contradiction he had found years earlier. He said no preacher or church had ever been able to clear up this contradiction in his understanding, so we set out to study about it. By the time it was over, he was amazed because there was an answer. During the course of the conversation, I began reminiscing about how years earlier we had a similar class in the local jail ministry and a fight broke out during it. The gentleman I was speaking with got real quiet and asked, "Whatever happened to the elderly gentleman who had his lip split?" I said that he had passed away, and the man began to cry. He said that he had been one of those young men, and had been planning on asking this question that night when the fight broke out. I was amazed, and encouraged him to consider that maybe Satan had instigated that fight years earlier to keep him from asking that question and finding God. Help addicts to see the amazing ways that God is working in the world, even in their difficult and trying circumstances.

6). Finally, have a system in place to help the addicts you work with in jail ministry-both within jail, and when they get out. When they remain incarcerated for a prolonged period of time, do what you can to help them function as members of the church in jail. Get them involved in Bible study, reaching out to fellow inmates and their families, doing what they can to do good and benevolent deeds to those they are in contact with. Have a plan in place also for when they get out. The temptation to relapse will be very high when they first get out of jail. Do what you can to help them have a place to go when they come out of jail (a rehab, a half-way house, etc.). Be prepared for the reality that their family may be the first ones to help them re-lapse, and do what you can to safeguard them from this. The challenges that you face will be difficult, but they can be step-ping stones to help them climb higher then they have been be-fore. In jail, Daniel looked for ways to do God's will and to over-come the obstacles he faced (Daniel 1:8-21). Do what you can to help those you minister to in jail ministry excel.

## Question: What Is A Good Curriculum That We May Use In Drug Outreach Ministry?

Answer: Newlife Behavior Ministry Curriculum.

For years, I have used the Newlife Behavior Ministry material. They are a brotherhood organization that has specialized course material on lots of topics, including CASA (Christian Against

Substance Abuse). The current phone number that I have for them is 361-855-3372. Buck Griffith is one of the principal founders and directors of It.

The grace of the Lord Jesus Christ, and the love of God, and the communion of the Holy Spirit, be with you all. Amen.

# APPENDIX ONE:
# THREE UNGETOVERABLE ARGUMENTS FOR THE EXISTENCE OF GOD

Theism is the belief system which states, "I know that God exists."

Atheism, on the other hand, is that system which claims, "I know that God does NOT exist."

*Atheist* is from the Greek word *theos* (god). The the word "*theos*" is then joined with the letter *alpha*. When this word combination occurs in Greek, the word *atheist* literally means "no God."

This is different from an agnostic, who claims uncertainty regarding whether God exists or not.

> "Accepting that theism is belief in the existence of God, what is atheism? Again, the answer is far from straightforward. A simple dictionary definition, based on the Greek words a (without) and theos (God) is 'disbelief in the existence of God or gods', 22 but the history and use of the word are much more complex. In ancient Greece the word 'atheist' was used to describe three groups of people: those who were impious or godless; those who were without supernatural help; and those who did not accept the prevalent Greek idea of deity. The earliest Christians were often called atheists by their contemporaries because they refused to accept the existence of the popular pagan deities of their time, and one religious group has sometimes accused another of atheism even when both claimed to believe in a supernatural Being of whom at least part of our outline of who and what God is would be true. Yet even

*these examples do not exhaust the uses of 'atheism'. Swami Vivekanada, an Indian who was instrumental in bringing Hinduism to the West, once said, 'Just as certain world religions say that people who do not believe in a personal God outside themselves are atheists, we say that a person who does not believe in himself is an atheist. Not believing in the splendour of one's own soul is what we call an atheist.' 23 It would simplify things if we could settle for the general idea that atheism is the rejection of theism, but the difficulty of pinning down the meaning of theism makes the issue a lot more complicated than that. As long as our concept of God is sufficiently vague, our first proposition— that only a minority of people are atheists—is already proved. However, if we define God in the way I have suggested, our second proposition, which says that most people in the world are atheists, comes into play. It will take us twelve chapters to discover whether this is the case. We will then prepare the way for our third proposition, and follow it by examining some of its implications." (John Blanchard, Does God Believe in Atheists?, 472-494 (Kindle Edition); Carlisle, PA; EP Books USA)*

We will begin by considering the cosmological argument for the existence of God.

## The Cosmological Argument

This argument argues from the fact of "cause and effect" in the universe. It may be stated in different forms, but usually it goes something like this:

1. If there was ever a time when there was absolutely nothing, there would be nothing now.

2. There is something now.

3. Therefore, something has always existed.

4. But the universe has not always existed.

5. Therefore, something beyond the universe has existed.

6. But the only cause sufficient for the existence of the universe is God.

7. Therefore, God exists.

Each step of the argument is evidentially true.

Let's examine each line of the argument.

## "If There Was Ever A Time When There Was Absolutely Nothing, There Would Be Nothing Now."

The first premise argument from the general law of causality, which states that every effect must be preceded by an adequate and antecedent cause. In other words, "nothing" cannot cause "something!"

This is an obvious fact, one that is historically and continually demonstrated by the findings of logic and science. Consider these words from William Lane Craig:

> *"1. Something cannot come from nothing. To claim that something can come into being from nothing is worse than magic. When a magician pulls a rabbit out of a hat, at least you've got the magician, not to mention the hat! But if you deny premise 1, you've got to think that the whole universe just appeared at some point in the past for no reason whatsoever. But nobody sincerely believes that things, say, a horse or an Eskimo village, can just pop into being without a cause. This isn't rocket science. In The Sound of Music,*

*when Captain Von Trapp and Maria reveal their love for each other, what does Maria say? "Nothing comes from nothing; nothing ever could." We don't normally think of philosophical principles as romantic, but Maria was here expressing a fundamental principle of classical metaphysics. (No doubt she had been well trained in philosophy at the convent school!) Sometimes skeptics will respond to this point by saying that in physics subatomic particles (so-called "virtual particles") come into being from nothing. Or certain theories of the origin of the universe are sometimes described in popular magazines as getting something from nothing, so that the universe is the exception to the proverb "There ain't no free lunch."... "This skeptical response represents a deliberate abuse of science. The theories in question have to do with particles originating as a fluctuation of the energy contained in the vacuum. The vacuum in modern physics is not what the layman understands by "vacuum," namely, nothing. Rather in physics the vacuum is a sea of fluctuating energy governed by physical laws and having a physical structure. To tell laymen that on such theories something comes from nothing is a distortion of those theories.... "Properly understood, "nothing" does not mean just empty space. Nothing is the absence of anything whatsoever, even space itself. As such, nothingness has literally no properties at all, since there isn't anything to have any properties! How silly, then, when popularizers say things like "Nothingness is unstable" or "The universe tunneled into being out of nothing"! When I first published my work on the kalam cosmological argument back in 1979, I figured that atheists would attack premise 2 of the argument, that the universe began to exist. But I didn't think they'd go after premise 1. For that would expose them as people not sincerely seeking after truth but just looking for an academic refutation of the argument. What a surprise, then, to hear atheists denying premise 1 in order to escape the argument!..."For it is, I repeat, literally worse than magic. If this is the alternative to belief in God, then unbelievers can never accuse believers of irrationality, for what could be more evidently irrational than this? 2. If something can come into being from nothing, then it becomes inexplicable why just anything or everything doesn't come into being from nothing. Think about it: Why don't bicycles and Beethoven and root beer just pop into being from nothing? Why is it only universes that can come into being from nothing? What makes nothingness so discriminatory? There can't be anything about nothingness that favors universes, for nothingness doesn't have any properties. Nor can anything constrain nothingness, for there isn't anything to be constrained!..."3. Common experience and scientific evidence confirm the truth of premise 1. Premise 1 is constantly verified and never falsified. It's hard to understand how anyone committed to modern science could deny that premise 1 is more plausibly true than false in light of the evidence. So I think that the first premise of the kalam cosmological argument is clearly true. If the price of denying the argument's conclusion is denying premise 1, then atheism is philosophically bankrupt." (William Lane Craig, On Guard: Defending Your Faith with Reason and Precision, 1179-1240 (Kindle Edition); Colorado Springs, CO; David C. Cook)*

Sometimes atheists try and claim that the subatomic world demonstrates that there may be effects without causes. However, as Craig and others have proven, that is simply not true! Instead, this principle actually demonstrates the existence of a cause in another dimension of reality that is empirically undetectable to creatures in a four-dimensional universe!

Geisler notes:

"Heisenberg's principle of uncertainty is a principle of quantum mechanics which states that "the position and speed of a particle cannot be simultaneously known with complete certainty. If one is known with high certainty, the other becomes very uncertain." For example, according to this theory, "it is possible to accurately predict what fraction of [uranium atoms] will radioactively disintegrate over the next hour, but it is impossible to predict which atoms will do so" (Lightman, 560). However, this principle of uncertainty does not support the view that events arise without a cause or that human actions are uncaused. Heisenberg's principle of uncertainty does not say there is no cause of the events, but simply that one cannot predict the course of a given particle. Hence, it is not to be understood as the principle of uncausality but the principle of unpredictability. The principle of causality affirms that there is a cause, even if we do not know precisely what it is. Were there no cause, there would be no effect or event. In fact, modern science was built on the principle that things do not arise without a cause (see ORIGINS, SCIENCE OF). Heisenberg's principle does not even deny predictability in general. It states only that "physical systems must be described in terms of probabilities" (Lightman, 553). That is, one can accurately predict what fraction of the particles will react in a certain way but not which atoms will do so (ibid.). Even though a particular particle's position cannot be predicted, the overall pattern can be predicted. That implies a causal connection. The point is that scientists, with their limited instruments and observational abilities cannot now predict the courses of individual subatomic particles. An infinite Mind could predict both course and speed. If I empty a sack of ping-pong balls above several open bins, it is not possible for me to predict which of the falling balls will fall into which bins. In practice it is not possible to know and properly calculate all the physical factors involved in the

> *falling and bouncing. We can only know that about twice as many will fall into the bins that are twice as large. This does not mean that, in principle, it is impossible to know which balls will fall in which bins. Heisenberg's principle describes the subatomic realm, which is not known without investigator interference. Electron microscopes, by which the subatomic realm is observed, bombard the subatomic particles in order to "see" them. As Mortimer Adler noted, "At the same time that the Heisenberg uncertainty principles were established, quantum physics acknowledged that the intrusive experimental measurements that provided the data used in the mathematical formulations of quantum theory conferred on subatomic objects and events interdeterminate character. ... It follows, therefore, that the indeterminacy cannot be intrinsic to subatomic reality" (Adler, 96-100). Hence, unpredictable behavior may result in part from the attempt to observe it. Not all physicists accept quantum physics and the uncertainty theory. In response to it, Albert \*Einstein complained, "God does not play dice with the universe."" (Norman L. Geisler, Baker Encyclopedia of Christian Apologetics (Baker Reference Library), 356 (Kindle Edition); Grand Rapids, Michigan; Baker Books)*

Clearly, if there was ever a time when there was absolutely nothing, there could be nothing now!

There Is Something Now

No one can deny their existence unless they first exist to deny their existence.

Therefore Something Has Always Existed

Following logically from the first two premises, it is undeniable that something has always existed!

But The Universe Has Not Always Existed

Here is where many begin to question the cosmological argument.

Acknowledging that something has always existed, isn't the most logical conclusion that the universe has always existed?

How do we know that the universe has not always existed?

## Numerous Contradictions With An Infinitely Old Universe

Consider how an infinitely old universe would lead to numerous contradictions. Peter Kreeft has well pointed out:

> *"Yes, there are," he replied. "If there is no Creator and therefore no moment of creation, then everything is the result of evolution. If there was no beginning or first cause, then the universe must have always existed. That means the universe has been evolving for an infinite period of time—and, by now, everything should already be perfect. There would have been plenty of time for evolution to have finished and evil to have been vanquished. But there still is evil and suffering and imperfection—and that proves the atheist wrong about the universe." (Lee Strobel, The Case for Faith: A Journalist Investigates the Toughest Objections to Christianity, 35 (Kindle Edition); Grand Rapids, Michigan; Zondervan)*

There are, of course, many other problems with the idea of the universe being eternal. Several scientific evidences confirm that the universe had a beginning.

> *"Robert Jastrow, founder and former director of NASA's Goddard Institute for Space Studies, has summarized*

*marized the evidence in his book God and the Astronomers, saying, "Now three lines of evidence-the motions of the galaxies, the laws of thermodynamics, and the life story of the stars-pointed to one conclusion: all indicated that the Universe had a beginning." (Norman Geisler & Ronald Brooks, When Skeptics Ask: A Handbook On Christian Evidences, 220 (Kindle Edition); Grand Rapids, Michigan; Baker Books)*

## The Laws Of Thermodynamics

The laws of thermodynamics indeed point to a beginning of the universe:

*"The biggest problem with this view is that it violates the First Law of Thermodynamics, sometimes known as the law of conservation of mass and energy. This fundamental law, which Isaac Asimov called 'the most powerful and most fundamental generalization about the universe that scientists have ever been able to make,' states that matter and energy can neither be self-created nor destroyed...The First Law of Thermodynamics clearly supports the idea that an expanding universe must have had a beginning but could not have created itself. The Second Law of Thermodynamics, which states that any isolated physical system becomes less ordered and more random over time, provides another piece for the cosmic jigsaw. Applied very simply and generally, it means that our entire universe is running down. As the rotation of the planets and their moons slows down, and as stars (and whole galaxies) burn themselves out, the matter in our universe is becoming more and more disorganized as its energy is dissipated. The logical consequence of this is that the universe cannot be eternal. If it were, the stars would have ceased to shine long ago and all the energy in our universe would have long since been evenly*

> *spread throughout space. At the same time, this suggests that if the universe is becoming less ordered, it must have been more ordered in the past, and have had a highly ordered beginning." (John Blanchard, Does God Believe In Atheists? 5601-5620 (Kindle Edition); Carlisle, PA; EP Books USA)*

The Laws of Thermodynamics clearly demonstrate that the universe had a beginning.

## The Expanding Universe

Writing of the research of the famous Edwin Hubble, Powell has noted:

> *"In the 1920s Astronomer Edwin Hubble discovered that our universe was bigger than previously thought. In fact, it was much bigger. Until he saw outside our galaxy, the prevailing thought was that our galaxy was the entire universe. Hubble was the first to recognize that ours was only one of billions of galaxies....Everywhere he looked in the universe he saw a red shift in the light. This meant the objects emitting the light—stars—are all moving away from each other. Thus the universe is expanding....So, because the universe had a beginning, something must have initiated it. It did not start itself. The cause of the universe must be found outside of the universe; it must be transcendent." (Doug Powell, Holman QuickSource Guide To Christian Apologetics, 697-741 (Kindle Edition); Nashville, TN: Holman Reference)*

There can be no doubt that the universe had a beginning!

## Why Not An Infinite Regress?

Why couldn't the universe have always existed in the form of an infinite regress?

An infinite regress is the idea that there has been an endless chain of causes and effects throughout eternity, without any initial "uncaused First Cause." It is what people are implying when they ask questions like, "Well, what made God?" They are suggesting that if everything has a cause, then God must have a cause.

Then, what caused that?

And what caused that?

And so on and so forth.

Ultimately, however, there are many problems with an infinite regress. The first (and most obvious) is that an infinite regress would lead to an infinite number of contradictions which would make existence impossible.

For example, an infinite regress would make mathematics impossible.

Craig demonstrated this in another interview with Lee Strobel:

> *"The early Christian and Muslim scholars, Craig explained, used mathematical reasoning to demonstrate that it was impossible to have an infinite past. Their conclusion, therefore, was that the universe's age must be finite—that is, it must have had a beginning. "They pointed out that absurdities would result if you were to have an actually infinite number of things," he said. "Since an infinite past would involve an actually infinite number of events, then the past*

*simply can't be infinite." It took a moment for that state-
ment to sink in. I have always been a reluctant student of
mathematics, especially such esoteric permutations as
transfinite arithmetic. Before we could venture into any
mathematical complexities, I reached over and pushed the
"pause" button on my tape recorder. "Hold on a minute,
Bill," I said. "If I'm going to track with you on this, you're
going to have to give me some illustrations to clarify
things." Craig already had some in mind. "Okay, no problem," he replied. When I turned the recorder back on, he
continued. "Let's use an example involving marbles," he
said. "Imagine I had an infinite number of marbles in my
possession, and that I wanted to give you some. In fact,
suppose I wanted to give you an infinite number of marbles. One way I could do that would be to give you the entire pile of marbles. In that case I would have zero marbles
left for myself. "However, another way to do it would be to
give you all of the odd numbered marbles. Then I would still
have an infinity left over for myself, and you would have an
infinity too. You'd have just as many as I would—and, in
fact, each of us would have just as many as I originally had
before we divided into odd and even! Or another approach
would be for me to give you all of the marbles numbered
four and higher. That way, you would have an infinity of
marbles, but I would have only three marbles left. "What
these illustrations demonstrate is that the notion of an actual infinite number of things leads to contradictory results.
In the first case in which I gave you all the marbles, infinity
minus infinity is zero; in the second case in which I gave you
all the odd-numbered marbles, infinity minus infinity is infinity; and in the third case in which I gave you all the marbles numbered four and greater, infinity minus infinity is
three. In each case, we have subtracted the identical number from the identical number, but we have come up with
nonidentical results. "For that reason, mathematicians are*

*forbidden from doing subtraction and division in transfinite arithmetic, because this would lead to contradictions. You see, the idea of an actual infinity is just conceptual; it exists only in our minds. Working within certain rules, mathematicians can deal with infinite quantities and infinite numbers in the conceptual realm. However—and here's the point—it's not descriptive of what can happen in the real world." I was following Craig so far. "You're saying, then, that you couldn't have an infinite number of events in the past." "Exactly, because you would run into similar paradoxes," he said. "Substitute 'past events' for 'marbles,' and you can see the absurdities that would result. So the universe can't have an infinite number of events in its past; it must have had a beginning." (Lee Strobel, The Case for a Creator: A Journalist Investigates Scientific Evidence That Points Toward God, 1816-1841 (Kindle Edition); Grand Rapids, Michigan; Zondervan)*

Mathematics would be impossible if there were an infinite number of causes and effects!

## Therefore Something Beyond The Universe Has Always Existed

This is the only possible conclusion from logic and science.

*"Here, then, is the problem: the Universe exists; it must, in some fashion, be explained. There are but three ways to account for it. (1) It is eternal. (2) It is not eternal; rather it created itself from nothing. (3) It is not eternal; it was created by something anterior, and superior, to itself. Let us now explore these ideas. First, it is now clear scientifically that the Universe is not eternal. Jastrow declares: "... in science, as in the Bible, the World begins with an act of creation. That view has not always been held by scientists. Only*

as a result of the most recent discoveries can we say with a fair degree of confidence that our Universe has not existed forever; that it began abruptly, without any apparent cause, in a blinding event that defies scientific explanation" (p. 2). The very fact that scientists attempt to assign an age to the Universe admits to its having an origin! Second, it is absurd to even suggest that matter could create itself. There is no known natural process whereby matter could, from nothing, fashion itself. Dr. George E. Davis, a physicist, has said: "No material thing can create itself" (1958, p. 71). The Universe is not self-explanatory. Third, the only remaining alternative is that the Universe was created by: (a) something that existed before it did, i.e., some eternal, uncaused Cause; (b) something superior to it, for the created cannot be superior to the Creator, and; (c) something of a different nature since the finite, dependent Universe of matter is unable to explain itself." (Wayne Jackson, Eric Lyons, Kyle Butt, Surveying The Evidence, 273-293 (Kindle Edition); Montgomery, Alabama; Apologetics Press, Inc.)*

## But The Only Cause Sufficient For The Existence Of The Universe Is God.

From the cosmological argument, we can see that there are several characteristics of this Being that can only be adequately described as "God."

First, the cause of the universe must be a Person. This is shown to be true for several reasons.

Powell has written:

> "At this point there are only two options: either the cause was personal or it was impersonal. Reflection on what this uncaused cause would look like leads us to a conclusion

*rather quickly. The first cause would require an ability to create. Without this ability nothing could be created. It would also require an intention to create, a will to initiate the universe. Without this will to create, nothing would be created. It would require a non-contingent being, one whose existence depends on nothing but itself. If it was contingent, then it would simply be one more effect in the chain of causes and effects. And it must be transcendent. The cause of the universe must be outside of and apart from the universe. Now add all these things together. What kind of thing relies on nothing for its existence, has the power to create something from nothing, has a will to do it or not do it and has the characteristic of existing outside of the creation? Does this sound like a personal or impersonal being? Personal, of course. Thus, the Kalam argument brings us to the conclusion that the universe had a beginning that was caused by a personal, powerful, transcendent being." (Doug Powell, Holman QuickSource Guide to Christian Apologetics (Holman Quicksource Guides), 633-642 (Kindle Edition); Nashville, TN: Holman Reference)*

Second, this Being is eternal, having no beginning and having no end. If it were not eternal, then it would just be part of the contingent universe and this would lead to an infinite regress, which is impossible.

Third, this Being must be non-contingent. This means that it is fully self-sufficient. If it depended on anything outside of itself, it would just be part of the created universe.

Fourth, this Being must be perfect in all of its' attributes. An imperfection is that which is lacking in some quality. But since this Being is fully self-sufficient, it cannot be imperfect.

Fifth, this Being must be immaterial (i.e., Spirit). The universe of matter had a beginning; and since this Being is transcendent to the universe of matter, it must be immaterial.

Sixth, this Being must be non-spatial (i.e., not bound or confirmed to space). Space itself had a beginning; and since this Being is transcendent to the universe of space, this Being must be non-spatial.

Seventh, this Being must be outside of time. We know from science that time is itself a real dimension, one that is measurable by different standards but which nonetheless exists.

> *"We think of time as the measurement of days, hours and seconds. It's what allows us to meet our friends at the café or start work and school in unison. We grow into adults if we are given enough time, and we might get the chance to grow old if we use it wisely. It's more than a mere idea, however: time is a physical property. That's not an obvious concept, but it's profoundly important to understand. We don't live our daily lives in three dimensions, but in four. This is why physicists always speak of "space-time" as a single term; space and time are inextricably tied together. The discoveries of physics during the past two centuries have given us insights not enjoyed by the generations of Bible scholars that went before us. The geometry of eternity is not a simple timeline down which we can run our fingers. Time is not linear and absolute, but-like space-it can flex. It can be stretched and contracted. This is why we often hear the metaphor, "the fabric of space-time." What we once thought of as a ruler is more like a rubber band....."This strange phenomenon of the speeding or slowing of time is known as time dilation. Time stretches as one travels closer to the speed of light. At the same time, spatial dimensions like length and width get shorter as one travels faster. This is why physicists refer to space-time rather than just space and time. Time is an additional dimension to our reality.*

*Time and space can stretch and bend, but they are as con-
nected as the width, length and height of a box." (Chuck
Missler, Beyond Time & Space, 44-128 (Kindle Edition);
Coeur d'Alene, ID; Koinonia House)*

Since time itself had a beginning, and this Being is eternal, It necessarily exists outside of the universe of time.

Eight, this Being must be changeless. Change is simply the pro-
gression of something from one moment to the next. However,
since this Being is outside of time, It must be therefore be tran-
scendental to the universe of change.

Nine, this Being must be immensely powerful. This is due to the
fact that it created the universe!

Now, add all of these factors together, and what can we conclude?

*"Using the clock analogy again, the further back in time,
the more wound up the clock. Far enough back in time, the
clock was completely wound up. The universe therefore
cannot be infinitely old. One can only conclude that the universe had a beginning, and that beginning had to have
been caused by someone or something operating outside
of the known laws of thermodynamics. Is this scientific
proof for the existence of a creator God? I think so. Evolutionary theories of the universe cannot counteract the
above arguments for the existence of God." (John M. Cim-
bala, 'Mechanical Engineering,' in John F. Ashton, PhD, In
Six Days: Why Fifty Scientists Choose To Believe In Creation, 3021-3026 (Kindle Edition); Green Forest, AR; Master
Books)*

The cosmological argument provides powerful evidence that
God exists.

## **The Teleological Argument**

The teleological argument for God's existence argues from the fact of design in the universe which points to the existence of the Designer (i.e., God).

Major Premise: Design implies Designer.

Minor Premise: The universe exhibits undeniable evidence of design.

Conclusion: Therefore the Universe has a Designer (i.e., God Exists).

As mankind has learned more about science, we have discovered that there are large number of universal factors in place which make life on Earth possible. If any of these factors were changed-even to the smallest degree-then life here would be impossible.

For example:

> *"Here's another illustration: the ratio of the electromagnetic force to the gravitational force is fine-tuned to one part in ten thousand trillion trillion trillion. Astrophysicist Hugh Ross said to understand that number, imagine covering a billion North American continents with dimes up to the moon—238,000 miles high. Choose one dime at random, paint it red, and put it somewhere in the piles. Blindfold a friend and have him pick out one dime from the billion continents. What are the odds he'd choose the red dime? One in ten thousand trillion trillion trillion...."These extraordinary cosmic "coincidences" have not escaped secular scientists. "There is, for me, powerful evidence that there is something going on behind it all," said Paul Davies, a professor of physics at Arizona State University. "It seems*

*as though somebody has fine-tuned nature's numbers to make the universe... The impression of design is over-whelming." 7 British cosmologist Edward R. Harrison doesn't hesitate to draw conclusions from the universe's razor-sharp calibration. "Here is the cosmological proof of the existence of God," he said flatly. "The fine-tuning of the universe provides prima facie evidence of deistic design." 8 And Strauss wasn't done yet. "Not only is our universe precisely calibrated to a breathtaking degree, but our planet is also remarkably and fortuitously situated so life would be possible." "In what way?" I asked. "To have a planet like ours where life exists, first you need to be in the right kind of galaxy. There are three types of galaxies: elliptical, spiral, and irregular. You need to be in a spiral galaxy, like we are, because it's the only kind that produces the right heavy elements and has the right radiation levels. "But you can't live just anywhere in the galaxy," he continued. "If you're too close to the center, there's too much radiation and there's also a black hole, which you want to avoid. If you're too far from the center, you won't have the right heavy elements; you'd lack the oxygen and carbon you'd need. You have to live in the so-called 'Goldilocks Zone,' or the galactic habitable zone, where life could exist." "Are you referring to intelligent life?" I asked. "Anything more complex than bacteria," he said. Then he continued, "To have life, you need a star like our sun. Our sun is a Class G star that has supported stable planet orbits in the right location for a long time. The star must be in its middle age, so its luminosity is stabilized. It has to be a bachelor star—many stars in the universe are binary, which means two stars orbiting each other, which is bad for stable planetary orbits. Plus, the star should be a third-generation star, like our sun.....*"Strauss paused, but I could tell he wasn't done yet. "There are so many parameters that have to be just right for our planet to support life," he said. "The distance from* *the sun, the rotation rate, the amount of water, the tilt, the right size so gravity lets gases like methane escape but allows oxygen to stay. "You need a moon like ours—it's very rare to have just one large moon—in order to stabilize Earth's tilt. As counterintuitive as it sounds, you even need to have tectonic activity, which experts said could be 'the central requirement for life on a planet.' 9 Plate tectonics drives biodiversity, helps avoid a water world without continents, and helps generate the magnetic field. Also, it's nice to have a huge planet like Jupiter nearby to act like a vacuum cleaner by attracting potentially devastating comets and meteors away from you." "Periodically, newspapers tout the discovery of what astronomers call an 'Earth-like planet,'" I said. "Yes, but generally all they mean is that it has a similar size as Earth or that it might be positioned to allow surface water. But there's so much more to Earth than those two factors." "How many conditions have to be met to create an Earth-like planet?" I asked. "Hugh Ross sets the number at 322," he replied. 10 "So if you run probability calculations, you find that there's a 10-304 chance you're going to find another planet that's truly like Earth." "Still, there are lots of potential candidates out there," I pointed out. "One estimate is there could be more than a billion trillion planets." "Granted," he said. "So let's factor that number into our probability equation. That still means the odds of having any higher life–supporting planet would be one in a million trillion trillion trillion trillion trillion trillion trillion trillion trillion trillion trillion trillion trillion trillion trillion trillion trillion trillion trillion trillion trillion." He let that astonishing number sink in. "In science," he said, "we have a phrase for probabilities like that." "Really? What is it?" There came a grin. "Ain't gonna happen."" (Lee Strobel, The Case for Miracles: A Journalist Investigates Evidence for the Supernatural, 178-181 (Kindle Edition); Grand Rapids, Michigan; Zondervan)*

As amazing as the evidence of design is through the macrouniverse, the evidence of the microuniverse is equally stunning.

Consider the sunning complexity of DNA:

> *"In fact, the chance of you being able to jump high enough to reach the moon is greater than the chance that DNA would form by chance....Sir Fredrick Hoyle vividly illustrates the probability of spontaneous generation like this: Supposing the first cell originated by chance is like believing a tornado could sweep through a junkyard filled with airplane parts and form a Boeing 747....This means that the odds of a single functional DNA molecule coming together at random are about the same odds that you could fill a billion universes with golf balls and put a small red dot on the bottom of one ball and somehow a blindfolded baby could find that ball while rummaging through the hundred billion galaxies on the very first try." (Joe White with Nicholas Comninellis, Darwin's Demise: Why Evolution Can't Take The Heat, 302-350 (Kindle Edition); Green Forest, AR; Master Books)*

The evidence from nature points undeniably to the existence of God.

One scientist, describing some aspects of this evidence, writes:

> *"In some respects I find that being a practicing scientist helps me in my understanding of God. The Trinity, the godhead, the three-in-one, may be a stumbling block for some, but to a physicist, who accepts the concept of the wave-particle duality of matter, the Trinity is a perfectly acceptable concept of the nature of God. In my own research area of nuclear astrophysics I am struck by the large number of cosmic "coincidences" which have occurred in order for the*

*universe to be as it is and for life to exist on planet Earth. Far from weakening my faith, science has in fact strengthened it." (John R. De Laeter, 'Physics,' in John F. Ashton PhD, On The Seventh Day: Forty Scientists And Academics Explain Why They Believe In God, 208-212 (Kindle Edition); Green Forest, AR; Master Books)*

More examples of the design of the universe will be brought forth in the following studies.

## **The Moral Argument**

The third argument for the existence of God which we will consider is known as the Moral Argument. It is based upon the existence of objective moral law. The argument may be summed up in this fashion:

1.  If objective moral law exists, then God exists.

2.  Objective moral law does exist.

3.  Therefore, God exists.

When we talk about "objective moral law," what do we mean?

Geisler has written:

*"Before the absolute nature of morality can be understood, morality must be defined. Several things are meant by a moral obligation. First, a moral duty is good in itself (an end), not merely good as a means. Further, it is something we ought to pursue, a duty. Morality is prescriptive (an "ought"), not merely descriptive (an "is"). Morality deals with what is right, as opposed to wrong. It is an obligation, that for which a person is accountable. An absolute moral obligation is: an objective (not subjective) moral duty—a*

*duty for all persons. an eternal (not temporal) obligation — a duty at all times. a universal (not local) obligation — a duty for all places. An absolute duty is one that is binding on all persons at all times in all places. Defense of Absolutes. Moral absolutes can be defended by showing the deficiency of moral relativism. For either there is a moral absolute or else everything is morally relative. Hence, if relativism is wrong, then there must be an absolute basis for morality. Everything is relative to an absolute. Simply by asking, "Relative to what?" it is easy to see that total relativism is inadequate. It can't be relative to the relative. In that case it could not be relative at all, ad infinitum, since there would be nothing to which it was relative, etc.". (Norman L. Geisler, Baker Encyclopedia of Christian Apologetics (Baker Reference Library), 501 (Kindle Edition); Grand Rapids, Michigan; Baker Books)*

Those who have carefully studied other cultures have come to learn that there are some identical moral precepts between each one. Former atheist, C.S. Lewis, discusses this in detail:

*"I know that some people say the idea of a Law of Nature or decent behaviour known to all men is unsound, because different civilisations and different ages have had quite different moralities. But this is not true. There have been differences between their moralities, but these have never amounted to anything like a total difference. If anyone will take the trouble to compare the moral teaching of, say, the ancient Egyptians, Babylonians, Hindus, Chinese, Greeks and Romans, what will really strike him will be how very like they are to each other and to our own. Some of the evidence for this I have put together in the appendix of another book called The Abolition of Man; but for our present purpose I need only ask the reader to think what a totally different morality would mean. Think of a country where*

*people were admired for running away in battle, or where a man felt proud of double-crossing all the people who had been kindest to him. You might just as well try to imagine a country where two and two made five. Men have differed as regards what people you ought to be unselfish to— whether it was only your own family, or your fellow coun- trymen, or every one. But they have always agreed that you ought not to put yourself first. Selfishness has never been admired. Men have differed as to whether you should have one wife or four. But they have always agreed that you must not simply have any woman you liked." (C.S. Lewis, Mere Christianity, 5-6 (Kindle Edition); HarperCollins E-Books)*

Another researcher points out some of these common moral precepts:

*"NDErs commonly experience two things in the presence of this Being of Light: an overwhelming love and compassion, and a life review where this God of light emphasizes the impact of their actions on others....People commonly say, "All religions basically teach the same things." There's some truth to this. It's actually uncanny how similar the moral laws are across cultures— in ancient China, Babylon, Egypt, Greece, and Rome; across Anglo- Saxon and Ameri- can Indian culture; through Buddhist, Hindu, Christian, and Muslim sacred writings— all basically agree in this area. Former Oxford scholar C. S. Lewis gives evidence of this common moral law summarized below: Don't do harm to another human by what you do or say (the Golden Rule). Honor your father and mother. Be kind toward brothers and sisters, children, and the elderly. Do not have sex with another person's spouse. Be honest in all your dealings (don't steal). Do not lie. Care for those weaker or less for- tunate. Dying to self is the path to life. 10 In just about*

*every culture and world religion since the beginning of rec-orded history, we see this common moral law. "They demonstrate that God's law is written in their hearts" (Romans 2:15 NLT)." (John Burke,* Imagine Heaven: Near-Death Experiences, God's Promises, And The Exhilarating Future That Awaits You, *160-161 (Kindle Edition); Grand Rapids, Michigan; Baker Books).*

Even if one were to deny objective moral reality, simple logic will show that he actually believes in and adheres to such!

*"In a sense, this argument also follows the principle of causality But moral laws are different from the natural laws that we have dealt with before. Moral laws don't describe what is; they prescribe what ought to be. They are not simply a description of the way men behave, and are not known by observing what men do. If they were, our idea of morality would surely be different. Instead, they tell us what men ought to do, whether they are doing it or not. Thus, any moral "ought" comes from beyond the natural universe. You can't explain it by anything that happens in the universe and it can't be reduced to the things men do in the universe. It transcends the natural order and requires a transcendent cause. Now some might say that this moral law is not really objective; it is nothing but a subjective judgment that comes from social conventions. However, this view fails to account for the fact that all men hold the same things to be wrong (like murder, rape, theft, and lying). Also, their criticism sounds very much like a subjective judgment, because they are saying that our value judgments are wrong. Now if there is no objective moral law, then there can be no right or wrong value judgments. If our views of morality are subjective, then so are theirs. But if they claim to be making an objective statement about moral law, then they are implying that there is a moral law*

*in the very act of trying to deny it. They are caught both ways. Even their "nothing but" statement requires "more than" knowledge which shows that they secretly hold to some absolute standard which is beyond subjective judgments.. Finally, we find that even those who say that there is no moral order expect to be treated with fairness, courtesy, and dignity. ty. If one of them raised this objection and we replied with, "Oh, shut up. Who cares what you think?" we might find that he does believe there are some moral "oughts." Everyone expects others to follow some moral codes, even those who try to deny them. But moral law is an undeniable fact."* (Norman L. Geisler & Ronald M. Brooks, When Skeptics Ask: A Handbook on Christian Evidences, 22-24 (Kindle Edition); Grand Rapids, Michigan; Baker Books)

Now, all of this quickly demonstrates that there must be a God!

*"My argument against God was that the universe seemed so cruel and unjust. But how had I got this idea of just and unjust? A man does not call a line crooked unless he has some idea of a straight line. What was I comparing this universe with when I called it unjust?"* (C.S. Lewis, *Mere Christianity*, 38-39 (Kindle Edition); HarperCollins E-Books)

Just as you cannot get a law without a lawgiver, so you cannot have a moral law without a moral Lawgiver.

God exists.

## **Conclusion**

When we compare the facts from the cosmological, teleological, and moral arguments, the evidence shows demonstrably that there is a Creator. More to the point, by looking at the characteristics of God revealed through nature, we can see that the God of Creation is the God revealed through the Judeo-Christian Scriptures.

Geisler summarizes:

> *"This God Who Exists Is Identical to the God Described in the Christian Scriptures. The God described in the Bible is said to be eternal (Col. 1 :16; Heb. 1:2), changeless (Mal. 3:6; Heb. 6:18), infinite (I Kings 8:27; Isa. 66:1), all-loving (John 3:16; I John 4:16), and all-powerful (Heb. 1:3; Matt. 19:26). But there cannot be two infinitely perfect, changeless, eternal beings. First, there can be only one infinite and necessary Being, as was shown above (p. 239f.). Second, there could not be two beings who have all possible perfections attributable to them. For in order to be two beings one would have to differ from the other; where there is no difference in being there is only one being. But there can be no difference unless one being has something the other does not. But if there is something that an infinite being can have but one lacks, then the one lacking it is not absolutely perfect. Hence, there is only one absolutely perfect being. But if there cannot be two such beings, then the God described in the Bible is identical to the God concluded from the above argument. Therefore, the God Described in the Bible Exists. If there is only one God and the God described in the Bible is identical in characteristics to him, then it follows logically that the God described in the Bible exists. For there cannot be two infinitely perfect beings; there cannot be two such ultimates or absolutes, and so forth. Hence, the God portrayed in Scripture does indeed exist." (Norman Geisler, Christian Apologetics, 249-250 (Kindle Edition); Grand Rapids, Michigan; Baker Books House)*

In recent world history, the name of Antony Flew is still well-

known. Being a defender of atheism for the last century and re-
ceiving world-renown fame in academia for his arguments
against God, Flew is perhaps well-known as being the mentor of
renowned skeptic, Richard Dawkins. Indeed, in many colleges
around the world, Flew's arguments uphold atheism are still
popular.

What many do not realize is that a few years before his death,
Flew came to believe that there is a God.

He wrote:

> *"I now believe that the universe was brought into existence
> by an infinite Intelligence. I believe that this universe's in-
> tricate laws manifest what scientists have called the Mind
> of God. I believe that life and reproduction originate in a
> divine Source. Why do I believe this, given that I expounded
> and defended atheism for more than a half century? The
> short answer is this: this is the world picture, as I see it, that
> has emerged from modern science. Science spotlights three
> dimensions of nature that point to God. The first is the fact
> that nature obeys laws. The second is the dimension of life,
> of intelligently organized and purpose-driven beings, which
> arose from matter. The third is the very existence of nature.
> But it is not science alone that has guided me. I have also
> been helped by a renewed study of the classical philosoph-
> ical arguments. My departure from atheism was not occa-
> sioned by any new phenomenon or argument. Over the last
> two decades, my whole framework of thought has been in
> a state of migration. This was a consequence of my contin-
> uing assessment of the evidence of nature. When I finally
> came to recognize the existence of a God, it was not a par-
> adigm shift, because my paradigm remains, as Plato in his
> Republic scripted his Socrates to insist: "We must follow the
> argument wherever it leads." (Antony Flew & Roy Abraham*

*Varghese, There Is a God: How the World's Most Notorious Atheist Changed His Mind by Antony Flew, 88-89 (Kindle Edition); New York, NY; Harper Collins Publishers, Inc.)*

In the conclusion of his book, Flew notes:

*"But the three items of evidence we have considered in this volume—the laws of nature, life with its teleological organization, and the existence of the universe—can only be explained in the light of an Intelligence that explains both its own existence and that of the world....I must say again that the journey to my discovery of the Divine has thus far been a pilgrimage of reason. I have followed the argument where it has led me. And it has led me to accept the existence of a self-existent, immutable, immaterial, omnipotent, and omniscient Being." (Antony Flew & Roy Abraham Varghese, There Is a God: How the World's Most Notorious Atheist Changed His Mind by Antony Flew, 155 (Kindle Edition); New York, NY; Harper Collins Publishers, Inc.)*

The grace of the Lord Jesus Christ, and the love of God, and the communion of the Holy Spirit, be with you all. Amen.

# APPENDIX TWO: EVIDENCE FROM ARCHAEOLOGY THAT THE BIBLE IS THE WORD OF GOD

(Note: This section is taken from my book, Old Apologetics For A New Age: Volume Two-The Inspiration Of The Bible (Kindle Edition): Charleston, AR: Cobb Publishing)

## Archaeology As Proof That The Bible Is The Inspired Word Of God

Archaeology is the study of ancient events, persons, peoples, and civilizations. There has been amazing evidence from archaeology in the last several decades which demonstrate and document that the Bible is historically accurate. In this chapter, we will notice some of these amazing discoveries.

Let's start at the beginning: with the Book of Genesis!

### Genesis Authorship And Archaeology

The first five Books of the Bible (Genesis, Exodus, Leviticus, Numbers, and Deuteronomy) are often referred to as the Pentateuch (literally, "Five Books"). They form the basic core of the Law of Moses. Indeed, several Scriptures indicate that Moses wrote these Books:

> *Exodus 17:14—Then the LORD said to Moses, "Write this for a memorial in the book and recount it in the hearing of Joshua, that I will utterly blot out the remembrance of Amalek from under heaven."*

*Exodus 24:4-4 And Moses wrote all the words of the LORD. And he rose early in the morning, and built an altar at the foot of the mountain, and twelve pillars according to the twelve tribes of Israel.*

*Exodus 34:27—Then the LORD said to Moses, "Write these words, for according to the tenor of these words I have made a covenant with you and with Israel."*

*Numbers 33:2—Now Moses wrote down the starting points of their journeys at the command of the LORD. And these are their journeys according to their starting points:*

*Deuteronomy 31:9—So Moses wrote this law and delivered it to the priests, the sons of Levi, who bore the ark of the covenant of the LORD, and to all the elders of Israel.*

*Deuteronomy 31:24-26—So it was, when Moses had completed writing the words of this law in a book, when they were finished, that Moses commanded the Levites, who bore the ark of the covenant of the LORD, saying: 26 "Take this Book of the Law, and put it beside the ark of the covenant of the LORD your God, that it may be there as a witness against you;*

---

There is considerable evidence from the Bible and the ancient rabbis that Moses wrote the Pentateuch. However, within the last few centuries, there have been those who have raised their voices and claimed that Moses could not have written the Books of the Pentateuch. The early arguments were that no one in the time when the Pentateuch was written knew how to write. However, that argument went out the window when it was discovered that people were not only writing during Moses' day, but long before! Indeed, the writing analysis of the Pentateuch shows that it indeed belongs to the time frame of 1500 B.C.

Later, the argument switched to try and claim that the Penta-teuch was actually based on Babylonian legends. Yet numerous evidences have demonstrated that the Book of Genesis espe-cially predates these Babylonian documents.

## The Fall In The Garden

Brad was a nice guy, when he wasn't trying to get his coven to come kill me.

We had met when he saw my former book, "I'm Back Again." Raising his hands in a gesture of worshiped to a demon known as Baphomet, Brad told me that he was a pagan. However, his roots went much deeper than that. He did not realize that he was actually serving Satan.

After cursing a friend of mine with a Satanic bible, Brad decided to get on someone's phone and texted his coven with specific instructions. He gave them my name, my phone number, my ad-dress, and said, "His church does food boxes: use that and lure him out." One of Brad's group members said, "What do you want us to do?"

Brad responded (and I quote): "I want him dead. I want his fam-ily dead. I want his house burnt to the ground lol."

(He did not realize that I was given a copy of all the text mes-sages).

What happened with Brad is something that the Bible describes in detail: there is a spiritual war going on, and we are all involved in it. In fact, we have all chosen our sides-and are choosing sides every day that we live.

---

*James 4:7—Therefore submit to God. Resist the devil and he will flee from you.*

*Ephesians 6:12—For we do not wrestle against flesh and blood, but against principalities, against powers, against the rulers of the darkness of this age, against spiritual hosts of wickedness in the heavenly places.*

The Bible tells us this war goes back to the Fall in the Garden of Eden:

*Genesis 3:1-6—Now the serpent was more cunning than any beast of the field which the LORD God had made. And he said to the woman, "Has God indeed said, 'You shall not eat of every tree of the garden'?" And the woman said to the serpent, "We may eat the fruit of the trees of the garden; but of the fruit of the tree which is in the midst of the garden, God has said, 'You shall not eat it, nor shall you touch it, lest you die.' " Then the serpent said to the woman, "You will not surely die. For God knows that in the day you eat of it your eyes will be opened, and you will be like God, knowing good and evil." So when the woman saw that the tree was good for food, that it was pleasant to the eyes, and a tree desirable to make one wise, she took of its fruit and ate. She also gave to her husband with her, and he ate.*

The account of the Fall was well-known in the ancient world, as demonstrated by the archaeological record. Examples include evidences from Babylon and China. Others could be cited.

Nephilim Giants

The Bible tells us about the nephilim (the offspring of the fallen angels and humanity).

*Genesis 6:1-4—Now it came to pass, when men began to multiply on the face of the earth, and daughters were born to them, that the sons of God saw the daughters of men, that they were beautiful; and they took wives for themselves of all whom they chose. And the LORD said, "My Spirit shall not strive with man forever, for he is indeed flesh; yet his days shall be one hundred and twenty years." There were giants on the earth in those days, and also afterward, when the sons of God came in to the daughters of men and they bore children to them. Those were the mighty men who were of old, men of renown.*

The word translated as "giants" is the Hebrew word "nephilim." This word includes two ideas, both related together in the ancient languages. First, the word Nephilim means "fallen ones." Second, it carries with it the idea of a "giant."

According to the Bible, these giants were the descendants of the the "sons of God" and the "daughters of men." The phrase "sons of God" had specific reference during the time Genesis was written to fallen angels:

*Job 1:6—Now there was a day when the sons of God came to present themselves before the LORD, and Satan also came among them.*

*Job 2:1—Again there was a day when the sons of God came to present themselves before the LORD, and Satan came also among them to present himself before the LORD.*

*Job 38:4-7—Where were you when I laid the foundations of the earth? Tell Me, if you have understanding. Who determined its measurements? Surely you know! Or who stretched the line upon it? To what were its foundations fastened? Or who laid its cornerstone, When the morning stars sang together, And all the sons of God shouted for joy?*

Many are offended by the Bible identification of the "sons of God" with "angels." However, the Bible testimony is clear on the matter. Furthermore, the most ancient Jewish and Christian sources   document that the "angel" view was the most ancient.

Now, the giants are also mentioned in numerous other passages throughout the Old Testament.

For example:

*Numbers 13:28—Nevertheless the people who dwell in the land are strong; the cities are fortified and very large; moreover we saw the descendants of Anak there.*

*Numbers 13:32-33—And they gave the children of Israel a bad report of the land which they had spied out, saying, "The land through which we have gone as spies is a land that devours its inhabitants, and all the people whom we saw in it are men of great stature. There we saw the giants (the descendants of Anak came from the giants); and we were like grasshoppers in our own sight, and so we were in their sight."*

*Deuteronomy 2:9-11—Then the LORD said to me, 'Do not harass Moab, nor contend with them in battle, for I will not give you any of their land as a possession, because I have given Ar to the descendants of Lot as a possession.' ". (The Emim had dwelt there in times past, a people as great and numerous and tall as the Anakim. They were also regarded as giants, like the Anakim, but the Moabites call them*

*Emim.*

*Deuteronomy 2:20-23—(That was also regarded as a land of giants; giants formerly dwelt there. But the Ammonites call them Zamzummim, a people as great and numerous and tall as the Anakim. But the LORD destroyed them before them, and they dispossessed them and dwelt in their place, just as He had done for the descendants of Esau, who dwelt in Seir, when He destroyed the Horites from before them. They dispossessed them and dwelt in their place, even to this day. And the Avim, who dwelt in villages as far as Gaza—the Caphtorim, who came from Caphtor, destroyed them and dwelt in their place.)*

*Deuteronomy 3:11—For only Og king of Bashan remained of the remnant of the giants. Indeed his bedstead was an iron bedstead. (Is it not in Rabbah of the people of Ammon?) Nine cubits is its length and four cubits its width, according to the standard cubit.*

*1 Chronicles 20:6—Yet again there was war at Gath, where there was a man of great stature, with twenty-four fingers and toes, six on each hand and six on each foot; and he also was born to the giant.*

Many reject the Bible teaching regarding the existence of the nephilim giants. However, the nephilim (giants) are mentioned not only throughout the Bible, but by other historians as well. Indeed, such historians as Pliny the Wilder, Josephus, the ancient Egyptians, and Herodotus all bear testament to the ancient giants. Indeed, Cooper has documented other examples from numerous ancient sources which document the existence and prevalence of the giants.

Furthermore, there is a great deal of evidence from our day and age regarding the existence of giants. Chief Joseph RiverWind was commissioned by his Native American tribe to document and chronicle their ancient traditions. Many of these share amazing similarities with the Bible, which is very interesting since many of these legends predate their exposure to the Bible! In this regard, there are many legends among the Native Americans regarding giants.   There are numerous accounts of newspaper headlines from America which document giant graves and skeletons being found.   Some researchers believe that the giant bones are being destroyed by those in positions of power since they are proof that the Bible is true and that Darwinian evolution is false.   Nevertheless, there is evidence-even from the ancient archives of the Smithsonian Institute-which confirms the existence and excavation of giant skeletons and accessories from America.

The giants were killed during the Flood and their spirits were left in the world to become demons;   yet we know through ancient sources they were brought back through sorcery   and twisted science.   Indeed, an interesting passage of Scripture from the Book of Ezekiel may shed some light on this subject:

---

*Ezekiel 13:17-18—Likewise, son of man, set your face against the daughters of your people, who prophesy out of their own heart; prophesy against them, and say, 'Thus says the Lord GOD: "Woe to the women who sew magic charms on their sleeves and make veils for the heads of people of every height to hunt souls! Will you hunt the souls of My people, and keep yourselves alive?"*

---

Delving into this text reveals some disturbing facts. Notice the phrase "magic charms," "sleeves," and "veils," and their connection to "hunting souls." These terms were used in the ancient world for occult rituals which were designed to try and bring back the spirits of the nephilim into the world of the living.

In numerous ways, we see how the findings of archaeology again confirm the Bible narrative.

## The Flood

The Bible teaches that there was a worldwide Deluge (Flood) that God brought upon the Earth because of the wickedness of humankind and mankind (Genesis 6:1-6). While the canon of the Old Testament Scripture was closed at 408 B.C. With our 39 Book Library, the Bible references non-inspired books.

For example, notice these quotations of the New Testament from non-inspired books:

Chart Of Non-Biblical Citations From The New Testament Scriptures

| Bible Reference And Quotation | Non-Biblical Source Referred To |
|---|---|
| Matthew 5:21- "You have heard that it was said to those of old, 'YOU SHALL NOT MURDER, and whoever murders will be in danger of the judgment.' (Cf. Matthew 5:31, 33, 38, 43) | "Jesus used the phrase 'You have heard that the ancients were told,' or a similar one, to introduce each of the six corrective illustrations He gives in this part of His sermon (see vv. 21, 27, 31, 33, 38, 43). The phrase has reference to rabbinical, traditional teaching, and in each illustration Jesus contrasts that human teaching with the divine Word of God. The examples show ways in which God's righteousness surpasses |

that of the scribes and Pharisees (see v. 20)...Jesus is not modifying the law of Moses, the teaching of the Psalms, the standards of the prophets, or any other part of Scripture. The essence of what He has just said in verses 17-20 is (1) that His teaching stands firmly in agreement with every truth, even every word, of the Old Testament, and (2) that the Jewish religious traditions did not...The rabbis of past generations were often called the 'fathers of antiquity,' or 'the men of long ago,' and it is to them that 'the ancients' (vv. 21, 33) refers. Jesus was contrasting His teaching0and the true teaching of the Old Testament Scriptures themselves-with the Jewish written and oral traditions that had accumulated over the previous several hundred years and that had so terribly perverted God's revelation." (John MacArthur, The MacArthur New Testament Commentary: Matthew 1-7, 7025-7066 (Kindle Edition); Chicago, Illinois; Moody Press)

| 1 Corinthians 15:33— Do not be deceived: "Evil company corrupts good habits." | "Paul now moves from a biblical text with an anti-Epicurean thrust (vs. 32 b) to a quotation from the third-to-fourth century Athenian dramatist Meander: 'Do no be misled; bad company corrupts good character.'...The epigram from Meander's |
|---|---|

| | |
|---|---|
| | Thais was a popular one in Paul's day and would probably have been known to any educated Corinthian." (Roy E. Ciampa & Brian S. Rosner, The First Letter To The Corinthians: The Pillar New Testament Commentary, 791-792 (Kindle Edition); Grand Rapids, Michigan; William B. Eerdmans Publishing Company) |
| Acts 17:26-28—And He has made from one blood every nation of men to dwell on all the face of the earth, and has determined their preappointed times and the boundaries of their dwellings, **27** so that they should seek the Lord, in the hope that they might grope for Him and find Him, though He is not far from each one of us; **28** for in Him we live and move and have our being, as also some of your own poets have said, 'For we are also His offspring.' | "The precise expression is found in the writings of Aratus (270 B.C.); and though not the exact words still the idea is found in the writings of Cleanthes (300-220 B.C.). Cleanthes was a Stoic philosopher, and the sentiment here quoted was directly at variance with the Epicureans' beliefs. Aratus was a native of Cilcia, the same country Paul was from. This quotation of the heathen poets would at once quicken the attention of the hearers. This was not an illiterate Jew, but a man of culture, acquainted with the thoughts of their own great poets." (Gareth Reese, Acts: New Testament History, 632; Joplin, Missouri; College Press) |
| Titus 1:12-13—One of | "This phrase is found in the Minos of |

| | |
|---|---|
| them, a prophet of their own, said, "Cretans *are* always liars, evil beasts, lazy gluttons." **13** This testimony is true. Therefore rebuke them sharply, that they may be sound in the faith, | the Cretan poet Epimenides, a sixth-century B.C. poet of Knossos, Crete, quoted by Callimachus (ca. 300-240 B.C.). Epimenides joked of his own people that the absence of wild beasts on the island was supplied by its' human inhabitants...Paul occasionally quoted Ancient Greek poets (Acts 17:28)." (Thomas C. Oden, First And Second Timothy And Titus: INTERPRETATION: A Bible Commentary For Teaching And Preaching, 65-66 (Kindle Edition); Louisville, KY; Westminster John Knox Press) |
| Jude 1:9—Yet Michael the archangel, in contending with the devil, when he disputed about the body of Moses, dared not bring against him a reviling accusation, but said, "The Lord rebuke you!" | "This phrase is found in the Minos of the Cretan poet Epimenides, a sixth-century B.C. poet of Knossos, Crete, quoted by Callimachus (ca. 300-240 B.C.). Epimenides joked of his own people that the absence of wild beasts on the island was supplied by its' human inhabitants...Paul occasionally quoted Ancient Greek poets (Acts 17:28)." (Thomas C. Oden, First And Second Timothy And Titus: INTERPRETATION: A Bible Commentary For Teaching And Preaching, 65-66 (Kindle Edition); Louisville, KY; Westminster John Knox Press) |
| Jude 1:14-15—Now Enoch, the seventh from Adam, prophesied about these men | First Enoch 1:9-"9Behold! He comes with ten thousands of His holy ones to execute judgment upon all, to destroy all the ungodly, to convict all |

| | |
|---|---|
| also, saying, "Behold, the Lord comes with ten thousands of His saints, **15** to execute judgment on all, to convict all who are ungodly among them of all their ungodly deeds which they have committed in an ungodly way, and of all the harsh things which ungodly sinners have spoken against Him." | flesh of all the works of their ungodliness which they have ungodly committed, and of all the harsh things which ungodly sinners have spoken against Him." Quoted in Jude 14-15 |

Again, notice how the Book of Revelation references many non-inspired works:

| The Book Of Revelation | Non-Canonical Books Referenced |
|---|---|
| Revelation 1:1-20; 9:1-21; 20:1-15 | 1 Enoch |
| Revelation 2:1-3:22; 18:1-24 | The Epistle Of Enoch |
| Revelation 4:1-11 | The Testament Of Levi |
| Revelation 5:1-14; 11:1-19; 13:1-18; 21:1-22:5 | 4 Ezra (Also Known As 2 Esdras) |

| Revelation 6:1-17 | 2 Maccabees |
| --- | --- |
| Revelation 7:1-17; 19:1-21 | Psalms Of Solomon |
| Revelation 8:1-13 | The Testament Of Adam |
| Revelation 10:1-11 | Book Of Jubilees |
| Revelation 12:1-17 | The Life Of Adam And Eve |
| Revelation 14:1-20 | The Damascus Document |
| Revelation 15:1-16:21 | Words Of The Luminaries |
| Revelation 17:1-18 | Joseph And Aseneth |
| Revelation 22:6-21 | The Apocalypse Of Zechariah |

According to the Bible and extra-biblical documents (such as 1 Enoch, Jasher, etc.), there were many reasons for the Flood. God gave people time to repent, but they refused to do so.

| Reason For Flood | Biblical And Extra-Biblical References |
| --- | --- |
| Sexual Sin Between Angelkind And Mankind | Genesis 6:1-4; 2 Peter 2:4-6; Jude 6-7 |

| Acceptance/Practice Of Homosexual Marriage And Bestiality | Genesis Rabbah 26:4-5; Leviticus Rabbah 23:9 |
|---|---|
| Wickedness | Genesis 6:5 |
| Sorcery And Various Forms Of Occultism/Astrology | Enoch 7:1-6; 8:1-4 |
| Sexual Sin | Enoch 7:1-6; 8:1-4 |
| Cannibalism And Vampirism | Enoch 7:1-6 |
| Genetic Experimentation Mixing Different Species With Mankind | Enoch 7:1-6; Jasher 4:18 |
| Warfare/Violence | Enoch 8:1-6; 69:69:4-6 |
| Abortion | Enoch 69:12 |

In the time leading up to the Flood, God apparently allowed the righteous people in the world to die.   This was so that the people would not see the devastation of the Flood. However, God saved Noah and his family in the Ark along with the animals (Genesis 6-9). Scripture affirms that the Ark landed on Mount Ararat (Genesis 8:4). There is, indeed, many evidence from around the globe which document the historical accuracy of the Flood.

## Eyewitness Testimony Of The Ark

There have been many eyewitnesses of Noah's ark on Mount Ararat. Here is a partial list:

Berosus (a historian who lived in Babylon, who wrote three books between 350-290 B.C.) wrote: "It is said there is still some part of this ship in Armenia, at the mountain of the Cordyaeans; and that some people carry off pieces of the bitumen, which they take away, and use chiefly as amulets for the averting of mischiefs."

Nicolas Of Damascus: "There is a great mountain in Armenia, over Minyas, called Baris, upon which it is reported that many many who fled at the time of the Deluge were saved; and that one who was caried in an ark came on shore upon the top of it; and that the remains of the timber were a great while preserved. This might be the man about whom Moses the legislator of the Jews wrote."

Josephus: "However, the Armenians call this place, The Place of Descent; for the ark being saved in that place, its' remains are shown there by the inhabitants to this day."

Bishop Theophilus: "And of the Ark, the remains are to this day to be seen in the Arabian mountains."

Bishop Epiphianus (a Christian who was defending the truthfulness of the Bible against skeptics around the year 380 A.D.)-""Do you seriously suppose that we are unable to prove our point, when even to this day the remains of Noah's Ark are shown in the country of the Kurds?"

Isidore Of Seville (560-636 A.D.)-Ararat is a mountain in Armenia, where the historians testify that the Ark came to rest after the Flood. So even to this day, wood remains of it are to be seen there."

William of Rubruck (a Franciscan monk who was sent by King Louis IX of France to the Mongolian Emperor, wrote the following when he travelled near Mount Ararat): "Near this city

(Naxua) there is a mountain of which it is said, 'Here lies Noah's Ark.' The one (is) larger than the others, and Araxes (River) flows at the foot of them; there is a city they call Cemanum, which, when translated, means 'eight,' and they say that it is named after the eight people that came out of the Ark and who built it on the great mountain.'

Sir John Madeville: "...and there beside is another mountain called Ararat, but the Jews call it Taneez, where Noah's ship rested, and still is upon that mountain; and men may see it afar in clear weather. That mountain is a full seven miles high; and some men say that they have seen and touched the ship, and put their fingers in the parts where the devil went out, when Noah said 'Benedicte.' "But they that say so speak without knowledge; for no one can go up the mountain for the great abundance of snow which is always on the mountain, both sum-mer and winter, so that no man ever went up since the time of Noah, except a monk, who, by God's grace, brought one of the planks down, which is yet in the monastery at the foot of the mountain."

Jan Janszoon Struys (a slave who was near Ararat travelled from 1647-1672.). Writing of a monk who was suffering from a hernia, he was encouraged by other monks to help him. After rendering service, he recorded:

> *"The brave hermit thanked me so profusely that I was em-barrassed. He added that his sacred vows prevented him from giving me rich presents and that he had nothing more precious than a cross attached to a little silver chain. He re-moved it from his neck and gave it to me. It consisted of a little fragment of reddish- brown wood, and with it he gave me a piece of the rock on which the Ark came to rest. Such a high value did he attribute to these pieces of wood and rock that, in his judgment, I would be too rich if I retained*

*them. If, on the other hand, I was willing to take them to St. Peter's Church in Rome, he assured me a recompense that would make my fortune. He had been born at Rome, and he said that his name was Domingo Alessandro, and he was the son of one of the richest and most influential families of Rome... When I was ready to depart, I thought that it might not be a bad idea to obtain from him an attestation as to my experience on Mt. Ararat. He willingly gave it to me in the following terms: 4 I have thought it unreasonable to refuse the request of Jan Janszoon (Struys) who besought me to testify in writing that he was in my cell on the holy Mt. Ararat, subsequent to his climb of some thirty- five miles. This man cured me of a serious hernia, and I am therefore greatly in his debt for the conscientious treatment he gave me. In return for his benevolence, I have presented to him a cross made of a piece of wood from the true Ark of Noah. I myself entered that Ark and with my own hands cut from the wood of one of its compartments the fragment from which that cross is made. I informed the same Jan Janszoon in considerable detail as to the actual construction of the Ark and also gave him a piece of stone which I had personally chipped from the rock on which the Ark rests. All this I testify to be true – as true as I am in fact, alive here in my sacred hermitage. Dated the 22nd of July, 1670, on Mt. Ararat."*

Haji Yearam is a man who grew up near Greater Mount Ararat. His family would take specially chosen individuals to see the remains of Noah's Ark. Once they were approached by a group of atheists who wanted to disprove the story of Noah and the worldwide Deluge. Years later, Haji reported the event to a close friend, Harold Williams, in 1952:

*"When Haji was a large boy, but not yet a man fully grown, there came to his home some strangers. If I remember*

*correctly there were three vile men who did not believe the Bible and did not believe in the existence of a personal God. They were scientists and evolutionists. They were on this expedition specifically to prove the legend of Noah's Ark to be a fraud and a fake. They hired the father of young Haji Yearam as their official guide...."It was an unusually hot summer, so the snow and glaciers had melted more than usual. The Armenians were very reticent to undertake any expeditions to the Ark because they feared God's displeasure, but the father of Haji thought that possibly the time had come when God wanted the world to know the Ark was still there and he wanted to prove to these atheists that the Bible story of the Flood and the Ark is true. "After extreme hardship and peril the party came to the little valley way up on Greater Ararat, not on the very top, but a little down from the top. This little valley is surrounded by a number of small peaks. There the Ark came to rest in a little lake, and the peaks protected it from the tidal waves that rushed back forth as the Flood subsided. "On one side of the valley the water from the melting snow and glacier spills over in a little river the rims deep mountain as they reach the spot there they found the crown of a mighty ship protruding out of the ice. They went inside the Ark and did considerable exploring. It was divided up into many floors and stages and compartments and had bars like animal cages of today. The whole structure was covered with a varnish or lacquer that was very thick and strong both outside and inside the ship. "The ship was built more like a great and mighty house on the whole of the ship without any windows there was a great doorway of immense size but the door was missing. The scientists were appalled and dumbfounded and went into a Satanic rage at finding with they hoped to prove nonexistent." They were so angry and mad that they said they would destroy the ship but the wood was more like stone than any wood we have now. They did not have tools or means to wreck so mighty a ship and had to give up. They did tear out some timbers and tried to burn the wood but it was so hard it was almost impossible to burn it. They held a council and then took a solemn and fearful death oath. Any man present who would ever breathe a word about what they found would be tortured and murdered. They told their guide and his son that they would keep tabs on them and that if they ever told him anyone and they found it out they would surely be tortured and murdered. For fear of their lives Haji and his father had never told what they found except to their best trusted and closest relatives. "Here Haji was in America, an old man about 75 years old by this time. The scientists were much older and he doubted if any of them were then living. To be sure the record was left he wanted his story recorded before he died. So I recorded it very carefully and he went over it again and again to make sure no mistakes had been made. He felt quite sure that the men who had threatened his life if he told were dead and gone by then..."One evening... I sat reading the daily paper in our apartment in Brockton. Suddenly I saw in very small print a short story of a dying man's confession. It was a news item one column wide and, as I remembered it, not more than 2 inches deep. It stated that an elderly scientist on his deathbed in London was afraid to die before making a terrible confession. It gave briefly the very date and facts that Haji Yearam had related to us his story. I got out the composition book containing the story he had me write. It was identical in every detail. "Haji Yearam had died in my parents home in Oakland California about the same time that the old scientist who died in London. We had never for one moment doubted Haji's story, but when this scientist on his deathbed on the other side of the world confessed the same story in every detail, we knew positively that the story was true in every detail." (As reproduced in Tim LaHaye and John*

*Morris, The Ark On Ararat, 43-49; (published jointly) Nash-ville, TN and New York, N.Y.; Thomas Nelson Publishers and Creation Life Publishers)*

Flood Legends

There are hundreds of Flood legends from around the world that provide further confirmation of the Bible.

> *"The story of the Flood permeates nearly every culture of the world in some way, shape, or form. While some of the details vary between the different cultural versions, the same basic plotline occurs in all of them: a god becomes angry and destroys the earth with a flood but preserves the human race by selecting a certain number of people to survive the catastrophe. These people are saved from the flood by a vessel, which carries them throughout the duration of the event. In the stories, it is this same group of people that is then responsible for repopulating the earth."* (Charles Martin, Flood Legends: Global Clues Of A Common Event, 83-89 (Kindle Edition); Green Forest, AR; Master Books).

One of the most amazing Flood legends comes from the Hmong:

> *"In remote times, ca 2000 BC, as the original Chinese settlers entered the country, they were joined by another group travelling up through Indo-China. They were soon dubbed the Miaotsu by the Chinese population, a somewhat derogatory term, the miao-element meaning 'barbarian' or 'outsider'. 5 They are more properly known as the Hmong, and today number some 12 million. They were a brave people. For nigh 4000 years they fought off all attempts by the Chinese to destroy them, but the interesting part of their story for our purpose is that, from the earliest*

*times, they meticulously kept their ancestral records and pedigrees, happily recording the fact that they are descended, not from Ham as the Chinese are, but from Jahphu, Japheth, the son of Nuah, Noah —no, I'm not making this up, really! The Miaotsu recollect other named patriarchs who appear also in the Book of Genesis: Lama (Lamech, the father of Noah); Cusah (the Cush of the Bible), and Mesay (the Biblical Mizraim), who are both descendants of Lo Han (Ham); Elan (the Elam of the Bible), and Ngashur (the Biblical Asshur), these being descended from Lo Shen (Shem, exactly as in Genesis); and we have Go-men (Gomer), the son of Jah-phu (Japheth, again exactly as in the Book of Genesis). 6 Six generations after Gomer, the Miaotsu record that eleven tribes were descended from a patriarch named Seageweng. 7 Five of these tribes became the ancestors of the Miaotsu themselves, whilst the other six intermarried with the surrounding Chinese population. Now that is a great deal —more, in fact, than modernism has ever been pleased to tell us about —but it is not all, not by any means. In an ancestral song recited since time immemorial by the Miaotsu at funerals, weddings and like occasions, and in which all the above details are included, we find the following remarkable account enshrined in that song. 8 Of great interest to us is the fact that the song is written in couplets, which not only aids the memory of those who have to recite it, but also ensures that additions and interpolations are impossible to insert. 9 It is also worth bearing in mind that this song was already of great antiquity when Christian missionaries first encountered the Miaotsu, a people so introverted and shut off from the outside world, that they had no idea that the earth was even round. But the writers of this ancient song knew it, and knew it of old. 10 They knew many other things too. Consider the opening lines: " On the day God created the heavens and earth, On that day He opened the gateway of light." 11 Compare this with Genesis 1:3. The two accounts are not a million miles removed from one another, are they? Nor are the other lines of the song removed from Genesis to any great degree. The song goes on to tell of the creation of the land, the plants, the animals and birds, and then lastly of man himself: " On the earth He created a man from the dirt, Of the man thus created, a woman He formed." It goes on to tell how the Miaotsu's Adam (named as in the Bible after the clay from which he was made) measured the earth's weight and the stars of heaven, and pondered the ways of God. The line of his children from Se-teh (Seth, Genesis 5:4) to Lama (Lamech, the father of Noah, Genesis 5:26) is also given (as is the name of Noah's wife, Gaw Bo-lu-en). Their three sons, Lo-Han, Lo-Shen and Jah-phu (Ham, Shem and Japheth) make their appearance at this point, and: " So the earth began filling with tribes and with families. Creation was shared by the clans and the peoples." 12 The song goes on to tell in great but independent detail (no rehash of Genesis this) how things then went between mankind and God: " These did not God's will nor returned His affection, But fought with each other defying the Godhead. But their leaders shook fists in the face of the Mighty..." So, the Miaotsu remembered things just as the Bible describes them (Genesis 6:1-12). The earth was filled with violence. Judgment must come, and judgment did come. The song recalls further that God determined to destroy all flesh from off the face of the earth, save righteous Nuah and his wife and family. They build a boat and come safely through the Flood, with male and female animals on board and birds mated in pairs. But it is the Miaotsu's graphic depiction of the Flood that is of particular interest to us, largely because of the fact that it radically departs from the commonly found 'seven days of rain' that most other cultures speak of: " So it poured forty days in sheets and in torrents, Then fifty-five days of misting and drizzle.*

*The waters surmounted the mountains and ranges. The deluge ascending leapt valley and hollow. An earth with no earth upon which to take refuge! A world with no foothold where one might subsist! The people were baffled, impotent and ruined, Despairing, horror-stricken, diminished and finished." 13 Forty days of torrential rain is exactly right and agrees with Genesis 7:4 precisely. But the added detail, which Genesis doesn't give, of a following fifty-five days of drizzle and mist rings true too. After the initial forty-day downpour, the air would have been unimaginably heavy with moisture producing constant drizzle and heavy mist, a detail that the occupants of the Ark were doubtless to pass on to their many hearers. Indeed, it may well account for the notable darkness that seems to have enveloped the earth during the Flood, and which is pointedly remembered in several Flood traditions. This fascinating song of the Miaotsu goes on to tell of Nuah releasing a dove to see if the waters had abated, and the sacrifice which he made after leaving the Ark. God blesses him and there follows the lineage of Nuah's grandsons, Cusah and Mesay (Cush and Mizraim), and Elan and Nga-shur (Elam and Asshur)." (Bill Cooper, The Authenticity Of The Book Of Genesis, 3979-4037 (Kindle Edition))*

It is amazing how this account confirms the Book of Genesis in numerous ways!

In fact, Cooper (investigating the numerous Flood legends from around the world) shows how these legends confirm the account in the Book of Genesis:

*"Well, we have reached the end of our enquiry. We have noted dozens of Flood traditions that are preserved by nations around the world, making sure that we have noted only those which date to times before any Christian*

*influence could have placed them there. We have listened to witnesses that have often been hostile, or indeed igno-rant of the issues involved. Some of the evidence heard, dates from the end of the third millenium BC; some of it to the 20th century CE, a span of 4000 years or more. It has come to us in languages as diverse as the many cultures of the world. But however old the testimony, and no matter where in the world it has come from, it has always proved remarkably consistent and faithful to the known facts as contained in the Book of Genesis. No other subject on earth has ever produced the like....When witnesses are few and their testimonies inconsistent and contradictory, then the court will invariably decide that the case is not proven. But if, in any given case, witnesses, hundreds of them (some of them hostile) from all parts of the world, turn up and give independent and consistent testimony to the fact that such and such took place at such a time, then the laws of prob-ability alone would compel the court to pronounce that the case is indeed proven. Men have been hanged on much less testimony than that of hundreds of witnesses. Would it therefore be reasonable, or just, to declare that the entire world's testimony to a Great Flood is worth nothing, and that it proves nothing? Hardly. To evaluate the quality of the evidence that we have heard, we would do well to con-sider the work of Dr John Morris in this field. Dr Morris had collected (by 2001) more than 200 Flood traditions from around the world, and dismantling them down to their component parts, he found that 88% of the traditions fea-ture a 'favored' family; 66% tell of the warning that that family received of the coming Flood; 66% tell how the com-ing Flood was due to man's wickedness; 95% mention that the Flood alone was responsible for the world's destruc-tion; 95% likewise testify to the universality (global extent) of the Flood; 70% testify to a boat being the means of sur-vival; 67% state that animals were also saved; 73% testify to the participation of animals (birds being sent out, and so on); 57% state that the survivors landed on a mountain; 82% name local places and peoples; 35% testify to the use of birds; 7% hark back to the rainbow; 13% state that the survivors offered a sacrifice; and 9% specifically state that eight persons were saved. It was a brilliant piece of research, and we may assume that the traditions we have looked at would yield a similar indication of evidential quality. Dr Morris remarks, concerning this data: "Putting them all back together, the story would read something like this: Once there was a worldwide flood, sent by God to judge the wickedness of man. But there was one righteous family which was forewarned of the coming flood. They built a boat on which they survived the flood along with the animals. As the flood ended, their boat landed on a high mountain from which they descended and repopulated the whole earth." 1...(Bill Cooper, The Authenticity Of The Book Of Genesis, 5490-5525 (Kindle Edition))*

With these things firmly in mind, Cooper has come to this powerful conviction:

*"That is surely reason enough for any man to believe the Book of Genesis. But God Himself, whose Word Genesis is, has gone the extra mile with us. He has given us a whole world of witnesses -a veritable cloud of witnesses -to persuade us of the Eternal Truth of His Word. Consider. That part of His Word that the world has learned to laugh at the most, the Flood, is the very part that has the most witnesses to its Truth." (Bill Cooper, The Authenticity Of The Book Of Genesis, 5557-5562 (Kindle Edition))*

Archaeology also confirms many other aspects of the Flood account, including the long lifespans of the patriarchs. It is also amazing how the science of Population Statistics confirms the timeline presented in the Book of Genesis regarding the Flood.

## The Table Of Nations

In Genesis 10-11, the Bible tells us about the Table of Nations and the Tower of Babel. The Table of Nations is a list of seventy nations that were descended from Noah's descendants. Bill Cooper spent years studying the Table of Nations to determine if it was accurate or a fabrication.

What did he learn?

> *"When I first came across this problem some fifty years ago, I found it most perplexing. On the one hand I had the Bible itself claiming to be the very Word of God, and on the other I was presented with numerous commentaries that spoke with one voice in telling me that the Bible was nothing of the kind. It was merely a hotch- potch collection of Middle- Eastern myths and fables that sought to explain the world in primitive terms, whose parts had been patched together by a series of later editors. Modem scientific man need have nothing whatever to do with it. Now, it simply was not possible for both these claims to be valid. Only one of them could be right, and I saw it as my duty, to myself at least, to find out which was the true account and which was the false....Either way, I would discover once and for all whether the Biblical record was worthy of my trust or not. It seemed a little irreverent to treat a book that claimed to be the very Word of God in such a fashion. But if truth has any substance at all, then that Book would surely be able to bear such a test. If Genesis contained any falsehood, error or misleading statement of fact, then a severe testing would reveal it and I would be the first to add my own voice to those of all the other scholars who declared the Book of Genesis to be little more than fable...What I had not*

*expected at the time was the fact that the task was to en-*
*gage my attention and energies for more than twenty- five*
*years. Nor had I expected the astonishing degree to which*
*Genesis, particularly the tenth and eleventh chapters, was*
*to be vindicated. These chapters are conveniently known to*
*scholars as the Table of Nations, and the sheer breadth and*
*depth of the historical evidence that was available for their*
*study astonished me....Today I can say that the names so*
*far vindicated in the Table of Nations make up over 99% of*
*the list, and I shall make no further comment on that other*
*than to say that no other ancient historical document of*
*purely human authorship could be expected to yield such a*
*level of corroboration as that!" (Bill Cooper, After The*
*Flood: The Early Post-Flood History Of Europe Traced*
*Back To Noah, 80-111 (Kindle Edition))*

Other archaeological evidences from this period of Genesis include the Ebla tablets (which confirm monotheism and Bible
names of that era) and the discovery of the remains of Sodom
and Gomorrah.

## Joseph

One of the most thrilling and heart-wrenching Bible stories is
that of Joseph and his "coat of many colors." Sold into slavery by
jealous brothers (who then took his coat of many colors and tore
it, dipped it in blood, and told their father he had been killed by
a wild beast), Joseph was taken to Egypt where he was then
falsely accused of rape and thrown into prison. Near the end of
two years, Joseph had developed quite a reputation as an inter-
preter of dreams. The Lord God warned Pharaoh (through his
dreams) that there would be seven years of great abundance in
the crops and fields of Egypt, followed by seven years of great
famine that would sweep through the entire Earth.

However, Pharaoh could not understand the meaning of the dreams! It was then that he was told about Joseph. When Joseph explained the meaning of the dreams, Pharaoh set him in charge to build and prepare great storehouses to stock with grain and flour so that when the seven years of famine finally hit, people would be able to come to Egypt for food. Indeed, Joseph was made the second most powerful man in Egypt at this time!

Yet the story gets deeper and more tangled. When the seven years of famine finally hit, guess who ends up coming to Egypt looking for food? Joseph's brothers! They don't recognize him, and the Book of Genesis tells us of the incredible and beautiful reconciliation that took place when Joseph finally forgave them of their horrible wickedness. So great is his mercy that Joseph allows his brothers to bring all of their families to the land of Egypt, to settle in the land of Goshen (Genesis 45:10).

Critics of the Bible, of course, have said for years that the Egyptians would never make a Hebrew the second most powerful man in the land. To many, the thought is preposterous, and the Bible is often dismissed out of hand as a reliable document at this point. Therefore, it is with this thought in mind that we will begin studying and learning of the findings of archaeology in regard to these matters.

Archaeology has recorded ample evidence of the seven years of abundance and famine.

> *"We dwelt at ease in this castle a long tract of time; nor had we a desire but for the region-lord of the vineyard. Hundreds of camels returned to us each day at evening, their eye pleasant to behold in their resting-places. And twice the number of our camels were our sheep, in comeliness like white does, and also the slow moving kine. We dwelt in this castle seven years of good life—how difficult*

*for memory its description! Then came years barren and burnt up: when one evil year had passed away, then came another to succeed it. And we became as though we had never seen a glimpse of good. They died and neither foot nor hoof remained. Thus fares it with him who renders not thanks to God: His footsteps fail not to be blotted out from his dwelling." (Charles Forster, Sinai Photographed (London: Richard Bentley, 1862); quoted in Jeffrey).*

Again:

*"In thy name O God, the God of Hamyar, I Tajah, the daughter of Dzu Shefar, sent my steward to Joseph, And he delaying to return to me, I sent my hand maid With a measure of silver, to bring me back a measure of flour: And not being able to procure it, I sent her with a measure of gold: And not being able to procure it, I sent her with a measure of pearls: And not being able to procure it, I commanded them to be ground: And finding no profit in them, I am shut up here. Whosoever may hear of it, let him commiserate me; And should any woman adorn herself with an ornament From my ornaments, may she die with no other than my death." (Rule and Anderson, Biblical Monuments, 9; also quoted in Jeffrey).*

Another amazing find of archaeology which confirms the Bible narrative regarding Joseph is the Joseph Coins.

*""Recent research conducted on previously overlooked Egyptian coins confirms the biblical story of Joseph and his role in government service in ancient Egypt. In 2009, archaeological authorities from the Egyptian National Museum announced that a cache of ancient coins had been "rediscovered." Initially discovered almost a century earlier, the coins had been in storage. They were uncovered in*

*the vast storage vaults of the national museum and the An-tiquities Authority. Cairo's Al Ahram newspaper reported that the coins bear the name and image of the biblical Jo-seph.21 The cache of more than five hundred coins had been set aside decades earlier in the belief that they were miscellaneous objects of worship and likely of no signifi-cance. However, scientists re-examined the coins using re-cently developed technology and discovered that a number of them dated to the time of ancient Egypt. Most of the coins were engraved with the year they were minted and their monetary value and the effigies or images of the phar-aohs ruling Egypt when the coins were minted. Researchers concluded that the "Joseph coins" originated in the period when Joseph served as Pharaoh's treasurer—during the seven years of plenty and seven years of famine (see Gen-esis 41:41–45). Biblical history suggests a date for Joseph's high position in the Egyptian government that coincides with the date of the minting of the coins in the cache (ap-proximately 2000 B.C.). Amazingly, some of the coins bear both Joseph's name and image." (Grant R. Jeffrey, The Sig-nature Of God: Conclusive Proof That Every Teaching, Every Command, Every Promise In The Bible Is True, 69-70 (Kindle Edition); Waterbrook Press)*

We should also make mention here of the "Joseph Canal."

*"And what shall we say of the common assertion amongst modernists that no Egyptian monument exists which bears the name of Joseph? Well, we can always point out the fact that about 80 miles south of Cairo, there lies the still-flour-ishing town of Medinet- el- Faiyum. It is a lush and fertile area, famed for its 'gardens, oranges, mandarines, peaches, olives, pomegranates and grapes'. It has been like this for well over 3,000 years, and owes its lush fertility to a 200 mile- long canal which still conveys to it the waters*

*of the Nile in a constant year- round flow. It is an astonish-*
*ing feat of engineering which to this day is known through-*
*out Egypt as the 'Bahr Yusuf' – the Joseph Canal. This has*
*always been its name. Moreover, the people of Egypt are*
*perfectly happy to tell you that it was built by the Joseph of*
*the Bible who once was Pharaoh's 'Grand Vizier'. 14". (Bill*
*Cooper, The Authenticity Of The Book Of Genesis, 2040-*
*2046 (Kindle Edition))*

Indeed, there is a great deal of evidence that during the time of
Joseph, there was a significant Semitic population in Egypt.

*"There is no doubt that there was a significant Semitic pop-*
*ulation throughout Egypt during the New Kingdom (see*
*chap. 3).Because of the preponderance of epigraphic evi-*
*dence for a Syro-Palestinian presence in Egypt from the mid*
*to late second millennium B.C., even the most skeptical his-*
*torian cannot dismiss the fact that both the Bible and Egyp-*
*tian sources agree on this situation.42 Even as far south as*
*Thebes there was a significant number of Semitic-speaking*
*people during the Empire period.43 The names of Semites*
*have even turned up among the workers of Deir el-Medineh*
*in western Thebes.44" (James K. Hoffmeier, Israel In Egypt:*
*The Evidence For The Authenticity Of The Exodus Tradi-*
*tion, 3689-3697 (Kindle Edition); New York, New York; Ox-*
*ford University Press)*

## The Hebrews In Egypt As Slaves

At the end of Genesis, the Hebrews are living in the land of
Egypt. At the beginning of Exodus, the people are now enslaved.
It is a common claim that the Bible depiction of the Hebrews
being slaves in Egypt is a myth invented by the Jewish people.
Yet there is strong evidence that the Bible is correct.

*"The Brooklyn Papyrus was acquired by the founder of the Brooklyn Museum, Charles Edwin Wilbour, during his winter travels in Egypt during the years 1881-1896. It was first understood in 1938 that this text mentioned "a list of slaves of foreigners." It was a tiresome work to put all the 500-600 fragments in order and interpret the ancient text, which was done in 1952. The total length of the papyrus is 182 cm. Above, an important section is shown representing a part of the list of foreign slaves in Egypt. The dating, based on information in the text, places the papyrus somewhere from the late 12th to the mid 13th dynasty, which is during the period when the Hebrews were enslaved in Egypt. The character of the papyrus is a business document used by Egyptian administrators to keep order in the family structures and duties of the slaves. A typical design of a section with slave names is: "The female Asiatic Siprah." One list contains 79 slaves, with 33 Egyptians and 45 Asiatics (and one unknown). In total 20 were males, 43 were females and the remaining were children. It is stated that the Asians probably were Semites of Syrian and Palestinian background. The Hebrews were Semites and came from areas of Syria and Palestine. A number, at least 30, of the slaves listed have names that are Semitic/ Hebrew to their character. Shiphrah is one slave name identical to the Hebrew midwife mentioned in Ex. 1:15. Other Hebrew related names are Dodihu, Hayabilu, Hayimmi, Munahhima, Yasaskir, Aduttu, Ahatu, Dodihuat, Sukrapati, Aser, Aqabtu, Abu, etc. Translation of other names clearly indicate foreigners, as the example "I-am-prayed-for-in-a-foreign-land" (102). It is of great interest to find an Egyptian source from the time of the Hebrews in Egypt, that lists slaves with Hebrew names, in particular one name that is identical to a Hebrew name found in the book of Exodus. This is a strong support to the history of the Hebrews." (Lennart Moller, The Exodus Case: New Discoveries Of The Historical*

*Exodus, 2168-2180 (Kindle Edition); Copenhagen NV, Den-mark; Scandinavia Publishing House)*

## The Ten Plagues

The Pharaoh of the Exodus would not let the people of Israel go, so the Lord brought Ten Plagues upon the Egyptians. There is an ancient Egyptian document known as the Ipuwer Papyrus.

Many believe that it is an account of the Ten Plagues.

> *"Though the evidence for the Exodus has been slow to be gathered, there is good reason to believe that it actually occurred as described in the Bible. This thinking is based on the biblical testimony, Egyptian extrabiblical sources, and archaeological excavation in Egypt and neighboring regions. For example, one of the most well-known documents in Egyptology is the Ipuwer papyrus (officially known as Papyrus Leiden 344), which records an account remarkably similar to the plagues described in the book of Exodus. The papyrus was obtained by Swedish diplomat, Giovanni Anastasi, and sold to the Leiden Museum in Holland in 1828. No one realized the exact significance of the contents of the document until the first full translation was done in 1909 by a British Egyptologist, Alan H.Gardiner, under the title The Admonitions of an Egyptian Sage from a Hieratic Papyrus in Leiden. In addition, there have been many later full translations made, including an Oxford edition (2009). Currently, the document is stored at the National Museum of Antiquities in the Netherlands. Its contents are widely regarded by Egyptologists as a lamentation over the catastrophic conditions in Egypt written by a high Egyptian official named Ipuwer sometime prior to the thirteenth century BC (which is consistent with either an early or late chronology for the Exodus).\* Ipuwer was known as one of*

*the great wise sages in Egyptian tian history. His astonishing description of the conditions, to the surprise of Egyptologists, appeared remarkably similar to the biblical account of the ten plagues recorded in the book of Exodus. The date of the Ipuwer manuscript approximately fits the Exodus date. The hieratic script style was in use at that time period, the events described are remarkably similar to the plagues, the location of the events (Egypt) matches the setting of the Exodus, and the odds of all these calamities occurring at the same time make them more than coincidental. There is no scientific, linguistic, or historical fact that Egyptologists can point to that would decisively preclude the content of the papyrus being a lament over the Exodus plagues. A simple comparison of the content in both the book of Exodus and the Ipuwer papyrus leaves little doubt to their similarities (see table below)." (Joseph M. Holden & Norman Geisler, The Popular Handbook Of Archaeology And The Bible: Discoveries That Confirm The Reliability of Scripture, 2555-2568 (Kindle Edition); Eugene, Oregon; Harvest House Publishers).*

Please note some of the ways in which the Ipuwer Papyrus confirms the biblical narrative:

Exodus 4:9—And it shall be, if they do not believe even these two signs, or listen to your voice, that you shall take water from the river and pour it on the dry land. The water which you take from the river will become blood on the dry land."

Ipuwer 7:5—Behold, Egypt is fallen to the pouring of water. And he who poured water on the ground seizes the mighty in misery."

Exodus 7:20-21—And Moses and Aaron did so, just as the LORD commanded. So he lifted up the rod and struck the waters that were in the river, in the sight of Pharaoh and in the sight of his servants. And all the waters that were in the river were turned to blood. 21 The fish that were in the river died, the river stank, and the Egyptians could not drink the water of the river. So there was blood throughout all the land of Egypt.

Ipuwer 2:10—The River is blood. If you drink of it, you lose your humanity, and thirst for water."

Exodus 9:6, 23, 31—So the LORD did this thing on the next day, and all the livestock of Egypt died; but of the livestock of the children of Israel, not one died....And Moses stretched out his rod toward heaven; and the LORD sent thunder and hail, and fire darted to the ground. And the LORD rained hail on the land of Egypt....Now the flax and the barley were struck, for the barley was in the head and the flax was in bud.

Ipuwer 6:3; 3:3; 7:13—Gone is the barley of abundance.... Food supplies are running short. The nobles hunger and suffer.... Those who had shelter are in the dark of the storm."

Exodus 10:15, 7—For they covered the face of the whole earth, so that the land was darkened; and they ate every herb of the land and all the fruit of the trees which the hail had left. So there remained nothing green on the trees or on the plants of the field throughout all the land of Egypt....Then Pharaoh's servants said to him, "How long shall this man be a snare to us? Let the men go, that they may serve the LORD their God. Do you not yet know that Egypt is destroyed?"

Ipuwer 3:13-"What shall we do about it? All is ruin! "

Exodus 12:29—And it came to pass at midnight that the LORD struck all the firstborn in the land of Egypt, from the firstborn of Pharaoh who sat on his throne to the firstborn of the captive who was in the dungeon, and all the firstborn of livestock.

Ipuwer 2:5, 6, 13; 4:3-"Behold, plague sweeps the land, blood is everywhere, with no shortage of the dead.... He who buries his brother in the ground is everywhere.... Woe is me for the grief of this time."

Exodus 12:30—So Pharaoh rose in the night, he, all his servants, and all the Egyptians; and there was a great cry in Egypt, for there was not a house where there was not one dead.

Ipuwer 3:14—Wailing is throughout the land, mingled with lamentations."

## The Apiru

One of the ancient names for the Hebrews among the Egyptians and Canaanites is the name Apiru.

> *"(2) The initial reed leaf in the caption of Sinai 115 is consonantal, and thus probably a glottal stop, rather than i. This option accepts as valid that the original spoken-Hebrew word for "Hebrew," whatever its initial consonant must have been, is synonymous with Akkadian ḫa-bi-ru and Egyptian apir(u), which used to be the time-honored view in scholarship. James Hoch (1994:63), whose treatment of WS foreign words in Egyptian was referred to by Redford (1997a: 59) as the most thorough study on the topic, stated that Egyptian ʿapiru and Akkadian ḫa-bi-ru is "very likely related to the Biblical term/ name עִבְרִי 'Hebrew'," while Waterhouse (2001:31) affirmed that "it is now agreed upon that indeed there is a valid etymological relationship between the term 'Habiru' and the biblical name 'Hebrew' (ʿibrî)." The potential validity of this view simply cannot be swept under a rug, even though the full range of meaning for Habiru/ Apiru is a matter that cannot be taken up here. With this second option of a glottal stop, Ḥebeded would*

*have departed from rendering into ME writing the same sound as the initial ḫ consonant of the Akkadian noun ḫa-bi-ru. However, neither was the Akkadian consonant rendered into ME with phonetic precision. Seemingly, no scholar disputes that apir(u) "Apiru" and ḫa-bi-ru "Habiru" are synonymous, that the term and the people originally came from Mesopotamia, or that their appearance in Egypt and Egyptian writings was a later phenomenon. If this is true, the Akkadian form is the earlier one. According to Huehnergard (2011:2), Caplice (2002), and Marcus (1978:1), Akkadian ḫ is pronounced ch, as in the Scottish word loch. Yet Hoch (1997:8) noted that in ME the unvoiced velar x (Aa1, unclassified sign [a circle with horizontal lines interspersed within]) is the consonant pronounced as ch in Scottish loch, not the a (D36, the forearm glyph) of apir(u). Akkadian ḫ is unvoiced, whereas ME a is "produced with a restriction in the pharynx and with voicing" (Hoch 1997:8). Even in proto-Northwest Semitic, the consonant ḫ is listed as an unvoiced velar fricative, whereas ʿayin traditionally is considered a voiced pharyngeal fricative. Plus, proto-Northwest-Semitic ḫ merges into ḥ in Hebrew (preserved in Ugaritic and Arabic), and ME ḥ (V28, wick thread or twisted flax: a pharyngeal aspirate) is the unvoiced counterpart of ʿayin (Hoch 1997:8). The point is that during the NK, ME's choice of a (ʿayin) to represent Akkadian ḫ is anything but a phonetic match, yet the connection between the Habiru and the Apiru has gone unchallenged, despite the linguistic incongruity. Evidently, the congruity between the third consonant of each word + the second consonant of each word, if the need for a b → p shift can be overcome (Petrovich 2016b: 73–74), has been enough to prevent scholars from contending that the association of the Habiru with the Apiru is invalid or flawed. In like manner, the present writer merely is appealing for the same allowance in this case, namely that the congruity in the final two consonants (i.e., the br of iBr/ jBr in Sinai 115 and the br in ḫa-bi-ru) is enough to establish the validity of the connection. The phonetic incongruity in the first consonant of iBr/ jBr with the ḫ of ḫa-bi-ru is no more objectionable than ME's rendering of the Akkadian unvoiced velar with the voiced pharyngeal. It also must not be forgotten that Sinai 115 dates to 1842 bc, whereas the consistent use of a in apir(u) dates to no earlier than the fifteenth century bc. What was standard and expected in the rendering of foreign words at one time in history cannot be expected to have been exactly the same 400 years earlier. Perhaps the use of ʿayin in ME and later Hebrew arose (i.e., between 1842 and 1500 bc) for some unknown but intricately-connected reason. This principle, and valid possibility, takes all of the sting out of Schneider's criticism. Kogan (2001:291) even stated that ḫāpiru is obviously a non-Akkadian term, while CAD (1956:84) calls it a "foreign (prob. WSem.) word." When discussing the lack of consistent correspondence between Akkadian ḫ and WS consonants, Huehnergard (2003:112) added that "[ w] hen confronted with such a situation, where two co-equal branches of a language family exhibit a large set of cognates in which one of the consonants differs consistently in the two branches, and yet no conditioning factors can be found to account for the difference, the historical linguist is justified in suggesting that the cognates reflect mergers in the two branches of an earlier, now lost, third consonant." Therefore, it seems that a number of consonants can actualize in Akkadian as ḫ, and that the reed leaf on Sinai 115 may preserve some hint of that third, now lost, consonant. Why should one consider as valid that the original spoken-Hebrew word for "Hebrew" is synonymous with Akkadian ḫa-bi-ru and Egyptian apir(u)? Among the texts from southern Mesopotamia of about 1850 bc is one that departs from the typical use of the Sumerian logogram SA.GAZ by supplying the Akkadian cuneiform ḫapiri.*

*According to biblical history/ chronology, Abram ventured from southern Mesopotamia in ca. 2091 bc. Therefore, if Abram was a historical figure, he undoubtedly would have spoken Akkadian as a resident of southern Mesopotamia, in addition to his own native Semitic tongue. If this was the case, why should one expect an initial voiced pharyngeal on the Semitic (Hebrew?) term that he used of his own ancestry (Eberite/Heberite → Hebrews, Habiru, Hapiru, Hapiri, Apiru, etc.), and before his offspring had been in Egypt for any considerable length of time? This matter is discussed more elsewhere (Petrovich 2016b: 24), but the point to emphasize here is that the second and third Hebrew consonants on Sinai 115's caption match perfectly with the br of ḥa-bi-ru/ ḥa-pi-ru, which should be viewed as no less tolerable than the accepted but linguistically imperfect match between Habiru/ Hapiru and Apiru." (Douglas Petrovich, Origins of the Hebrews: New Evidence of Israelites in Egypt from Joseph to the Exodus, 186-190 (Kindle Edition); Nashville, TN: New Creation)*

## The Amarna Tablets

The Amarna Tablets are a series of records that were kept by the Canaanites, many of them from the time the Bible says that Joshua lived. Found therein is a very interesting word, Apiru. Cooper points out that this is an Akkadian form of the word "Hebrew," and that the Amarna Tablets tell us a great deal about the Hebrew invasion of Canaan. He writes:

*"It is therefore with considerable surprise that we read about Joshua and his people, not just once in some ambiguous, fragmentary inscription of dubious date and interpretation, but plainly and at least 85 times in that 15th-century BC Canaanite archive known as the Tell El Amarna Tablets. The critics don't like to mention the fact, but*

*Joshua himself is sometimes obliquely referred to in the Tablets. There is one man in particular who is referred to as 'that Hebrew'; 'that Hebrew dog'; at least three times as the 'chief of the Hebrews'; and, it seems, in one inscription he is called 'Ilimilku,' which name is the Akkadian cognate of the Hebrew name Elimelech, God is my King. It is a nickname which would have suggested itself to Canaanite observers after it became clear to them that Joshua was not a king, but that he fought under the God of Israel. Though not a name that the Bible specifically gives him, it is one that the Canaanites seem to have known him by, and they accordingly wrote it down in their correspondence - 'Ilimilku!' 1 The Hebrews themselves are referred to in the Amarna Tablets as slaves —'runaway dogs' in some of the Tablets —'slaves that have become Habiru' in another -recalling the history of their escape from slavery in Egypt. This again is entirely natural and to be expected....What has been made available is the somewhat inaccurate notion that a couple of the tablets mention some 'Apiru,' a name which, we are asked to believe, may be derived from the Assyrian word habbatu, meaning robber, and that these occurrences must therefore refer to some troublesome bandits that were roaming the area at that time. Nothing could be more distorted and inaccurate. It is a forced and false derivation which misleads the reader. The Canaanite kings were certainly strong enough and well enough organized to see off any such bands of robbers, whom they would have hunted to extinction. It is what they did, and they were very good at it. Canaan could never have become a land flowing with milk and honey had it been a land in which lawless bands of cutthroats carried the day. Neither do bands of robbers capture whole swathes of territories along with their walled and fortified cities which were protected by regiments of disciplined and armed soldiers. No. The term Apiru, which appears throughout the archive, is merely the Akkadian cognate of the word Hebrew (Habiru), Akkadian being the diplomatic language in which most of the tablets are written." (Bill Cooper, The Authenticity Of The Book Of Joshua, 240-249 (Kindle Edition).*

With this knowledge, look at how the Canaanite Amarna Tablets confirm the teachings of the Bible the fact that the Hebrews invaded the land of Canaan.

Cooper (Bill Cooper, The Authenticity Of The Book Of Joshua, 255-294, Kindle Edition) tells us of some of the concern that the Canaanite kings and leaders had about the Jewish people:

"Now he is like the Hebrew, a runaway dog...' (EA 67:17).

"The war of the Hebrew hosts against me is most severe...". (EA 68:18).

"Through the Hebrews his auxiliary force is strong!....Let him not gather together all the Hebrews....". (EA 71:21 & 29).

"Kill your lord and join the Hebrews...and all the lands will be joined to the Hebrews...." (EA 73:29 & 33).

"They were won over following his message, and they are like Hebrews....that the entire country be joined to the Hebrews." (EA 74:29 & 36).

"The war, however, of the Hebrews against me is severe...The Hebrews killed Aduna, the king of Irqata, and so they go on taking territory to themselves." (EA 75:10 & 27).

"He has just gathered together all the Hebrews against Sigata and Ampi, and he himself has taken these two cities." (EA 76:18).

"...speak to your lord so that he will send you at the head of the archers to drive off the Hebrews..." (EA 77:24 & 29).

"....all the Hebrews...have turned against me...If there are no archers, then all lands will be joined to the Hebrews. Listen!" (EA 79:10 & 20).

"He said to the men of Gubla, 'Kill your lord, and be joined to the Hebrews like Amiya.'" (EA 81:13).

"All the Hebrews are on his side...he is strong." (EA 82:9).

"The Hebrews have taken the entire country!" (EA 83:17).

"...the Hebrews have gone to Yapah-Hadda in Beirut so an alliance might be formed....the lands have been joined to the Hebrews...lest he gather together all the Hebrews and they seize the city." (EA 85:41, 73 & 78).

"Let an elite force, together with chariots, advance with you, that I may drive the Hebrews from the gate." (EA 87:21).

"But if the king my lord does not give heed to the words of his servant...all the lands of the king as far as Egypt will be joined to the Hebrews." (EA 88:34).

"You yourself have been negligent of your cities, so that the Hebrew dog takes them." (EA 90:25).

"Why have you sat idly by and done nothing, so that the Hebrew dog takes your cities?...I hav just heard that he has gathered all the Hebrews to attack me!" (EA 91:5 & 24).

"They would attack me and I would be unable to get out, and Gubla would be joined to the Hebrews. They have gone to Ibirta, and an agreement has been made with the Hebrews." (EA 104:49-54).

"If this year there are no archers, then all lands will be joined to the Hebrews. Behold, members of the (Hebrew) army have entered Akka..." (EA 11:21).

"I paid 13 shekels of silver and a pair of mantles as the hire of the Hebrews..." (EA 112:46).

"...all my towns have been joined to the Hebrews...". (Ea 116:38).

"There is treachery against me...all the lands will belong to the Hebrews...What am I to do? May the king send a garrison and men from Meluhha to guard me. May the city not be joined to the Hebrews!" (EA 117:58 & 94).

"Behold...the Hebrews will seize the city!" (EA 118:38).

"...the sons of Abdi-Asiata have said to the Hebrews and the men who have joined them...". (EA 121:21).

"Should Gubla be joined to the Hebrews..." (EA 127:22).

"They have won the lands for the Hebrews...". (EA 129.94).

"They are like dogs, and there is no one who wants to serve them. What am I, who live among the Hebrews, to do?" (EA 130:38).

"Now Aziru has gathered all the Hebrews..." (EA 132:21).

"All the cities that the king put in my charge have been joined to the Hebrews...a man that will lead the archers of the king to call to account the cities that have been joined to the Hebrews, so you can restore them to my charge....". (EA 144:26 & 30).

"The king of Hasura has abandoned his house and has aligned himself with the Hebrews...He has taken over the land of the king for the Hebrews." (EA 148:43 & 45).

"He has made Amurru an enemy territory, and has turned over all the men in the cities of the king....to the Hebrews." (EA 179:22).

There are, indeed, many other references that could be cited.

## Conclusion: The Testimony Of Titus Kennedy

There are many, many other examples of archaeological evidence which could be cited that confirm the accuracy and authenticity of the Bible. However, I would like to conclude this section by sharing with you the testimony of a Bible archaeologist named Titus Kennedy.

"Because the Bible contains stories from the ancient world, written in a style different than the method of modern historians and paired with theology, many have assumed that the narratives in the Bible are myth, legend, and propaganda instead of accurate history. In fact, the majority of scholars, most media and educational sources, and many in the general public regard the Bible as a fairy tale and frequently portray it as unimportant or irrelevant beyond literary and religious studies. For years, the Bible has been routinely attacked and disregarded on the basis of history or archaeology. And yet when people look into what archaeologists have unearthed, a different story comes to light, showing that instead of fiction and fairy tales, archaeology indicates that the Bible preserves an accurate recounting of the history addressed in its pages. Specifically, hundreds of artifacts from the distant past have demonstrated the events, people, and places in the Bible to be historical." (Titus M. Kennedy, Unearthing the Bible: 101 Archaeological Discoveries That Bring the Bible to Life, 9 (Kindle Edition); Eugene, Oregon; Harvest House Publishers)

Indeed, the contributions of archaeology to the veracity of the Bible continue to abound.

*"Artifacts related to the Bible specifically have illuminated or confirmed events, chronologies, practices, terminology, locations, and individuals that would otherwise have remained a mystery. As an example, there are currently about 70 individuals mentioned in the Old Testament who have been confirmed by archaeological artifacts, and about 32 individuals in the New Testament so far confirmed by archaeology, with several more people from the Bible tentatively identified by archaeological artifacts. Many artifacts have also illuminated obscure words and practices in the Bible, from times long ago in lands far away, that would be misunderstood or unknown otherwise....*"The fallacious arguments claiming that the archaeological data shows the Bible to be unhistorical myth, legend, or propaganda are demonstrated to be sensationalism and falsehood by the artifact evidence presented in this book. Although 101 objects were presented, there might have been around 500 artifacts noted if there were no space restrictions and the scope was more comprehensive! Further, every year new and significant discoveries connected to the Bible are being made, suggesting that the amount of archaeological evidence will increase as time goes on and as ancient sites are found and excavated. Pass on this information to others, visit archaeological sites and museums to see these artifacts with your own eyes, and be on the lookout for these new exciting finds, which are usually announced in press releases, archaeology journals, and documentaries. Only time will tell what else lies buried, and the mysteries that will be revealed as more artifacts of the past are rediscovered." (Titus M. Kennedy, Unearthing the Bible: 101 Archaeological Discoveries That Bring the Bible*

*to Life, 238-239 (Kindle Edition); Eugene, Oregon; Harvest House Publishers)*

*"The term archaeology is a compound word (from the Greek archaios and logos) meaning the "study of ancient things...In modern times, when we speak of archaeology, in general we are referring to the discipline typically within the field of anthropology and history that draws upon an investigation of current material human remains in order to understand past customs, cultures, and civilizations.. These remains include pottery, graves, buildings, coins, tools, weapons, clothing, jewelry, literature, inscriptions, and more. "Archaeology of the Bible" exists as a specific field of inquiry within this discipline; its primary goal is the excavation of areas associated with the Bible and its socie-ties and cultures, such as Jerusalem,, Sodom, Jericho, Egypt, Israel, the Levant as a whole, and Mesopotamia." (Joseph M. Holden & Norman Geisler, The Popular Hand-book Of Archaeology And The Bible: Discoveries That Confirm The Reliability Of Scripture, 2023-2031 (Kindle Edition); Eugene, Oregon; Harvest House Publishers)*

*"It may be stated categorically that no archaeological dis-covery has ever controverted a Biblical reference. Scores of archaeological findings have been made which confirm in clear outline or in exact detail historical statements in the Bible. And by the same token, proper evaluation of Biblical descriptions has often led to amazing discoveries. They form tesserae in the vast mosaic of the Bible's almost in-credibly correct historical memory." (Nelson Glueck, Rivers in the Desert: A History of the Negev (New York: Farrar, Straus and Cudahy, 1959), 31)*

*"Of the hundreds of thousands of artifacts found by the archeologists, not one has ever been discovered that contradicts or denies one word, phrase, clause, or sentence of the Bible, but always confirms and verifies the facts of the biblical record." (Quotation from J. O. Kinnaman found at www.geocities.com/Heartland/7234/quotes.html (accessed October 26, 2009).*

*"There are several lines of evidence to indicate that Moses, the great lawgiver and deliverer of Israel who wrote the other four books of the Law, was the author of Genesis. (1) The earliest and continual tradition of the Jewish people, as recorded in the Talmud, attributes this book to Moses. (2) Moses is the only person we know of from this early time period who had the ability to write this book. The rest of the Israelites were a nation of uneducated slaves, whereas Moses was a highly educated son of the king (Acts 7:22). (3) Moses was the only one who had both the interest and information to write Genesis. Being Jewish Moses would have had access to the family records of his ancestors (cf. Gen. 5:1; 10:1; 25:19; etc.) which were no doubt brought down to Egypt by Jacob (Gen. 46). Since Moses was bent on delivering his people from Egypt, it is natural to assume that he was familiar with the promises of God passed down by his forefathers that God would indeed deliver them (cf. Gen. 46:3-4; Exod. 2:24). (4) Citations from Genesis show that the rest of the Old Testament regards it as part of the Law of Moses (Deut. 1:8; II Kings 13:23; I Chron. 1:1ff.). Since Moses was the author of the other "books of Moses," as we will see later, it is reasonable to attribute the first book of Moses to him as well. (5) Jesus and the New Testament writers clearly regard Moses as the author of an essential part of Scripture (cf. Matt. 19:8; Luke 16:29; 24:27). We can conclude that Moses, using the family records which had been passed on to him, compiled the Book of*

*Genesis." (Norman Geisler, A Popular Survey Of The Old Testament, 610-623 (Kindle Edition); Grand Rapids, Michigan; Baker Books)*

*"1B. R.H. Rfeiffer writes: 'There is no reason to doubt that the Pentateuch was considered the divine revelation to Moses when it was canonized about 400 B.C.' (Pfeiffer, JOT, 133) 1C. Ecclesiasticus, one of the books of the Apocrypha, written about 180 B.C., gives this witness: 'All this is the covenant book of God Most High, the law which Moses enacted to be the heritage of the assemblies of Jacob' (Ecclesiasticus 24:23 NEB). 2C. The Talmud (Baby Bathra, 146), a Jewish commentary on the Law (Torah) dating from 200 B.C., and the Mishnah (Pirqe Aboth, I, 1), a rabbinic interpretation and legislating dating from 100 B.C., both attribute the Torah to Moses. 3C. Likewise, Philo, the Jewish philosopher theologian born approximately A.D. 20, held Mosaic authorship: 'But I will...tell the story of Moses as I have learned it, both from the sacred books, the wonderful monuments of his wisdom which he has left behind him and from some of the elders of the nation.' (Philo, WP, 279) 4C. The first century A.D. Jewish historian Flavius Josephus writes in his Josephus Against Apion (11:18): 'For we have not an innumerable multitude of books among us, disagreeing from and contradicting one another (as the Greeks have) but only 22 books (our present 39), which are justly believed to be divine; and of them, five belong to Moses, which contain his laws, and the traditions of the origin of mankind till his death.' (Josephus, WFJ, 609)" (Josh McDowell, The New Evidence That Demands A Verdict, 458-459; Nashville, TN; Thomas Nelson Publishers).*

*"These Old Testament verses record that the Torah or "the Law," was from Moses: Joshua 8:32 speaks of "the Law of Moses, which he had written." (The verses marked by an*

*asterisk refer to an actual written "Law of Moses," not simply an oral tradition): Joshua 1:7,8\*; 8:31\*,34\*; 23:6\* 1 Kings 2:3\* 2 Kings 14:6\*; 23:25 1 Chronicles 22:13 2 Chronicles 5:10; 23:18\*; 25:4\*; 30:16; 33:8; 34:14; 35:12\* Ezra 3:2; 6:18\*; 7:6 Nehemiah 1:7,8; 8:1\*,14\*; 9:14; 10:29; 13:1\* Daniel 9:11,13\* Malachi 4:4 WITNESS OF THE NEW TESTAMENT The New Testament held that the Torah or "law" came from Moses: The apostles believed that "Moses wrote for us a law" (Mark 12:19). John was confident that "the Law was given through Moses" (John 1:17). Paul, speaking of a Pentateuchal passage, asserts "Moses writes" (Romans 10:5). Other passages which insist on this include: Luke 2:22; 20:28 John 1:45; 8:5; 9:29 Acts 3:22; 6:14; 13:39; 15:1,21; 26:22; 28:23 1 Corinthians 9:9 2 Corinthians 3:15 Hebrews 9:19 Revelation 15:3 Jesus believed the Torah to be from Moses: Mark 7:10; 10:3-5; 12:26 Luke 5:14; 16:29-31; 24:27,44 John 7:19,23 Notice especially John 5:45-47: Do not think that I will accuse you before the Father; the one who accuses you is Moses, in whom you have set your hope. For if you believed Moses, you would believe Me; for he wrote of Me. But if you do not believe his writings, how will you believe My words? Eissfeldt states: The name used in the New Testament clearly with reference to the whole Pentateuch—the Book of Moses— is certainly to be understood as meaning that Moses was the compiler of the Pentateuch. 27/158" (Josh McDowell &* Bill Wilson, *The Best Of Josh McDowell: A Ready Defense: 148-149 (Kindle Edition); Nashvillee, TN; Thomas Nelson Publishers)*

*"Critics have also suggested that Moses could not have written his account in the fifteenth century before Christ because, they claim, writing had not yet been invented. However, the discovery of numerous ancient written inscriptions, including the famous black stele containing the*

*laws of Hammurabi written before 2000 B.C., prove that writing was widespread for many centuries before the time of Moses." (Grant Jeffrey,* The Signature Of God, *42 (Kindle Edition); Waterbrook Press @ Books)*

*"Perhaps the massive accumulation of inscriptions on stone, clay, and papyrus that have been exhumed in Mesopotamia and Egypt might have been questioned as necessarily proving the extensive use of writing in Palestine itself—until the 1887 discovery of the archive of Palestinian clay tablets in Tell el-Amarna, Egypt, dating from about 1420 to 1380 B.C. (the age of Moses and Joshua). This archive contained hundreds of tablets composed in Babylonian cuneiform (at that time the language of diplomatic correspondence in the Near East), which were communications to the Egyptian court from Palestinian officials and kings. Many of these letters contain reports of invasions and attacks by the Ha-bi-ru and the so-called SA.GAZ (the oral pronunciation of this logogram may well have been Habiru also) against the city-states of Canaan. Wellhausen himself chose to ignore this evidence almost completely after the earliest publication of these Amarna Tablets came out in the 1890s. He refused to come to terms with the implications of the now-established fact that Canaan even before the Israelite conquest was completed contained a highly literate civilization (even though they wrote in Babylonian rather than their own native tongue). The later proponents of the Documentary Hypothesis have been equally closed-minded toward the implications of these discoveries. The most serious blow of all, however, came with the deciphering of the alphabetic inscriptions from Serabit el-Khadim in the region of Sinai turquoise mines operated by the Egyptians during the second millennium B.C. These consisted of a new set of alphabetic symbols resembling Egyptian hieroglyphs but written in a dialect of Canaanite*

*closely resembling Hebrew. They contained records of min-*
*ing quotas and dedicatory inscriptions to the Phoenician*
*goddess Baalat (who was apparently equated with the*
*Egyptian Hathor). The irregular style of execution precludes*
*all possibility of attributing these writings to a select group*
*of professional scribes. There is only one possible conclu-*
*sion to draw from this body of inscriptions (published by*
*W.F. Albright in The Proto-Sinaitic Inscriptions and Their*
*Decipherment [Cambridge: Harvard University, 1966]): Al-*
*ready back in the seventeenth or sixteenth centuries B.C.,*
*even the lowest social strata of the Canaanite population,*
*slave-miners who labored under Egyptian foremen, were*
*well able to read and write in their own language."*
*(Gleason L. Archer Jr., New International Encyclopedia of*
*Bible Difficulties, 98-100 (Kindle Edition); Grand Rapids,*
*Michigan; Zondervan)*

*"These higher critics maintained that some of Genesis, es-*
*pecially the material in the first eleven chapters, had been*
*derived from myths of the ancient Babylonians...Today it is*
*beyond question that writing was practiced widely, and in*
*many forms, long before the time of Moses...Similarly, ar-*
*chaeologists now recognize that the cultural indications in*
*Genesis, at least from the time of Abraham onward, are ex-*
*actly what would be expected of eyewitness records from*
*those times....In similar fashion, linguistic studies by nu-*
*merous first-rate Biblical scholars have repeatedly shown*
*that there is no real substance to the claims of the higher*
*critics that the language of Genesis was much later than*
*the time of Moses." (Henry Morris,* The Genesis Record:
A Scientific & Devotional Commentary On The Book
Of Beginnings, *7-8 (Kindle Edition); Grand Rapids, Michi-*
*gan; Baker Books).*

*"Besides this, there are several reasons why conservative scholars do not believe Moses was dependent upon these earlier creation myths. First, the critical scholars' overemphasis on similarities has blinded their eyes to the many differences that set the accounts apart as unique. Unlike the mythic stories, the Genesis account offers one monotheistic God as the creator of all things. The Mesopotamian epic speaks of a pantheon of gods involved in creation. Genesis offers a loving and all-powerful Lord as creator, unlike the Enuma Elish, which portrays the gods as conspiring, vengeful monsters who are seeking ill for one another. In the Enuma Elish, human beings are created from the blood of a rebel god and are seen as lowly slaves created to serve and feed the gods. This is in stark opposition to the Genesis account, which records that man was made in the image of God and meant to be like His creator-the highest of His creation. Moreover, in the epic, creation was made out of something evil (Tiamat's body) and pre-existing (that is, ex deo or ex materia), whereas Genesis describes a creation from a good source (that is, God) and out of nothing (ex nihilo). Second, the similarities may be accounted for by the fact that different groups were writing about the same original historical event (creation). If the creation of the world actually occurred, and various civilizations later reinterpreted the story within the contexts texts of their polytheistic religions and purposes, it would account for the basic similarities in content. Moses would have received his monotheistic creation account directly from God or from oral tradition that was passed down through Noah and his descendants. Third, we now know the Genesis account is not dependent on or identified with any earlier Mesopotamian, Egyptian, or Assyrian creation tradition because of the recognized direction of myth. Near-Eastern scholar D.J. Wiseman and others familiar with myth literature (for example, C.S. Lewis) have understood that an early myth can*

*become even more mythical over time, and that earlier his-*
*torical events can become embellished with myth over*
*time. But never do we see earlier myth traditions (such as*
*these Mesopotamian and Egyptian creation accounts) be-*
*come more historical-sounding, believable, and simpler*
*over time. The Genesis record is more simple, historical,*
*natural,, and believable than these early myth traditions,*
*and therefore it cannot possibly be dependent on them or*
*classified as just another Near-Eastern creation account.*
*The mythical tone is obvious in the Enuma Elish, but it is*
*absent in the Genesis account. The epic tells of Marduk kill-*
*ing Tiamat and splitting her in two parts like a "shellfish"*
*and creating the sky from her body. However, Genesis*
*simply opens with the statement: "In the beginning, God*
*created the heavens and the earth" (Genesis 1:1). It contin-*
*ues with the simple and natural formula, "Then God said,*
*`Let there be.....' (Genesis 1:3,6,11,14). Fourth, some criti-*
*cal scholars forget that early creation myths are not neces-*
*sarily concerned with creation per se; rather, they are at-*
*tempts to justify or elevate the standing of particular dei-*
*ties or cities in the eyes of the people. For example, creation*
*is not the main story of Enuma Elish; it is the relatively un-*
*known Babylonian god Marduk. It appears now that the*
*story is an effort by its author to elevate Marduk as the*
*chief god of Babylon, though prior to this story he was not*
*given prominence among the multitude of other deities. In*
*the above example of the Egyptian account, most scholars*
*recognize that the creation elements present are not the*
*main theme, but the raising of the city of Memphis and its*
*god (Ptah) to prominence in order to justify Memphis as the*
*location of the capital city of Egypt. For these reasons, we*
*must consider the Genesis account as an independent his-*
*torical tradition, without dependency on the earlier Meso-*
*potamian or Egyptian myth literature." (Joseph M. Holden*
*& Norman Geisler, The Popular Handbook of Archaeology*

*and the Bible: Discoveries That Confirm the Reliability of Scripture, 2314-2355 (Kindle Edition); Eugene, Oregon; Harvest House Publishers)*

*"In some cases, however, the early Babylonian seals, which contained devices taken from these legends, more closely approached the Genesis story. One striking and important specimen of early type in the British Museum collection has two figures sitting one on each side of a tree, holding out their hands to the fruit, while at the back of one is stretched a serpent. We know well that in these early sculptures none of these figures were chance devices, but all represented events or supposed events, and figures in their legends; thus it is evident that a form of the story of the Fall, similar to that of Genesis, was known in early times in Babylonia."
(George Smith, The Chaldean Account Of Genesis: Containing The Description Of The Creation, The Fall Of Man, The Deluge, The Tower Of Babel, The Times Of The Patriarchs , And Nimrod; Babylonian Fables And Legends Of The Gods, From The Cuneiform Inscriptions, 1364-1368 (Kindle Edition); Global Grey)*

*"My personal study into the history of the written Chinese language through various treatises in English found in Harvard's Chinese-Japanese Yenching Library gave its approximate time of origin as 2500 B.C. This dating is provocative, for it coincides quite closely with the time (2218 B.C.) of the great dispersion of races from the tower of Babel, as calculated from the Biblical genealogies in a recent chronological study...When the Chinese, very early in their history as a separate people, found a need to communicate with a written language, a system of word-pictures was invented in keeping with the characteristic calligraphy of the ancient world. True to all primitive written languages, these so-called pictographs were satisfactory for representing*

*objects but carried limitations in expressing abstract con-cepts. The early graphic symbols, therefore, were com-bined in meaningful ways to convey ideas, called ideo-grams, and these "picture stories" of necessity had to con-tain common knowledge in order to be understood. It would have been only natural to use as a basis for some of the ideograms the history of the ancient beginnings of hu-manity with which all were familiar by oral tradition. Con-sequently, the written Chinese language is composed of characters uniquely adapted to the possibility of containing the stories of Genesis." (C.H.Kang & Ethel R. Nelson, The Discovery Of Genesis: How The Truths Of Genesis Were Found Hidden In The Chinese Language, 844-181 (Kindle Edition); St. Louis, Missouri; Concordia Publishing House)*

*"From the Chinese writing, we learn that in the beginning (B)1 (), there were just two persons on earth. Furthermore, another bronzeware rendition of beginning (B)2 reveals that the original couple had sinless characters. They were reflectors of God, heaven ()....The man was named Adam, meaning "the ground," from which he had been created by God. We learned that the Chinese radicals for ground, earth (B), , , (O) () all have reference to Adam (review p. 36). And we learned that "Adam called his wife's name Eve, be-cause she was the mother of all living....Thus we find a rec-ord of the first two ancestors , (O)4 (). Comparing and above, representing Adam arising from the earth, we find not only Adam, but two persons, he and his wife, Eve, "the mother of all living." The ancestors are found with the God radical , indicating that ShangTi is, of course, the ultimate ancestor in whose image Adam and Eve had been created. This character denotes not only ancestor, but also the founder, prototype, original, beginning." (Ethel Nelson & Richard Broadberry, Genesis And The Mystery Confucius*

*Couldn't Solve, 665-684 (Kindle Edition); Saint Louis, Mis-
souri; Concordia Publishing House)*

"Let us once more take some time to bridge some of the
Mysteries and background of this mythical antediluvian period, concerning those legendary heroes of renown. The
word Nephilim derives from the Hebrew language, and
specifically the Hebrew word nopelim or nepelim. The root
word for nopelim is npl, meaning "fall." The suffix im translates as "the ones." 1 Therefore, by piecing these two
words together alongside their literal translation, we find
the definition of nopelim as "fallen ones," just as Josephus
described the infamous ones, the fallen angels, those who
procreated with the daughters of men. Additionally, Nephilim is also the root Aramaic word for Nephila, for the
"Orion" constellation suggesting to me that Nephilim are
somehow directly connected to Orion. 2 In legend, Orion is
the constellation where the fallen angel Shemyaza/ Azazel
is believed to be hung; therefore suggesting Nephilim
somehow derive from Shemyaza/ Azazel. Remember, Nephilim were considered giant demigods, the unnatural offspring of the daughters of men and fallen angels, violating
God's natural order of creation." (Gary Wayne, The Genesis
6 Conspiracy: How Secret Societies and the Descendants of
Giants Plan to Enslave Humankind, 1749-1760 (Kindle Edition); Deep River Books)*

"One of the great debates over Genesis 6:1–4 is the meaning of the word nephilim. We've seen from the Mesopotamian context that the apkallus were divine, mated with human women, and produced giant offspring. We've also
seen that Jewish thinkers in the Second Temple period
viewed the offspring of Genesis 6:1–4 in the same way—as
giants. Any analysis of the term nephilim must account for,
not ignore or violate, these contexts. Interpretation of the*

*term nephilim must also account for another Jewish phe-
nomenon between the testaments—translation of the Old
Testament into Greek. I speak here of the Septuagint. The
word nephilim occurs twice in the Hebrew Bible (Gen 6:4 ;
Num 13:33 ). In both cases the Septuagint translated the
term with gigas ("giant"). 15 Given the backdrop we've
covered, it would seem obvious that nephilim ought to be
understood as "giants." But many commentators resist the
rendering, arguing that it should be read as "fallen ones"
or "those who fall upon" (a battle expression). These options are based on the idea that the word derives from the
Hebrew verb n-p-l (naphal , "to fall"). More importantly,
those who argue that nephilim should be translated with
one of these expressions rather than "giants" do so to avoid
the quasi-divine nature of the Nephilim. That in turn makes
it easier for them to argue that the sons of God were human. In reality, it doesn't matter whether "fallen ones" is
the translation. In both the Mesopotamian context and the
context of later Second Temple Jewish thought, their fathers are divine and the nephilim (however translated) are
still described as giants. 16 Consequently, insisting that the
name means "fallen" produces no argument to counter a
supernatural interpretation." (Michael S. Heiser, The Unseen Realm: Recovering the Supernatural Worldview of the
Bible, 1942-1965 (Kindle Edition); Bellingham, WA; Lexham
Press)*

*"Jewish targums (Aramaic translations of the Old Testa-
ment) flirt with the human view but do not completely
move away from a supernatural view until roughly the
same time period as the Christian departure (the third century AD ). Newman writes in this regard: "It is difficult to
know where to place the targumim. These Aramaic translations of Scripture (often paraphrases or even commentaries) have an oral background in the synagogue services*

*of pre-Christian times, but their extant written forms seem to be much later. Among these, the Targum Pseudo-Jonathan [ Tg. Ps.-J.] presents at least a partially supernatural interpretation. Although in its extant form this targum is later than the rise of Islam in the 7th century A.D., early materials also appear in it.... [Its translation] 'sons of the great ones' may reflect a non-supernatural interpretation, but the reference to Shamhazai and Azael falling from heaven certainly does not. The names given are close to those in 1 Enoch , considering that the latter has gone through two translations to reach its extant Ethiopic version. Notice also that the Nephilim are here identified with the angels rather than their offspring as in Enoch , Jub., and Josephus.... Targum Neofiti [ Targ. Neof.] is the only complete extant MS of the Palestinian Targum to the Pentateuch. The MS is from the 16th century, but its text has been variously dated from the 1st to the 4th centuries A.D. In place of the Hebrew* בני האלהים *is the Aramaic* בני דיינא *, 'sons of the judges,' using a cognate noun to the verb* ידון *appearing in the MT of Gen 6:3. Nephilim is rendered by* גיבריה *, 'warriors.' The text of the targum seems to reflect a nonsupernatural interpretation, unless we press the last sentence of 6:4—'these are the warriors that (were there) from the beginning of the world, warriors of wondrous renown'—so as to exclude human beings. However, the MS has many marginal notes, which presumably represent one or more other MSS of the Palestinian Targum. One such note occurs at 6:4 and reads: 'There were warriors dwelling on earth in those days, and also afterwards, after the sons of the angels had joined (in wedlock) the daughters of the sons.' Thus the text of Targ. Neof. seems to be nonsupernatural while a marginal note is clearly supernatural.... The Targum of Onqelos [ Tg. Onq.] became the official targum to the Pentateuch for Judaism. According to the Babylonian Talmud [ Bab. Talm.] (Meg. 3a ) it was* *composed early in the 2nd century A.D., but this seems to be a confusion with the Greek translation of Aquila. Although the relations between the various targumim are complicated by mutual influence in transmission, Onq. was probably completed before A.D. 400 in Babylonia using Palestinian materials as a basis. In our passage Onq. reads* בני רברביא *, 'sons of the great ones,' probably referring to rulers." See Newman, "The Ancient Jewish Exegesis of Genesis 6:2, 4," 21 , 23–24. It should be noted that the first-century writer Philo reflects both views. Newman also notes: "In his treatise On the Giants , the Alexandrian Jewish philosopher Philo (20 B.C.–A.D. 50) quotes the Old Greek version of this passage with the readings ἄγγελοι τοῦ θεοῦ and γίγαντες. Unfortunately Philo is not always a clear writer. Apparently he takes the literal meaning of the verses to refer to angels and women since, immediately after quoting Gen 6:2, he says: 'It is Moses' custom to give the name of angels to those whom other philosophers call demons [or spirits], souls that is which fly and hover in the air. And let no one suppose that what is here said is a myth.' After a lengthy discussion arguing for the existence of non-corporeal spirits, however, Philo proceeds to allegorize the passage: 'So, then, it is no myth at all of giants that he [Moses] sets before us; rather he wishes to show you that some men are earth-born, some heaven-born, and some God-born.'" See Newman, "Ancient Jewish Exegesis," 19." (Michael S. Heiser, Demons: What the Bible Really Says About the Powers of Darkness, 9900-9935 (Kindle Edition); Bellingham, WA; Lexham Press)*

*"The "angel" view of this classic Genesis text is well documented in both ancient Jewish rabbinical literature and Early Church writings. In addition to the Septuagint translation, the venerated (although non-canonical) Book of Enoch, the Syriac Version of the Old Testament, as well as*

*the Testimony of the 12 Patriarchs234 and the Little Gene-*
*sis, 235 confirm the lexicological usage and the extant be-*
*liefs of ancient Jewish scholars. Clearly the learned Philo Ju-*
*daeus understood the passage as relating to angels. 236*
*Josephus Flavius also represents this view: "They made God*
*their enemy; for many angels of God accompanied with*
*women, and begat sons that proved unjust, and despisers*
*of all that was good, on account of the confidence they had*
*in their own strength, for the tradition is that these men did*
*what resembled the acts of those whom the Grecians call*
*giants." 237 In accordance with the ancient interpretation,*
*the Early Church fathers understood the expression "sons*
*of God" as designating angels. These included Justin Mar-*
*tyr, 238 Irenaeus, 239 Athenagoras, 240 Pseudo-Clemen-*
*tine, 241 Clement of Alexandria, 242 Tertullian, 243 Com-*
*modianus, 244 and Lactantius, 245 to list a few. This inter-*
*pretation was also espoused by Luther and many more*
*modern exegetes including Koppen, Twesten, Dreschler,*
*Hofmann, Baumgarten, Delitzsch, W Kelly, A. C. Gaebelein,*
*and others." (Chuck Missler and Mark Eastman, Alien En-*
*counters, 207-208 (Kindle Edition); Coburn d'Alene, ID; Koi-*
*nonia House)*

*"A mountain of the island of Crete having been burst asun-*
*der by the action of an earthquake, a body was found there*
*standing upright, forty-six cubits in height; by some per-*
*sons it is supposed to have been that of Orion; while others*
*again are of opinion that it was that of Otus. It is generally*
*believed, from what is stated in ancient records, that the*
*body of Orestes, which was disinterred by command of an*
*oracle, was seven cubits in height. It is now nearly one*
*thousand years ago, that that divine poet Homer was un-*
*ceasingly complaining, that men were of less stature in his*
*day than they had formerly been. Our Annals do not inform*
*us what was the height of Nævius Pollio; but we learn from*

*them that he nearly lost his life from the rush of the people to see him, and that he was looked upon as a prodigy. The tallest man that has been seen in our times, was one Gabbaras by name, who was brought from Arabia by the Emperor Claudius; his height was nine feet and as many inches. In the reign of Augustus, there were two persons, Posio and Secundilla by name, who were half a foot taller than him; their bodies have been preserved as objects of curiosity in the museum of the Sallustian family." (Pliny The Wlder, Translated by John Bostock and Henry Thomas Riley, Complete Works of Pliny the Elder, 6064-6075 (Kindle Edition); Hastings, East Sussex; Delphi Classics)*

*"The body of Orestes which Pliny mentions, was measured at seven cubits, which equals some 12 feet in our terms; 6 whilst those of Pusio and Secundilla were some 10 feet 3 inches in height. It is a great pity that Pliny did not discuss them at greater length, though it is worth mentioning that the Romans were very exact in measuring things. If they tell us that Gabbara stood at 9 feet 9 inches, and Pusio and Secundilla at 10 feet 3, then we can rely on the exactness of those measurements. The Romans were not fools, and Pliny treasured his own reputation as a scholar too much to be caught out in a lie. After all, when he wrote his account, there were many hundreds in Rome still living who would have seen and spoken with these giants -and many rival scholars (Pollio and Livy among them) who would have delighted in exposing Pliny as a fraud or a fool had he got his facts wrong. The fact that that never happened should tell us something.". (Bill Cooper, The Authenticity Of The Book Of Judges, 694-700 (Kindle Edition)).*

*"For many angels of God accompanied with women, and begat sons that proved unjust, and despisers of all that was good, on account of the confidence they had in their own*

*strength; for the tradition is, that these men did what re-sembled the acts of those whom the Grecians call giants. But Noah was very uneasy at what they did; and being dis-pleased at their conduct, persuaded them to change their dispositions and their acts for the better: but seeing they did not yield to him, but were slaves to their wicked pleas-ures, he was afraid they would kill him, together with his wife and children, and those they had married; so he de-parted out of that land." (The Complete Works Of Flavius Josephus, One of the best known translations of Josephus's work, translated by William Whiston in 1737 Formatted by E.C. Marsh 2010, 1103-1108 (Kindle Edition); ecmarsh.com)*

*"For which reason they removed their camp to Hebron; and when they had taken it, they slew all the inhabitants. There were till then left the race of giants, who had bodies so large, and countenances so entirely different from other men, that they were surprising to the sight, and terrible to the hearing. The bones of these men are still shown to this very day, unlike to any credible relations of other men." (Flavius Josephus, The Complete Works Of Flavius Jose-phus, translated by William Whiston in 1737 Formatted by E.C. Marsh 2010, 4571 (Kindle Edition); ecmarsh.com)*

The testimony of the ancient Egyptians is equally incredible. In describing the warrior campaigns against the Canaanites, we read:

*"23,5 ones to look. Their eyes are good, thy hand grows weak(?)". 25: T\' Q "^ /Q3 rn2«*'. Thou makest the name of every Maher, officers of the land of Egypt". Thy name becomes like (that of) K-dr-d-y ^ the chief of *I-s-r ^* ^ when the hyena" found him in the balsam-tree'*. —The(r) narrow defile'* is infested (?) with Shosu concealed*

*beneath the bushes; some of them are of four cubits or of five cubits, from head(??) to foot(?)'", fierce of face, their heart is not mild, and they hearken not to coaxing. Thou art alone, there is no helper(?)" with thee, no army"". (Alan Henderson Gardiner, Egyptian Hieratic Texts, 1068-1086 (Kindle Edition))*

The Egyptians here record their battles against the Shosu, who were a race of giants that lived in the land of Canaan. The cubit mentioned here is an Egyptian royal cubit of 20.62 inches, which means that the Shosu were anywhere from 7-10 feet tall!

*For as there were at that time dealings under truce with the men of Tegea, he had come to a forge there and was looking at iron being wrought; and he was in wonder as he saw that which was being done. The smith therefore, perceiving that he marvelled at it, ceased from his work and said: "Surely, thou stranger of Lacedemon, if thou hadst seen that which I once saw, thou wouldst have marvelled much, since now it falls out that thou dost marvel so greatly at the working of this iron; for I, desiring in this enclosure to make a well, lighted in my digging upon a coffin of seven cubits in length; and not believing that ever there had been men larger than those of the present day, I opened it, and I saw that the dead body was equal in length to the coffin: then after I had measured it, I filled in the earth over it again.""". (Herodotus, The Histories, 527-537 (Kindle Edition); Start Publishing LLC)*

*"But why should we be surprised at these things? Like dragons -like the Great Flood itself -giants are known to every culture under the sun. Virtually every nation on earth remembers a time when they were neighbours to, or lived amongst giant populations, and the Israelites were no exception. Giant peoples were known to them under various*

*names: The Nephilim, the Rephaim, the Tzuzim, the Ana-kim, to name a few, all of whom were noted by the Israel-ites for their great stature; and even amongst later scholars and writers of the classical world we find mention of similar gigantic peoples. Homer, Lucretius, Virgil, Juvenal, Pliny, and even po-faced Augustine of Hippo all write of them. Whether they were writing truth or fable, however, may be judged by the mention of gigantic peoples which have ap-peared in more modern times, and which have been writ-ten about and lectured upon by 'establishment' anthropol-ogists and archaeologists. Note the following report which appeared in The Princeton Union, on October 11th 1894: "In a prehistoric cemetery recently uncovered at Montpel-lier, France, while workmen were excavating a waterworks reservoir, human skulls were found measuring 28, 31 and 32 inches in circumference. The bones which were found with the skulls were also of gigantic proportions. These rel-ics were sent to the Paris academy, and a learned 'savant' who lectured on the find says that they belonged to a race of men between ten and fifteen feet in height." 10 The 'learned savant' of the article was Dr Georges Vacher de Lapouge (1854-1936), and his findings were corroborated in full by Dr Paul Valéry, a colleague of his at the University of Montpellier between 1886 -1891.11 Would these men - these revered figures of the establishment –have willingly thrown away their careers and reputations for a stupid hoax? It seems not, for six months later, this same report appeared again in another journal, there having been plenty of time for the facts to be checked. 12 And then, out of Castelnau in France appeared this report: "In the year 1890, some human bones of enormous size, double the or-dinary in fact, were found in the tumulus of Castelnau (Herault) [France], and have since been carefully examined by Prof. Kiener, who, while admitting that the bones are those of a very tall race, nevertheless finds them abnormal in dimensions and apparently of morbid growth. They un-doubtedly re-open the question of 'giants' of antiquity, but do not furnish sufficient evidence to decide it." 13...The photo taken of the bones at the time of their discovery (see Fig. 19 above) shows clearly the immense difference in size between them and the 'normal' modern human femur placed between them. Kiener's staid and learned paper on the remains may be read to this day, 14 and it is notable that neither in the case of the Montpellier remains, nor yet those of Castelnau, has any serious attempt been made by anthropologists or archaeologists to dispute the simple facts of the case. In other words, the facts are unarguable. These are indeed the bones of gigantic human beings who stood up to 15 feet in height. As for the most famous giant in all history -Goliath -what can we say of him other than this? -his name has been discovered inscribed on a pot-sherd in the ruins of his hometown of Gath (Tel es-Safi, Is-rael) dating to within 70 years of his slaying by David, i.e. to about 950 BC (see Fig. 20 below). 15 Interesting, isn't it, when we consider what the critics have been saying all these years.". (Bill Cooper, The Authenticity Of The Book Of Judges, 751-776 (Kindle Edition))*

*"Rarely do we hear why the Creator destroyed the earth with water. I turned my attention back to PipeCarrier, whose war scarred face was showered with moonlight as it cascaded down his back as if tracing the length of his long black hair and asked him, "What do you know of the star people?" PipeCarrier focused his gaze beyond the moon into the deep evening sky full of shining stars. He pointed to The Warrior constellation's belt and said. "They fell from the heavens in the ancient times. They took our women. They were not washte [good]." PipeCarrier confirmed what I have heard from many other tribal elders. My father told me that there was a great battle in the Sky World where*

*good spirit and bad spirits were fighting one another. The bad spirits were thrown from the heavens down to the earth below where they made themselves out to be gods. These star people took our women by force and the resulting children became the race of giants that we read about in historical accounts from cultures around the world, including the Bible. Interestingly enough, the repeating similarity is these beings came from the sky, took the human women, and produced a race of giants....When I served in the U.S. Army, I met a traditional Navajo woman whose family was of the Bitter Water and Towering House Clans. We were on guard duty together one evening when we were deployed out in the desert, and we began talking about the star people. The most famous of the Southwestern star people is Kokopelli. This figure is well-known in pan-Indian Native American art and even common art that can be found in national retail stores although its origin is in Southwest United States. Kokopelli is one of the star people who fell from the heavens to the desert region of the Southwest, according to native tradition. He quickly made himself out to be a god of rain and fertility demanding worship and tribute of a young woman in exchange for bringing the rains to the fields or fertility to women by playing his flute. In the older renditions of him, he is often depicted with a hunched back, four protrusions sticking out of his back and two arms holding a flute which he would play to lure women to himself. Sometimes in more modern depictions, the four protrusions are what look like four crazy dreadlocks poking out from the top and back of his head. There are even many of the ancient drawings that depict him with an erect phallus, alluding to the sexual nature and focus of this false god. His portraits are not just found in the Southwest; there is even a petroglyph carving of Kokopelli on the island of Puerto Rico where he visited the Taino Native Americans. The stories of Kokopelli are vast across many Native cultures. It is strange to me that this seducing spirit could have grown in such popularity across the country. It is crucial that we know the origins of the things that we have or decide to pass along to another generation. For some time as a child, my wife lived on the Navajo reservation in Shonto, Arizona where an old song is occasionally sung: "Fathers, hide your daughters; Kokopelli is coming!" Kokopelli is just one of many "star people" that fell to the earth and made themselves out to be "gods." There are numerous accounts of giant tribes that sprung forth as a direct result of these fallen ones mixing with the human women. The common thread in the many cross-cultural stories across the globe is that these beings taking human women and breeding a race of giants. It is found throughout the world; so many cultures have stories that have been passed down for thousands of generations centering on these giants." (Chief Joseph RiverWind Assisted by Laralyn RiverWind, That's What The Old Ones Say: Pre-Colonial Revelations Of God, 122-129 (Kindle Edition); Marble, NC; Word Branch Publishing)*

*"On the upper terrace, within the corporate limits of Monongahela City, are situated the garden and greenhouse of Mr. I.S. Crall. Two ravines on the east and west sides open directly south into Pigeon Creek, and their erosion has lowered the ground until it is surrounded by higher land on every side except along the bluff next to the creek....In excavating for foundation walls and other purposes, Mr. Crall has, at different times, <u>unearthed skeletons of large size</u>: the ground is strewn with mussel shells, flint chips etc. On the eastern side of this levee, near the break of the ravine, and close to a never-failing spring, stands the largest mound above the one at McKee's rocks, measuring 9 feet in height and 60 feet in diameter... at the center a hole measuring 3 feet across the top and 2 feet into the original*

*soil. In this were fragments of human bones too soft to be preserved. They indicated an adult of large size. The gray clay was unbroken over this hole. Directly over this, above the clay and resting upon it, were portions of another large skeleton, with which was found part of an unburned clay tube or pipe." (The Wichita Daily Eagle - November 17, 1891)*

*"There has just been received at the Maryland Academy of Sciences, the skeleton of an Indian seven feet tall. It was discovered near Antietam. There are now skeletons of three powerful Indians at the Academy who at one time in their wildness roamed over the state of Maryland armed with such instruments as nature gave them or that their limited skill taught them to make. Two of these skeletons belonged to individuals evidently of gigantic size. The vertebrae and bones of the legs are nearly as thick as those of a horse and the length of the long bones exceptional. The skulls are of fine proportions, ample and with walls of moderate thickness and of great strength and stiffened beyond with a powerful occipital ridge. The curves of the forehead are moderate and not retreating, suggesting intelligence and connected with jaws of moderate development.". (BALTIMORE AMERICAN, NOVEMBER 15, 1897)*

*"The skeleton of a giant Indian, maybe seven or more feet in height, who died and was buried about the time Christ was born, has been unearthed from prehistoric burial grounds along the Potomac River near Point of Rocks recently. Nicholas Yinger, who has been excavating at this and other sites of early Indian villages along the Potomac River in recent years, discovered the skeleton of the giant Indian, along with the other artifacts buried with the body, on Saturday, April 28, just a few weeks ago." (MORNING HERALD, MAY 14, 1956)*

*"Along the Susquehanna River in Indiana County, Pennsyl-vania a major Indian burial site was uncovered. All to-gether, forty-nine skeletons were exhumed, the tallest be-ing eight feet tall. These skeletons were reportedly taken to the Harrisburg Museum for reassembly and then shipped to the Smithsonian for further study. However, the Smith-sonian denies any knowledge of them. On the site of the William H. Rhea farm (circa 1871–1880) in Conemaugh Township just west of the mouth of Black Legs Creek, skel-etons of men, probably Indians, were found. Noted local historian Clarence Stephenson says, "One of the skeletons is of a giant nearly eight feet tall. The giant's skeleton measured 89 inches from the top of the skull to the phalan-ges of the feet. It was covered with small stones, lay on the back, and measured 26 inches across the chest."". (CHAR-LEROI MAIL, MAY 7, 1953)*

*"On July 13, Professor Skinner of the American Indian Mu-seum, excavating the mound at Tioga Point, near Sayre, Pennsylvania, uncovered the bones of 68 men, which he es-timates had been buried at least seven or eight hundred years. The average height indicated by the skeletons was seven feet, but many were taller. Evidence of the gigantic size of these men was seen in huge axes found beside the bones." (CHARLESTON DAILY MAIL, SEPTEMBER 20, 1916)*

*"In my opinion it becomes clear that those at the helm of the Smithsonian were engaged in the deliberate obfusca-tion of evidence that would offer another paradigm than the accepted Darwinian one that then and now permeate all of science and academia. The question is why would men of science deliberately engage in this? And, I believe I have an answer. If these skeletons exist, and by all of the overwhelming evidence both from the written record found in newspapers and accounts from scientists, as well as the*

*oral traditions from Native Americans, they pose a direct threat to the pervading world view, Darwinism.". (L.A. Mar-zulli, On The Trail Of The Nephilim-Volume One-Giant Skel-etons & Ancient Megalithic Structures,1341-1350 (Kindle Edition); Spiral Of Life Publishing)*

*"The following is a brief list of documented findings, all rec-orded in the Annual Report of the Board of Regents of the Smithsonian Institution Showing the Operations, Expendi-tures, and Condition of the Institution for the Year […] se-ries (each book title ending with the year the discovery was made): · One skull measuring "36 inches in circumfer-ence."[ 152] Anna, Illinois, 1873. (The average circumfer-ence measurement for the human skull is between twenty-one and twenty-three inches, depending on varying factors such as sex, ethnicity, etc.) · One full skeleton with double rows of teeth, buried alongside a gigantic axe, referred to in the report as a "gigantic savage."[ 153] The skeleton— with a colossal skull—fell apart after exhumation, so an ex-act height/ head circumference was not reported, but the record states that "its height must have been quite [mean-ing "at least"] seven feet." Amelia Island, Florida, 1875. · Giant axes and "skinning stones."[ 154] One weighed over fifteen pounds, had an ornately carved handle, and was of such mass that it was documented: "Only a giant could have wielded this." Kishwaukee Mounds, Illinois, 1877. · One jawbone that easily slipped around the entire face of a large man on the research team; one thigh bone measur-ing "four inches longer than that of a man six feet two inches high"; one "huge skeleton, much taller than the cur-rent race of men."[ 155] Kishwaukee Mounds, Illinois, 1877. According to the Fifth Annual Report of the Bureau of Ethnology to the Secretary of the Smithsonian Institution 1883–1884, shortly following the discoveries in this bullet list, the Smithsonian team found ten more skeletons in*

*mounds and burial sites in Wisconsin, Illinois, West Virginia, North Carolina, and Georgia. Not every one of them was measured for height, but each was documented as much larger than the skeletons of our current race; those that were measured ranged between seven to seven and a half feet long.[ 156] Similarly, in the Twelfth Annual Report of the Bureau of Ethnology to the Secretary of the Smithsonian Institution 1894, two enormous skulls, several baffling femur bones, and seventeen full skeletons also measuring between seven to seven and a half feet long (one in East Dubuque, Illinois, measured almost eight feet) were unearthed in Illinois, Mississippi, Georgia, North Carolina, Tennessee, Ohio, Pennsylvania, and West Virginia.[ 157] The West Virginia dig report contains an additional claim of "many large skeletons," generically.[ 158] From these reports listed, more than forty thousand artifacts were found, including weapons, tools, jewelry, and various utensils that could not have feasibly been used by regular-sized humans." (Stephen Quayle & Dr.Thomas R. Horn, Unearthing the Lost World of the Cloudeaters: Compelling Evidence of the Incursion of Giants, Their Extraordinary Technology, and Imminent Return, 4911-4937 (Kindle Edition); Defender Publishing)*

*2 Enoch 15:8-12—My judgment for the giants is that since they are born from flesh they will be called evil spirits and will remain on the earth. Because they were created from above, from the holy Watchers, at death their spirits will come forth from their bodies and dwell on the earth. They will be called evil spirits. The heavenly spirits will dwell in heaven, but the terrestrial spirits who were born on earth will dwell on earth. The evil spirits of the giants will be like clouds. They will afflict, corrupt, tempt, battle, work destruction on the earth, and do evil ; they will not eat nor drink, but be invisible. They will rise up against the children*

*of men and against the women, because they have pro-
ceeded from them.*

*Jubilees 10:1-6—And in the third week of this jubilee the
unclean demons began to lead astray the children of the
sons of Noah; and to make to err and destroy them. 2. And
the sons of Noah came to Noah their father, and they told
him concerning the demons which were, leading astray and
blinding and slaying his sons' sons. 3. And he prayed before
the Lord his God, and said: God of the spirits of all flesh,
who hast shown mercy unto me, And hast saved me and
my sons from the waters of the flood, And hast not caused
me to perish as Thou didst the sons of perdition; For Thy
grace hath been great towards me, And great hath been
Thy mercy to my soul; Let Thy grace be lift up upon my sons,
And let not wicked spirits rule over them Lest they should
destroy them from the earth. 4. But do Thou bless me and
my sons, that we may increase and multiply and replenish
the earth. 5. And Thou knowest how THY WATCHERS, THE
FATHERS OF THESE SPIRITS, acted in my day: and as for
these spirits which are living, imprison them and hold them
fast in the place of condemnation, and let them not bring
destruction on the sons of thy servant, my God; for these
are malignant, and created in order to destroy. 6. And let
them not rule over the spirits of the living; for Thou alone
canst exercise dominion over them. And let them not have
power over the sons of the righteous from henceforth and
for evermore."*

*"The story of Nimrod in the book of Genesis may illustrate
how this could happen through genetic engineering or a
retrovirus of demonic design that integrates with a host's
genome and rewrites the living specimen's DNA, thus making it a "fit extension" or host for infection by the entity.
Note what Genesis 10:8 says about Nimrod: And Cush*

*begat Nimrod: he began to be a mighty one in the earth. Three sections in this unprecedented verse indicate something very peculiar happened to Nimrod. First, note where the text says, "he began to be." In Hebrew, this is chalal, which means "to become profaned, defiled, polluted, or desecrated ritually, sexually or genetically." Second, this verse tells us exactly what Nimrod began to be as he changed genetically—" a mighty one" (gibbowr, gibborim), one of the offspring of Nephilim. As Annette Yoshiko Reed says in the Cambridge University book, Fallen Angels and the History of Judaism and Christianity, "The Nephilim of Genesis 6:4 are always… grouped together with the gibborim as the progeny of the Watchers and human women." And the third part of this text says the change to Nimrod started while he was on "earth." Therefore, in modern language, this text could accurately be translated to say: "And Nimrod began to change genetically, becoming a gibborim, the offspring of watchers on earth."[ 75] Bible commentator Adam Clarke seems to agree with Dr. Horn's conclusions by quoting the Syraic Targum regarding Nimrod: "The Syriac calls him a warlike giant."[ 76] Then Clarke continues to share about Nimrod and the building of the Tower of Babel and its connection to giants: On this point Bochart observes that these things are taken from the Chaldeans, who preserve many remains of ancient facts; and though they often add circumstances, yet they are, in general, in some sort dependent on the text. 1. They say Babel was built by the giants, because Nimrod, one of the builders, is called in the Hebrew text גבור gibbor, a mighty man; or, as the Septuagint, γιγας, a giant. 2. These giants, they say, sprang from the earth, because, in Genesis 10:11, it is said, He went, מןהארץההוא min haarets hahiv, out of that earth; but this is rather spoken of Asshur, who was another of the Babel builders. 3. These giants are said to have waged war with the gods, because it is said of Nimrod, Genesis 10:9,*

*He was a mighty hunter before the Lord; or, as others have rendered it, a warrior and a rebel against the Lord. See Jarchi in loco. 4. These giants are said to have raised a tower up to heaven, as if they had intended to have ascended thither.[ 77] Nimrod achieved something that only the Watchers of old had accomplished, yet he took it to a whole new level. In fact, no one has been able to reproduce this highly revered occult achievement. This cutting-edge breakthrough of Nimrod has been the goal of all secret societies, alchemists, wizards, sorcerers, warlocks, and Illuminati elite throughout the millennia. You see, he was a fully grown man who was able to become a gibborim (another type of Nephilim)—he was not born that way. It would appear that Nimrod took the arcane knowledge of his family line and pushed it beyond what the Watchers themselves could do: He was able to alter his DNA and become a Nephilim. This transmogrification must have thrilled the kingdom of darkness. The fallen angels of Genesis 6 required the use of women in their genetic breeding program. Nimrod accomplished this alchemical feat without the use of a woman's womb. This is important to note, because the Word of God in Daniel gives us a hint that the Antichrist will be able to reproduce the dark magic of Nimrod. Neither shall he regard the God of his fathers, nor the desire of women, nor regard any god: for he shall magnify himself above all. (Daniel 11:37) Some have speculated that this refers to the Antichrist being a homosexual. Although it is true that most within the occult are bisexual (for use in ritual magic), I believe this is a prophetic clue linking the coming man of sin with Nimrod. This powerful working of dark magic and esoteric wisdom will be reproduced one more time in human history."* (Michael Lake & Thomas Horn, The Shinar Directive: Preparing the Way for the Son of Perdition's Return, 1446-1482 (Kindle Edition); Crane, MO; Defender)

*"Jubilees 10.1-12 informs us that after the flood evil spirits began afflicting many of Noah's descendants. Noah prayed to God to bind all of the demons away from men. God bound nine-tenths of the demons, leaving only one-tenth to tempt and torment man. Revelation 9 tells that the other nine-tenths will be released during the Great Tribulation. If the angels are bound, and the Nephilim are disembodied spirits, where did the giants after the flood come from? A third rebellion? No. The story continues: Genesis tells us that after the flood Noah divided the planet among his three sons. Ham was given what we call Africa and Shem, the middle east. Canaan, Ham's son, left his territory and ventured North along the Mediterranean Sea. Why did Canaan travel all the way up the cost to found Sidon, his first city, in an area he knew was not his territory, then quickly settle another city (Tyre)? The map at the right shows that those two locations are the closest he could get to mount an expedition to Mount Hermon. He wanted to find information about the pre-flood giants! And Canaan grew, and his father taught him writing, and he went to seek for himself a place where he might seize for himself a city. And he found a writing which former (generations) had carved on the rock, and he read what was thereon, and he transcribed it and sinned owing to it; for it contained the teaching of the Watchers in accordance with which they used to observe the omens of the sun and moon and stars in all the signs of heaven. And he wrote it down and said nothing regarding it; for he was afraid to speak to Noah about it lest he should be angry with him on account of it. Jubilees 8.1-5 After finding the writing containing the science of the Watchers, Canaan sought to create a race of warrior giants using the same type of genetic tampering which was done before the flood. This explains how the giants came to be, but with a few problems. Second Samuel 21:20 describes giants with six fingers on each hand and six toes on each*

*foot. Moses led the children of Israel into battle with Og, the king of Bashan, who being a true giant, stood at least twelve feet tall (Deuteronomy 3:11). Bashan was anciently called the Land of the Giants. Og actually reigned from Mt. Hermon (Joshua 12:4-5), the place where the angels descended. Even up to King David's time, Goliath remained (1 Samuel 17:4). He was one-quarter giant and three-quarters Philistine and reached only nine feet, nine inches tall. Another race of giants were the Anakim (Numbers 13:21-33). Some of the Amorites were as tall as a cedar tree (Amos 2:9), probably referring to the sons of Anak. Other giant races found in the Old Testament included the Emim (Deuteronomy 2:9-11), and the Zamzummim (Deuteronomy 2:20-21). The Anakim, Emim, and the Zamzaummim were all equally tall. The valley of Hinnom was anciently called the Valley of Giants (Joshua 15:8; 18:16). Joshua destroyed all the Anakim except for a giant that escaped to Gaza (Joshua 11:21-22), the later home of Goliath. David's men killed Goliath's brother and one other son of the giant (2 Samuel 21:20-21). In four hundred years time the giant out bred, so that Goliath and his brothers were only nine feet tall instead of thirteen feet tall. The Genesis 6 word for giants (Nephilim) occurs in only one other place: Numbers 13:33. These same post-flood giants who are called Nephilim in Numbers, are referred to as Rephaim in Deuteronomy 2:11 and Genesis 14:5. These passages show that the post-flood giants were a special kind of Nephilim called Raphaim. This means they were not the procreation of another angelic rebellion, but a genetic tampering by man in a similar fashion as the angels did in the pre-flood world."* (Ken Johnson, Ancient Book of Enoch, 182-184 (Kindle Edition)).

*"The Hebrew prophet Ezekiel made an important statement about "magic bands" (kesatot), which were*

*cryptically used to dispel (magically eject) the souls of men in order to replace those spirits with resurrected ones from the dead (as in the Rephaim or dead Nephilim). Will ye hunt the souls of my people, and will ye save [Hebrew, chayah, "restore to life"] the souls alive that come unto you... to slay the souls that should not die, and to save [restore to life] the souls alive that should not live...? Wherefore thus saith the Lord God; Behold, I am against your [Kesatot, "magic bands" used for binding and loosing souls], wherewith ye there hunt the souls to make them fly [Parach, "to fly away," or alternatively "to sprout up from out of the ground"] and I will tear them from your arms, and will let the souls go, even the souls that ye hunt to make them fly (Ez[ ekiel] 13:18b–20). (emphasis added) The kesatot was a magic arm band used in connection with a container called the kiste. Wherever the kiste is inscribed on sarcophagi, it is depicted as a sacred vessel (a spirit prison?) with a snake peering through an open lid. How the magic worked and in what way a spirit was ejected and replaced with a spirit from the dead is a mystery (unless, again, modern occultists have these demonic incantations in their possession today). Pan, the half-man/ half-goat god that guarded the entrance to the "gates of hell" at the base of Mount Hermon—beyond which the Rephaim (dead Nephilim) were imprisoned—is sometimes pictured kicking the lid open and letting the snake (spirit?) out. Such loose snakes were then depicted as being enslaved around the limbs and bound in the hair of the Bacchae women, the servants of the demonic god Dionysus. Whatever this imagery of Pan, the serpents, the imprisoned spirits, and the magic kesatot and kiste actually represented, a noteworthy verification of the magical properties represented by them is discussed in the scholarly book Scripture and Other Artifacts by Phillip King and Michael David: In the closing verses of Ezekiel 13 the prophet turns his attention to magic practices whose details remain obscure. Two key terms are kesatot and mispabot.... The kesatot are worn on the arms, while the mispabot are made "on the head of every height" (?), which has been understood to mean "on the heads of persons of every height" [including those of great height; giants, offspring of the Watchers].... In modern times archaeological discoveries and texts from Babylonia in particular have shed further light on what might be involved: G. A. Cooke cited Hellenistic figurines from Tell Sandahannah (Mareshah) in Palestine with wire twisted around their arms and ankles... and a magical text from Babylonia that speaks of white and black wool being bound to a person or to someone's bed.... J. Herrmann [notes] that both words can be related to Akkadian verbs, kasu and sapabu, which mean respectively "to bind" and "to loose." Herrmann also drew attention to texts in which these verbs were used in a specifically magical sense.... This indicates that, whatever the objects were, their function was to act as "binders" and "loosers" in a magical sense, in other words as means of attack and defense [of spirits] in sorcery.[ 48]". (Thomas R. Horn & Josh Peck, Abaddon Ascending: The Ancient Conspiracy at the Center of CERN'S Most Secretive Mission, 118-120 (Kindle Edition))*

*"Many such Jewish and Christian apocalypses have been studied for millennia, but it was not until the first half of the nineteenth century that this literature was authoritatively identified as a distinct group of writings. 12 This advancement coincided with the discoveries of several ancient Jewish manuscripts and the publication of their critical editions, especially of 1 Enoch and the Ascension of Isaiah. The bulk of these and other works—including some that do not take the form of an apocalypse yet still can be described as apocalyptic because they share constitutive traits of the genre13—were studied and made accessible in*

*English around the turn of the twentieth century by British scholar R. H. Charles, who drew heavily on them in his own scholarship on Revelation. Charles maintained that these sources offer such valuable contextual insight for exegesis that "the New Testament Apocalypse cannot be understood apart from Jewish Apocalyptic literature." 14 In fact, Charles credited much of his newfound respect for the theological profundity of Revelation to his contextual studies. "The first ground for such a revolution in my attitude to the Book," Charles explained, "was due to an exhaustive study of Jewish Apocalyptic. The knowledge thereby acquired helped to solve many problems, which could only prove to be hopeless enigmas to scholars unacquainted with this literature." 15 Charles is not alone in his appreciation for this body of texts and its significance for unlocking Revelation. 16 In the decades that have followed, his contention has come to be shared by many others, including Bauckham, who remarks, "The tradition of apocalyptic literature is the living literary tradition to whose forms and content [John of Patmos] is most indebted."" (Ben C. Blackwell, John K. Goodrich, & Jason Maston, Reading Revelation in Context: John's Apocalypse and Second Temple Judaism 22-23 (Kindle Edition); Grand Rapids, Michigan; Zondervan Academic)*

*Jasher 4:20-20 And all men who walked in the ways of the Lord, died in those days, before the Lord brought the evil upon man which he had declared, for this was from the Lord, that they should not see the evil which the Lord spoke of concerning the sons of men.*

*Jasher 5:5—And all who followed the Lord died in those days, before they saw the evil which God declared to do upon earth.*

*Jasher 5:21—And all the sons of men who knew the Lord, died in that year before the Lord brought evil upon them; for the Lord willed them to die, so as not to behold the evil that God would bring upon their brothers and relatives, as he had so declared to do.*

Unless otherwise noted, the following historical accounts are from: Henri Nissen (translated from Danish by Tracy Jay Skondin, Bruce Steuer, Dorthe Orbesen and Irene Kjaedegaard), Noah's Ark-Ancient Accounts And New Discoveries; Copenhagen, Denmark; Scandinavia Publishing House)

*"Along with American composer George Gershwin, many people find it difficult to believe that Methuselah lived to be 969 years old. Nevertheless, the Bible teaches quite plainly that the early patriarchs often lived to be nearly 1,000 years old and even had children when they were several hundred years old! Similar claims of long life spans are found in the secular literature of several ancient cultures (including the Babylonians, Greeks, Romans, Indians, and Chinese). But even a life span of nearly 1,000 years is sadly abbreviated when we consider that God initially created us to live forever." (Dr. David Menton & Dr. Georgia Purdon, 'Did People Like Adam And Noah Really Live Over 900 Years Of Age?' in Ken Ham,* The New Answers Book 2; Over Thirty Questions On Creation/Evolution & The Bible, *2812-2819 (Kindle Edition); Green Forest, AR; Master Books)*

*"The Sumerian King List is of interest to students of the Bible for at least two reasons: its mention of a major flood and the incredibly long reigns attributed to the kings. The brief mention of the flood in the Sumerian King List is reminiscent of the biblical flood story involving Noah (Genesis 6). Admittedly, the Sumerian King List gives no details of*

*the flood, but the Sumerian flood, like the biblical flood, was viewed as an event of tremendous proportions, covering the land. The flood serves as a dividing line: the institution of kingship had to be reinstated after the flood, and kings are listed as being prior to the flood or after the flood...At most, one can say that the idea of a massive, ancient flood was widespread spread in antiquity...The other connection between the Sumerian King List and the Bible is the listing of the reigns of the kings, comparable to the genealogies in Genesis 5 and n. In both the Sumerian and biblical lists, approximately ten generations are listed prior to the flood. In both, the reigns or life spans are exceptionally long...In both traditions the time spans decline and generally are longer before the flood than after." (Clyde E. Fant & Mitchell D. Reddish, Lost Treasures Of The Bible: Understanding The Bible Through Archaeological Artifacts In World Museums, 490-502 (Kindle Edition); Grand Rapids, Michigan; William B. Eerdmans Publishing Company)*

*"Because Noah and his family were the only human survivors of the Flood approximately 4,500 years ago, all people today are descended from them. This is consistent with population statistics. Indeed, starting with Noah's family and calculating the population growth using a generation span of 40 years and an average of 2.5 children per family, the present world population of more than six billion people would be obtained in those 4,500 years. Since the parameters used are conservative, this would allow for even more people to have lived and then died early in wars or of disease." (Andrew Snelling, 'The Geological Evidence For Creation' in John Ashton & Michael Westacott, The Big Argument: Does God Exist? Twenty-Four Scholars Explore How Science, Archaeology And Philosophy Haven't Disproved God, 2172-2179 (Kindle Edition); Green Forest, AR; Master Books)*

292    *Christians Helping Addicts Pursue Sobriety*

*"One of the strongest arguments for a young Earth comes from the field of human population statistics. According to historical records, the human population on Earth doubles approximately every 35 years. If you break down that figure, it represents an annual increase of 20,000 people per every million. Let's suppose that humankind started with just two individuals (we will call them Adam and Eve for the sake of our argument). And suppose that they lived on the Earth one million years ago (some evolutionists suggest that man, in one form or another, has been on the Earth 2-3 million years). Suppose, further, that an average generation was 42 years, and that each family had an average of 2.4 children. (They probably had many more than that, but we will use a conservative estimate that would allow for at least some population growth; if a family unit had only two children, there would be zero population growth, since each parent simply would replace himself or herself, providing no net increase.) Allowing for wars, famine, diseases, and other devastation, there would be approximately 1 x 10 5000 people on the Earth today! That number is a 1 followed by 5,000 zeroes. But the entire Universe (at an estimated size of 20 billion light- years in diameter) would hold only 1 x 10 100 people. Evolutionary time scales simply cannot account for the present, relatively small human population. However, using young- Earth figures (of eight people having survived the Noahic Flood), the current world population would be around 6- 8 billion people. The question is— which of the two figures is almost right on target, and which could not possibly be correct?" (Eric Lyons & Kyle Butt, The Dinosaur Delusion: Dismantling Evolution's Most Cherished Icon, 1917-1927 (Kindle Edition); Montgomery, Alabama; Apologetics Press)*

*"Sixteen thousand clay tablets from the third millennium B.C. were discovered at Ebla in modern Syria, beginning in*

*1974. Biovanni Pettinato dates them 2580–2450 B.C. and Paolo Matthiae suggests 2400–2250 B.C. Either period pre-dates any other written material by hundreds of years. Apologetic Importance of the Tablets. The importance of the Ebla tablets is that they parallel and confirm early chapters of Genesis. Although clouded by subsequent polit-ical pressure and denials, the published reports in reputa-ble journals offer several possible lines of support for the biblical record (see ARCHAEOLOGY, OLD TESTAMENT). Tab-lets reportedly contain names of the cities Ur, Sodom and Gomorrah, and such pagan gods mentioned in the Bible as Baal (see Ostling, 76–77). The Ebla tablets reportedly con-tain references to names found in the book of Genesis, in-cluding Adam, Eve, and Noah (Dahood, 55–56). Of great importance is discovery of the oldest known creation ac-counts outside the Bible. Ebla's version predates the Baby-lonian account by some 600 years. The creation tablet is strikingly close to that of Genesis, speaking of one being who created the heavens, moon, stars, and earth. Parallels show that the Bible contains the older, less embellished version of the story and transmits the facts without the cor-ruption of the mythological renderings. The tablets report belief in creation from nothing, declaring: "Lord of heaven and earth: the earth was not, you created it, the light of day was not, you created it, the morning light you had not [yet] made exist" (Ebla Archives, 259). There are significant implications in the Ebla archives for Christian apologetics. They destroy the critical belief in the evolution of monothe-ism (see MONOTHEISM, PRIMITIVE) from supposed earlier polytheism and henotheism. This evolution of religion hy-pothesis has been popular from the time of Charles *Dar-win (1809–1882) and Julius *Wellhausen (1844–1918). Now monotheism is known to be earlier. Also, the force of the Ebla evidence supports the view that the earliest chap-ters of Genesis are history, not mythology." (Norman*

*Geisler, Baker Encyclopedia Of Christian Apologetics, 208 (Kindle Edition); Grand Rapids, Michigan; Baker Books)*

*"In spite of its limitations and shortcomings, this book has attempted to present a true narrative representation of the discovery of Sodom, in a manner that reflects the true narrative representational nature of the source of the site's history, the Bible. The existence of a significant Middle Bronze Age city at Tall el- Hammam is now confirmed beyond any doubt. In terms of the biblical Sodom criteria, it's in the right place, at the right time, with all the right stuff." (Dr. Steven Collins & Dr. Latayne C. Scott, Discovering The City Of Sodom: The Fascinating True Account Of Of The Discovery Of The Old Testament's Most Infamous City, 3440-3442 (Kindle Edition); Nashville, TN; Howard Books)*

*"Collins has identified Sodom's location as Tall el-Hammam, which is situated on the eastern edge of the Jordan disk, eight miles northeast of the mouth of the Jordan (hayarden). It is the largest tell in the southern Levant, measuring 1,000 meters long and containing within its walls 85 acres, a much smaller area than the general occupational spread beyond the walls of 240 acres....After eight seasons of excavation at the site, Collins has discovered several key indicators that confirm the city as Sodom. First, an abrupt occupational gap of several centuries immediately after the Middle Bronze Age II (1800-1550 BC) offers a perfect fit for the timing of the destruction of Sodom....Second, Tall el-Hammam contains a massive destruction and ash layer (one meter thick in some areas) distributed at various locations of the Middle Bronze Age layer of the city. The site reveals extensive destruction by fire of architectural features such as roofs, dwellings, walls, fortification barriers, as well as personal items such as jewelry, tools, and pottery. In addition to these, one of the most*

*sobering and striking features involves human remains that depict catastrophic destruction. It appears that many of the inhabitants' bones are charred and distorted, like those pictured, and are situated in a way that indicates a violent high-heat heat flash event that may have thrown inhabitants to the western side of their dwellings, showing that the destruction could have originated from the east....Third, in addition to the architectural destruction, distorted human remains, and pottery environmental analysis of the site has revealed high-heat indicators that are consistent with the biblical description of Sodom's fiery destruction. For example, one sample of Middle Bronze Age pottery had its surface transformed into glass. After visual and scientific testing of the shard, its transformation could only be explained by an extreme high-heat flash event; only a temperature of thousands of degrees Fahrenheit (much hotter than kilns of that day could heat pottery) could achieve such a process. Related to this, samples of area soil and sand have been examined. These samples give evidence of a high-heat event that was hot enough to turn desert sand into "desert glass," a phenomenon more associated with lightning, airbursts, or atomic explosions in the deserts of New Mexico than the once fertile tile Jordan River valley....In support of these archaeological finds are the many geographical reasons why Tall el-Hammam fits the biblical account of Sodom. As mentioned, Dr. Steven Collins has compiled a massive assortment of geographical data, some of which is adapted in the chart below." (Joseph M. Holden & Geisler, The Popular Handbook Of Archaeology And The Bible: Discoveries That Confirm The Reliability Of Scripture, 2473-2515 (Kindle Edition); Eugene, Oregon; Harvest House Publishers)*

# OTHER BOOKS BY MARK TABATA

*Old Apologetics for a New Age (Vol. 1):*
*The Existence of God*

*Old Apologetics for a New Age (Vol. 2):*
*The Inspiration of the Bible*

*Reincarnation: Fact or Fiction?*

*UFOs: A Study Guide*

*Paganism: A Study Guide*

*Don't Stay a Baby: A Study Guide for New Christians*

All these books and more can be found at
CobbPublishing.com

www.ingramcontent.com/pod-product-compliance
Lightning Source LLC
Chambersburg PA
CBHW070909120626
46546CB00001B/199